ENTERPRISE JAVABEANS COMPONENT ARCHITECTURE

Designing and Coding Enterprise Applications

GAIL ANDERSON • PAUL ANDERSON

Sun Microsystems Press
A Prentice Hall Title

Prentice Hall PTR, Upper Saddle River, NJ   07458
www.phptr.com

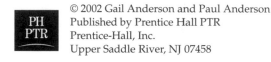

© 2002 Gail Anderson and Paul Anderson
Published by Prentice Hall PTR
Prentice-Hall, Inc.
Upper Saddle River, NJ 07458

The publisher offers discounts on this book when ordered in bulk quantities.
For more information, contact Corporate Sales Department, Prentice Hall PTR,
One Lake Street, Upper Saddle River, NJ 07458. Phone: 800-382-3419; FAX 201-236-7141.
E-mail: corpsales@prenhall.com.

Editorial/Production Supervision: *Wil Mara*
Acquisitions Editor: *Gregory G. Doench*
Associate Editor: *Eileen Clark*
Editorial Assistant: *Brandt Kenna*
Marketing Manager: *Debby vanDijk*
Buyer: *Alexis R. Heydt-Long*
Cover Design: *Anthony Gemmellaro*
Cover Design Direction: *Jerry Votta*
Art Director: *Gail Cocker-Bogusz*
Series Design: *Meg VanArsdale*

Sun Microsystems Press Publisher: *Michael Llwyd Alread*

Printed in the United States of America

10 9 8 7 6 5 4 3 2 1

ISBN 0-13-035571-2

Sun Microsystems Press
A Prentice Hall Title

Contents

CHAPTER 2   ENTERPRISE JAVABEANS OVERVIEW 12

CHAPTER 4   SESSION BEANS WITH JDBC 84

CHAPTER 5   STATEFUL SESSION BEANS 136

CHAPTER 7   ENTITY BEANS WITH CMP 276

CHAPTER 8   MESSAGE-DRIVEN BEANS 368

Preface

T he vision for this project began with the idea to write an example-driven book on Enterprise JavaBeans. We wanted to create a text that was not too long, yet one that contains enough substance to satisfy the enterprise architect. We looked for examples that apply to real-world requirements but are not overly complicated. We aimed for robust solutions that readers could adapt to their own particular needs. We applied industry-standard patterns to our designs with the hope that readers would have more success in applying a newly learned technology. Furthermore, we wanted our examples to show a complete solution, from the underlying database structure to the web component front end.

About the Front Cover

The front cover photograph shows the Roman aqueduct of Segovia, Spain. It is approximately 2,000 years old and delivers potable water to Segovia from the Frio River about 18 kilometers away. Its age alone is a testament to its exquisite engineering. Consisting of two tiers of arches and over 20,000 stone blocks (bonded with neither mortar nor concrete), the aqueduct's durability comes from its ingenious design and construction.

While recognizing the relatively recent emergence of computer science, we also appreciate that solid engineering is not new and is a goal well worth attaining.

Acknowledgments

The completion of this project is the culmination of the vision, effort, advice, hard work, sleuthing abilities, compassionate understanding, and feedback of many people. We'd first like to thank our editor at Prentice Hall, Greg Doench. He believed we could write and deliver a book on schedule, even when previous projects lasted much longer than planned. Thank you also to the staff at Prentice Hall, especially Eileen Clark, who was always available to answer questions. We also appreciate the consultations with Wil Mara (Production), Julie Bettis (Copy Editing), and Patricia Parkhill (FrameMaker expert).

Our reviewers did a wonderful job. We subjected them to reading chapters in chopped up parcels because we couldn't wait until the whole thing was written. They were understanding and accommodating to our schedule, giving us feedback in the midst of Thanksgiving and the Christmas holidays. Because of them, we added more diagrams, cleared up fuzzy explanations, moved sections to better places, wrote better code, and attempted as many improvements as scheduling would allow. And they didn't just suggest improvements; they also encouraged us and told us when they thought we were doing something right! Good technical reviewers are worth their weight in gold. Thank you to Bruce Englar, Rob Gordon, Christian Knecht, Dave Wilson, and Bob Zalusky.

Last but not least, we'd like to thank our family, for understanding that missed soccer games, skipped summer vacations, shortened holiday celebrations, and less family leisure time are temporary but worthwhile sacrifices. Thanks to our children Sara and Kellen, Paul's mother Jane Anderson, and Gail's brother Scott Campbell.

ENTERPRISE JAVABEANS COMPONENT ARCHITECTURE

Designing and Coding Enterprise Applications

INTRODUCTION

Topics in This Chapter

- The Enterprise JavaBeans™ Architecture
- How This Book Is Organized
- Our Vision
- Reader Audience
- About the Examples
- Source Code Online

Chapter 1

Distributed computing has always had tough problems to solve: security, concurrency, database transactions, data integrity, and performance requirements, to name a few. How does the Java 2 Platform, Enterprise Edition (J2EE) address these issues and what is the role of the Enterprise JavaBeans architecture?

As we describe the Enterprise JavaBeans component architecture, let's define where we hope to go, how we hope to get there, and who we hope to take with us. The software industry has exciting offerings right now and in the near future. The architecture of loosely coupled components promises to offer flexibility, scalability, and portability. There is no better time than now to delve into the world of distributed component computing!

1.1 What Is the Enterprise JavaBeans Architecture?

The Enterprise JavaBeans (EJB) architecture is a specification developed at Sun Microsystems. It describes a component-based architecture that provides for the development and deployment of distributed applications. The specification details the services and requirements of an application server which manages EJB components. It also describes coding requirements that bean developers must follow to create portable applications. The lofty and worthwhile goal is for bean developers to write EJB components once and deploy them on any application server that is compliant with Enterprise JavaBeans technology. Furthermore, the EJB architecture makes enterprise applications scalable, secure, and transactional.

Enterprise JavaBeans are components that execute within an "EJB container," under the supervision of an application server. There are three main EJB types: session, entity, and message driven. Furthermore, session beans come in two flavors: stateless and stateful. The application server and EJB container provide system services for EJBs, such as data persistence, transactions, security, and resource management. The EJB container maintains pools of database connections, as well as pools of EJB instances that can be assigned to clients as needed.

The Java 2 Platform, Enterprise Edition (J2EE) is an industry-standard suite of Java APIs for enterprise computing from Sun Microsystems. It includes the Enterprise JavaBeans architecture and a set of related packages that make everything work together. For example, a Java client may use the Java Naming and Directory Interface (JNDI) to look up the location of an EJB component. The application server, which provides the system services that make EJBs work, uses Java Remote Method Invocation (RMI) and RMI-IIOP to implement remote calls across a network. Message-driven beans, a new type of EJB, use the Java Message Service (JMS) to provide a bean capable of responding to messages. So, while Enterprise JavaBeans technology provides specific services in the realm of enterprise computing, it is part of a larger picture. This picture is inscribed by J2EE and its many independent packages that provide specific services.

Why should developers care about J2EE and EJB? Because the application server manages an EJB and provides the system services we mentioned, bean developers can concentrate on designing enterprise applications that adhere to specific business requirements. Instead of writing transactional database code, bean developers can pay attention to business rules, business processes, and how to best keep track of business data. Furthermore, as J2EE technology matures, commercial application servers that support this specification will become more numerous. Better still, as these J2EE application server products improve, the same enterprise application written today will perform better tomorrow—unchanged—because the application server will provide a better implementation.

1.2   How This Book Is Organized

The chapters follow a gradual progression from the simplest type of EJB (stateless session with no database access) to a complete enterprise application with eight EJBs, one web component, and multiple application clients. It's best to read the chapters in this order.

Chapter 2 begins with an overview of the Enterprise JavaBeans architecture. This chapter introduces the J2EE components and explains the role of the application server and container in managing EJBs and the system services they use. You should read this material first if you are new to enterprise beans, but even experienced developers may find it necessary to return to this chapter from time to time. By doing this, you discover how everything fits into the big picture.

Chapter 3 introduces the simplest EJB component, the stateless session bean. Our example, Loan EJB, is a component that produces amortization tables and monthly payment amounts for long term fixed-rate loans. We introduce the Value Object Pattern. After giving you an overview of Java Server Pages (JSP), we also present our first web component client.

Chapter 4 presents Java Database Connectivity (JDBC) with EJBs. In this example, we use a stateless session bean as a database reader. After introducing the basics of JDBC, we show you how to use an EJB for read-only database access. We implement the Data Access Object (DAO) Pattern and explain how to customize an application with a deployment descriptor. The chapter also presents a Swing application client (complete source listing found in Appendix A) and a JSP web component client.

Chapter 5 presents stateful session beans and contrasts them with stateless session beans. This is the beginning of our online shopping application example. Our stateful session bean, MusicCart EJB, is a virtual shopping cart that holds items selected by customers running a JSP web component client. We also introduce the Value List Iterator Pattern and explain EJB local interfaces.

Chapter 6 introduces entity beans. Although our example uses Bean-Managed Persistence (BMP), the reader should be familiar with the material in this chapter because much of it applies to entity beans in general. We present entity bean finder and home methods. Our example is Customer EJB, an isolated "customer" entity bean with BMP. We use the DAO pattern for the persistence implementation. We introduce the very important Session Facade Pattern and local interfaces with entity beans. We enhance our JSP web component client to perform customer lookup and verification against the persistent datastore.

Chapter 7 continues with entity beans. We now explore Container-Managed Persistence (CMP) and Container-Managed Relationships (CMR). We introduce EJB QL, the J2EE query language required to specify custom finder semantics and select methods. Our example includes three related entity beans: Customer EJB, Order EJB, and LineItem EJB. We describe the expanded role of local interfaces and revisit the Session Facade Pattern. The JSP web component client creates customer orders using the data collected in the stateful session MusicCart EJB presented in Chapter 5. The full application now contains seven EJBs, one web component, and an administrative client to inspect the database.

Chapter 8 introduces message-driven beans, the newest EJB component. We begin with an overview of the Java Message Service (JMS) and explain the Publish-Subscribe and Point-to-Point messaging models. Messaging provides a loosely coupled architecture that can enhance the performance of enterprise applications. Our first example is a Message-Driven Bean (MDB) that provides a response mechanism to a client. Our final example is a Java client which sends a message to a ShipOrder MDB. The ShipOrder MDB interfaces with the previously written Session Facade to request the shipment of certain customer orders.

1.3   Our Vision

Enterprise JavaBeans technology is not an easy topic. Yet we believe EJB to be a significant offering in the enterprise computing arena. For the first time, there exists a specification that allows bean developers to write transactional, multi-user, scalable enterprise applications without being experts in transactions, multithreaded programming, security, or database programming. Pulling the enterprise system services out of the components and standardizing them within an application server has tremendous benefits. The most obvious benefit is that we leave the implementation of these system services to developers who *are* experts in enterprise issues. As the technology matures, the application servers will get better, and our enterprise applications will in turn run better.

Does this make EJB authoring simplistic? Not hardly. But it makes EJB authoring accessible and portable across multiple platforms. Our vision is to create a text with examples that teach, not just how to create an EJB, but how to design components that work best within the framework of a particular application. We strive to create examples that show you when to use an entity bean, not as an isolated entity bean example, but as a component within a whole, real-world application.

The industry is learning as pockets of developers here and there build on experiences. We learn what works and what doesn't. And from these battles with reality emerge design patterns that address common problems. So, along with our examples, we've also attempted to attack some of these problems. We show you how to apply commonly accepted design patterns to your enterprise designs (and why). Our hope is that you can take our examples and build your own solutions more quickly with an understanding of the design trade-offs that you'll make.

As you wind your way through these examples, we hope your EJB journey will be both exciting and rewarding.

1.4 Reader Audience

We are writing to an audience of Java programmers. If you're reading this book, then you're interested in enterprise computing. A complete enterprise application entails many parts: one or more clients, an application server to manage the EJBs you write and deploy, and a Java Virtual Machine (JVM) to execute Java bytecode. Clients come in many flavors: a command-line Java program, a Java Server Pages (JSP) web component, or even a client that uses Java's Swing GUI are all common types of clients. Some familiarity with database software is helpful. Java Database Connectivity (JDBC) is the Java API for portable database operations. While we don't assume you know JSP or JDBC, we do provide only an overview of these subjects—enough so that you can follow and understand our examples.

We take a similar approach with our overviews of the Java Message Service (JMS) and the EJB Query Language (EJB QL). JMS underlies the implementation of message-driven beans. Bean developers use EJB QL to compose custom queries for CMP entity beans.

1.5 About the Examples

Enterprise JavaBeans Component Architecture is an example-driven book. Our goal is to show you how to design effective EJB components through our examples. Each example teaches you some aspect of EJB design. For instance, our first example (Loan EJB) illustrates the design and use of a stateless session bean (see "The Loan Enterprise Bean" on page 36).

The enterprise computing community has developed a rich set of design patterns. Where possible, we apply accepted design patterns within our examples, explaining the benefit that each pattern brings, as well as presenting its complete implementation. See, for example, the Session Facade Pattern implemented in several examples ("Session Facade Pattern" on page 250 as well as "Session Facade Pattern" on page 329).

We've attempted to bring an element of real-world problem solving to our program examples. At the same time, we avoid solutions that entail layers and layers of abstraction. We hope the developer can recognize the types of enterprise applications our examples represent and use our code as a starting point for further development. For example, we've written a JSP web component client that allows a user to log into a "system" based on a user name and a password. An underlying database stores "customer data," and several enterprise Java beans provide the database lookup and verification steps. There's hardly a customer-based web site that doesn't need a similar capability (see "Web Component Client" on page 262).

Note that besides presenting code for all our EJB examples, we also present complete code for the clients. It may be surprising to see JSP programs in a book about EJB, but our belief is that the examples become more useful when you see how they work within a complete application. Also, an EJB is a component—and components can have all sorts of clients. Thus, we show you a JSP client and a stand-alone Java client with the same EJB.

We've developed and deployed all our examples using the Sun Microsystems Reference Implementation. We run the J2EE server on a Solaris Machine, but have tested our clients on several platforms including Windows and Red Hat Linux.

Table 1.1 describes the different examples. Some chapters include a single application (one or more clients with one or more EJBs). Other chapters include multiple examples built on earlier ones. This table will be helpful as you install and run the examples on your own system.

Table 1.1 Examples by Chapter

Chapter and Topics	*Example Components*	*Source Directory*
Chapter 3: Stateless Session Beans		`loanSession`
Stateless Session Bean	Loan EJB	
Application Exceptions	LoanObjectException	
Value Object Pattern	LoanVO	
Stand-alone Java client	AmortClient	
JSP web component client	paymentGet	
	paymentPost	
Chapter 4: Session Beans with JDBC		`musicSession`
Session Beans with JDBC	Music EJB	
Database Reader		
Application Exceptions	NoTrackListException	
Value Object Pattern	RecordingVO	
	TrackVO	
Java Swing client	MusicApp	(see Appendix A)
JSP web component client	musicGet	
	musicPost	

Table 1.1 Examples by Chapter *(continued)*

Chapter and Topics	Example Components	Source Directory
Chapter 4: *Session Beans with JDBC* ** *Data Access Object Pattern***		`musicDAO`
DAO Pattern	Music EJB with DAO	
Factory Pattern	MusicDAOFactory	
System Exceptions	MusicDAOSysException	
Naming Environment Entry		
Chapter 5: *Stateful Session Beans*		`musicVL`
Stateful Session Bean	MusicCart EJB	
Value Object Pattern	CustomerVO	
Value List Iterator Pattern	MusicIterator EJB	
	MusicPage EJB	
JSP web component client	login	
	loginPost	
	musicCart	
	shoppingPost	
Chapter 5: *Stateful Session Beans* ** *Local Interfaces***		`musicLocal`
Local interfaces	MusicPage EJB	
Local vs. Remote interfaces	MusicIterator EJB	
Stateful vs. Stateless		
Chapter 6: *Entity Beans with BMP*		`customerDAO`
Bean-managed persistence	Customer EJB	
Finder/Home methods		
Transactions		
Local Interfaces		
DAO Pattern	CustomerDAO	
Session Facade Pattern	CustomerSession EJB	
Value Object Pattern	CustomerVO	
Test Client	CustomerTestClient	

Table 1.1 Examples by Chapter *(continued)*

Chapter and Topics	Example Components	Source Directory
JSP web component client	signUp	
	signUpPost	
	loginPost	
Chapter 7: Entity Beans with CMP		`ordersCMP`
Container-managed persistence	Customer EJB	
Relationship fields	Order EJB	
EJB Query Language	LineItem EJB	
Finder/Select Methods		
Session Facade Pattern	CustomerSession EJB	
Value Object Pattern	OrderVO	
	LoanVO	
JSP web component client	processOrder	
	submitOrder	
Administrative client	AdminClient	
Chapter 8: Message-Driven Beans		
JMS message queues	PingServer	
Publish/Subscribe Pattern	SchoolApp client	`School`
	Student MDB	
Point-to-Point Pattern	OrderApp client	`ShipOrders`
EJB integration	ShipOrder MDB	

1.6 Source Code Online

We maintain all the source code in this book at an FTP site. You can reach this site through our web site at **http://www.asgteach.com.**

ENTERPRISE JAVABEANS OVERVIEW

Topics in This Chapter

Chapter 2

This chapter presents an overview of the J2EE architecture and Enterprise JavaBeans architecture. We'll begin with the concepts behind the J2EE architecture and how the J2EE components help you design distributed applications. Next, we'll discuss the J2EE application server and the role of the container in each server. This helps you understand how enterprise beans fit into the big picture.

There's a lot of terminology that goes along with enterprise beans, so this chapter is a good place to define terms. We'll start with the concepts behind session beans (stateless and stateful), entity beans, and message-driven beans. We'll help you understand how entity beans with bean-managed and container-managed persistence interact with a database. You'll also learn about bean life cycles, entity relationships, interfaces (home, local home, remote, and local) and asynchronous messaging.

This chapter is meant as an overview, so some of the topic discussions will be brief. Others will be explained in more detail. There will, of course, be much more to talk about when we start designing enterprise systems in later chapters. Let's start with the J2EE architecture, which is the foundation of enterprise beans.

2.1   The J2EE Architecture

The J2EE platform gives you a multitiered application model to develop distributed components. Although any number of tiers is possible, a three-tier architecture is typical. Figure 2–1 shows the approach.

The client machine supports web browsers, Java applets, and stand-alone applications. A client application may be as simple as a command line program running as an administrator client or a graphical user interface created from Java Swing or AWT (Abstract Window Toolkit) components. Regardless, J2EE applications encourage *thin clients* in the presentation tier. A thin client is a lightweight interface that does not perform database queries, implement business logic, or connect to legacy code. These types of "heavyweight" operations preferably belong to other tiers.

The J2EE server machine is the center of the architecture. This middle tier contains web components and business objects managed by the application server. The web components dynamically process user requests and construct responses to client applications. The business objects implement the logic of a business domain. Both components are managed by a J2EE application server that provides important system services for these components, such as security, transaction management, naming and directory lookups, and remote connectivity. By placing these services under control of the J2EE application server, client components focus only on presentation logic. And, business objects are easier for developers to write. Furthermore, the architecture *encourages* the separation of business logic from presentation logic (or model from view).

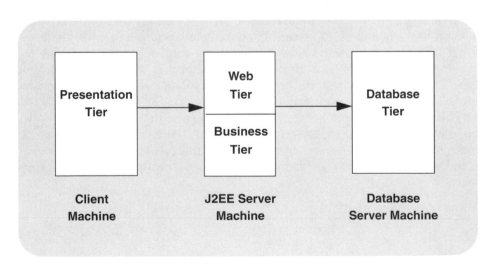

Figure 2–1 Three-Tier J2EE Architecture

The database server machine handles the database back end. This includes mainframe transactions, databases, Enterprise Resource Planning (ERP) systems, and legacy code. Another advantage of the three-tier architecture is that older systems can take on a whole new "look" using the J2EE platform. This is the approach many businesses are taking as they migrate their legacy systems to the web in a modern distributed computing environment.

2.2 The J2EE Components

To develop distributed components for the J2EE architecture, you need component technologies, APIs, and administrative tools. Let's take a look at each of these categories as they apply to the J2EE architecture and see what they offer to developers.

Enterprise JavaBeans (EJB)

EJB is a component technology that helps developers create business objects in the middle tier. These business objects (enterprise beans) consist of fields and methods that implement business logic. EJBs are the building blocks of enterprise systems. They perform specific tasks by themselves, or forward operations to other enterprise beans. EJBs are under control of the J2EE application server.

Java Servlets

This component technology presents a request-response programming model in the middle tier. Servlets let you define HTTP-specific servlet classes that accept data from clients and pass them on to business objects for processing. Servlets run under the control of the J2EE application server and often extend applications hosted by web servers.

JavaServer Pages (JSP)

A JSP page is a text-based document interspersed with Java code. A JSP engine translates JSP text into Java Servlet code. It is then dynamically compiled and executed. This component technology lets you create dynamic web pages in the middle tier. JSP pages contain static template data (HTML, WML, and XML) and JSP elements that determine how a page constructs dynamic content. The JSP API provides an efficient, thread-based mechanism to create dynamic page content. We provide several JSP clients as example clients to our EJB components in this book. See "Introducing Servlets and JSP" on page 64 in Chapter 3 for a more detailed JSP overview.

Java Naming Directory Interface (JNDI)

JNDI is a standard Java API for accessing different directory and naming services in the presentation tier or middle tier. JNDI lets you access databases and administered objects (queues, topics, etc.) without knowing their specific names or protocols. This makes JNDI an important step in the design of portable enterprise systems. J2EE application servers use JNDI so that clients can "find" needed distributed components or access environment information (such as database resource names or class names) used to customize EJB behavior.

Java Database Connectivity (JDBC)

JDBC is an API that lets you invoke SQL commands from Java methods in the middle tier. You can use the JDBC API to access a database from either an enterprise bean or from a servlet or JSP page. The JDBC API has an application-level interface for database access, and a service provider interface to attach JDBC drivers to the J2EE platform. In support of JDBC, J2EE application servers manage a pool of database connections. This provides business objects efficient access to database servers. We provide an overview of database fundamentals and JDBC (see "Database Fundamentals" on page 87 and "Introducing JDBC" on page 88 in Chapter 4).

Java Message Service (JMS)

The JMS API lets you perform asynchronous messaging in the presentation and middle tiers. Asynchronous messaging means that clients do not have to wait for a business method to complete. A JMS server stores messages with topic objects for publish-subscribe broadcasts and queue objects for point-to-point communications. JMS lets you implement push/pull technologies in enterprise designs. See "Introducing JMS" on page 372 in Chapter 8 for a JMS overview.

Java Transaction API (JTA)

Under control of the J2EE application server, the JTA provides a standard interface for demarcating transactions in the middle tier. When multiple clients access the same database, it's important to update the data correctly for each read and write operation. The JTA is useful for marking where dependent database operations occur so that they may be committed (written to the database) if successful or rolled back (undone) when there are errors. The J2EE architecture provides defaults for transaction auto commits and rollbacks.

Java API for XML (JAXP)

JAXP lets you read and write text-based XML programs in the presentation and middle tiers. XML is a portable language known to a large number of tools and applications on the web. In the J2EE platform, XML is used extensively with deployment descriptors for J2EE components. As more system services are provided by the J2EE application server (and not coded by developers), developers *customize* component behavior declaratively using XML.

JavaMail

The JavaMail API lets you send and receive e-mail in the presentation and middle tiers. JavaMail has a service provider interface and an application-level interface for application components to send mail. JavaMail is a valuable part of the J2EE platform because it allows J2EE components to send and receive e-mails with different protocols.

J2EE Connector API

The Connector API defines a standard for connecting the J2EE platform to systems in the database tier. This includes mainframe transaction processing, database systems, ERP, and legacy applications that are not written in Java. J2EE vendors and systems integrators use the Connector API to create resource adapters, which allow J2EE components to access and interact with a resource manager of another system.

Java Authentication and Authorization Service (JAAS)

JAAS extends the Java 2 platform security architecture to support user-based authorization. This provides a way for a J2EE application to authenticate a specific user or a group of users that wish to run an application.

J2EE Reference Implementation

The Reference Implementation is a noncommercial product from Sun Microsystems that provides a J2EE application server, web server, relational database (Cloudscape), the J2EE APIs, and a set of development and deployment tools. This implementation is made freely available by Sun for demonstrations, prototyping, and educational use. All of the examples in *Enterprise JavaBeans Component Architecture* have been developed and tested with the Reference Implementation.

Remote Method Invocation (RMI)

RMI, introduced in the Java Development Kit (JDK) 1.1, lets Java programs find and use Java classes residing on remote machines across networks. RMI makes the use of distributed objects within Java programs transparent and easy to use. RMI provides support for the network calls used by Enterprise JavaBeans in the J2EE architecture. RMI hides the nitty-gritty details of network sockets and TCP/IP. It also marshals and unmarshals method arguments and handles exceptions across the network.

Java Interface Definition Language (IDL)

The EJB specification includes a mapping for EJBs to communicate with each other using Common Object Request Broker Architecture (CORBA). Developers use an Interface Definition Language (IDL) to specify interfaces in a Java IDL file. This file defines the methods and fields that must be platform and language independent. The IDL file is compiled with a special compiler that generates the classes necessary to communicate over the network. CORBA and IDL enable Java programs and EJBs to call legacy code written in other languages. This makes it possible, for example, to call member functions in a C++ program running on a Windows machine from an EJB executing on a UNIX system across a network.

2.3   The J2EE Application Server

Now that we've introduced the J2EE components, let's take a closer look at the J2EE platform. Figure 2–2 shows a more detailed view of the J2EE architecture.

Containers and Services

Both the presentation and middle tiers use *containers*. An application client container runs on the client machine and manages the execution of client programs. In the J2EE server machine, a web container manages JSP and servlet components. The EJB container, which also runs on the J2EE server machine, manages the execution and life cycle of all enterprise beans. The browser is an applet container and runs on the client machine.

Why are containers important in the J2EE application server? Rather than have client programs handle the complex details of transaction and state management, multithreading, and resource pooling, the web and EJB containers provide these services in the middle tier. This arrangement makes thin clients

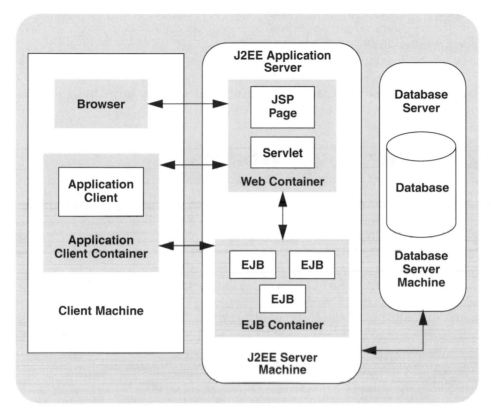

Figure 2–2 J2EE Application Server and Containers

possible and centralizes the important aspects of distributed computing in a dedicated server or cluster of servers.

All J2EE components, regardless of whether they are web components, enterprise beans, or application components, must be assembled into a J2EE application and deployed in their containers before executing. This assembly process involves specifying container settings for each component that is to be deployed.

Part of the packaging of EJB components involves the creation of a *deployment descriptor*. Deployment descriptors are XML-based files that describe how the container configures a bean to run on a server. In the deployment descriptor, you may specify settings for security, transactions, JNDI lookups, environment resources, and much more. The deployment descriptor is important because it affects the behavior of an EJB. By changing an EJB's deployment descriptor, you can make an EJB behave differently. We show you how to customize EJBs through the deployment descriptor (see "Naming Environment Entry" on page 124 in Chapter 4).

The containers also manage other types of services, such as EJB and servlet life cycles, database connection resource pooling, data persistence, transaction management, and security.

With this introduction to the J2EE architecture and its components, let's take a closer look at EJB components in the middle tier. We'll discuss the different types of enterprise beans and how the EJB container manages them in enterprise designs.

2.4   Enterprise JavaBeans

Enterprise JavaBeans are server-side components that encapsulate an application's business logic. An enterprise bean, for example, might calculate interest payments for a loan application or access a relational database for banking applications. A client that needs information calls business methods in the EJB, which may result in a remote invocation across a network.

EJBs have several benefits. First of all, they help bean developers write large applications with distributed components more easily. Recall that the EJB container provides system-level services to each bean deployed in a J2EE application server. This means bean developers do not have to handle complex issues such as transaction management, resource pooling, security, and multi-threaded programming. Instead, they focus only on business logic in their bean methods.

EJBs also benefit clients in the presentation tier. Clients become thinner, since they implement only presentation logic and use EJBs for their business methods. EJBs are also portable components, which means you can build different enterprise applications with the same EJBs and run them on any J2EE application server.

There are three types of enterprise beans: session beans, entity beans, and message-driven beans. Let's give you a brief overview of each enterprise bean and discuss how they might be used in an enterprise application. We'll also discuss bean life cycles and how the EJB container manages each bean.

Session Beans

Session beans represent an interactive session with one or more clients. Session beans may maintain state, but only during the time a client interacts with the bean. This means session beans do *not* store their data in a database after a client terminates. Session beans, therefore, are not persistent.

Session beans come in two flavors: stateless and stateful. Let's discuss the characteristics of each session bean and suggest when they might be appropriate in an enterprise application.

Stateless Session Beans

The values of any object's instance variables (fields) define the state of an object. Usually, method calls change an object's state. A stateless session bean, however, does *not* keep track of client-specific data. In fact, no instance variable in a stateless session bean stores client-specific data. This unique property allows the EJB container to create a pool of instances, all from the same stateless session bean. Why is this important?

When a client invokes a method of a stateless session bean, the EJB container fetches an instance from the pool. Any instance will do, since the bean does not store any client-specific information. As soon as the method finishes executing, the instance is available for another client's request. This arrangement makes stateless session beans highly scalable for a large number of clients (a small number of instances can service many clients). It also means better performance. The EJB container does not have to move stateless session beans from memory to secondary storage to free up resources—it simply regains memory and other resources by destroying the instances.

All enterprise beans have different states that they go through during their lifetimes. The life cycle of a bean is managed by the EJB container. Figure 2–3 shows the life cycle for a stateless session bean.

There are only two states in a stateless session bean: a *Does Not Exist* state and a *Ready* state. After the container creates an instance of a stateless session bean with `Class.newInstance()`, the container invokes the `setSessionContext()` and `ejbCreate()` methods in the bean. This makes the bean transition

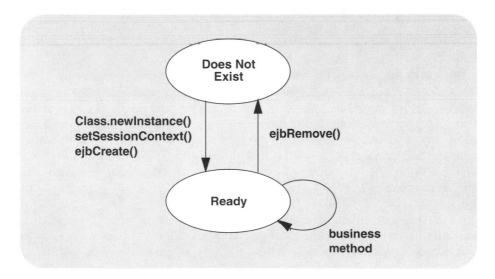

Figure 2–3 Stateless Session Bean Life Cycle

to the *Ready* state. The bean developer uses the `setSessionContext()` method to access the bean's context from the container. The container invokes the `ejb-Create()` method to initialize the bean and access resources. Once the bean is in the *Ready* state, a client may call its business methods. The container calls the bean's `ejbRemove()` method when it no longer requires a bean instance. This makes the bean return to the *Does Not Exist* state.

When should you use stateless session beans? Stateless session beans are appropriate when a task is not tied to a specific client. You could, for instance, use a stateless session bean to send an e-mail confirmation or calculate interest payments for loan applications. You could also use a stateless session bean to *read* data from a database. Such a bean would be useful for generating reports or viewing a collection of items.

Stateful Session Beans

In a stateful session bean, the instance variables store client-specific data. Each stateful session bean, therefore, stores the **conversational state** of one client that interacts with the bean. This conversational state is maintained by the bean while clients call its business methods. The conversational state is not saved when the client terminates the session.

The EJB container manages stateful session beans differently from stateless beans. Note that with stateful session beans, it's not possible for the container to create a pool of instances and share them among multiple clients. Since a stateful session bean stores client-specific data, the container creates a separate bean instance for each client. So that conversational state is not lost, the container saves and restores stateful session beans when moving them between memory and secondary storage. All this means that stateful session beans have more overhead associated with them and are not as scalable as stateless session beans.

The life cycle of a stateful session bean is also more involved, as Figure 2–4 shows. Stateful session beans have three states: a *Does Not Exist* state, a *Ready* state, and a *Passive* state. When a client calls `create()`, the EJB container instantiates the bean with `Class.newInstance()` and calls its `setSessionContext()` and `ejbCreate()` methods. This makes the bean transition to the *Ready* state where it can accept calls to its business methods. When the client terminates a session, the container calls the `ejbRemove()` method in the bean. The bean returns to the *Does Not Exist* state where it is marked for garbage collection.

A stateful session bean transitions to the *Passive* state when the container *passivates* the bean; i.e., the container moves the bean from memory to secondary storage. The container calls the bean's `ejbPassivate()` method just before passivating a bean. If the bean is in the *Passive* state when a client calls one of its business methods, the container *activates* the bean. The container restores

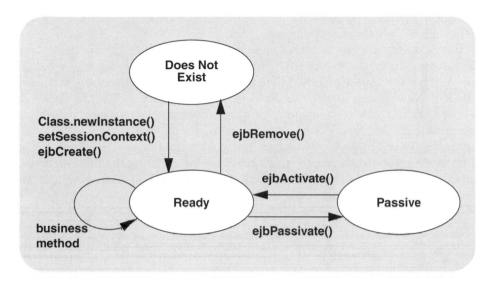

Figure 2–4 Stateful Session Bean Life Cycle

the bean in memory before calling the bean's ejbActivate() method. This makes the bean return to the *Ready* state.

When should you use stateful session beans? In general, any situation where a bean must remember client information *between method invocations* is a candidate for stateful session beans. A good example on the web is a virtual shopping cart in an online store. When clients log on to the system, a stateful session bean can maintain the items in the shopping cart. Each client has its own instance of a stateful session bean, which maintains a separate shopping cart for each client.

Note that with stateful session beans, client-specific information is stored in memory, not to a database. Therefore, you should use stateful session beans in situations where losing session data is not a problem when a client terminates a session. In our hypothetical online store, for instance, we discard the virtual shopping cart if a client decides not to buy the items. Saving the shopping cart contents comes under the application and use of entity beans, our next topic.

Entity Beans

Entity beans are in-memory business objects that correspond to data in persistent storage. An entity bean typically corresponds to a row in a relational database. The bean's instance variables represent data in the columns of the database table. The container must synchronize a bean's instance variables with the database. Entity beans differ from session beans in that instance variables are stored persistently. Entity beans also have primary keys for identification and may have relationships with other entity beans. Another key concept is that clients may share entity beans.

The EJB container locates an entity bean by its primary key. Primary keys are unique identifiers. Database software prevents you from inserting new data if the primary key is not unique. If multiple clients attempt to access the same data in an entity bean, the container handles the transaction for you. Through an entity bean's deployment descriptor, the developer specifies the transaction's attributes associated with entity bean methods. The container performs the necessary rollbacks if any step in the transaction fails. This is one of the most vital services that the container provides for entity bean developers. We provide an overview of transactions and entity beans. See "Transaction Overview" on page 246 in Chapter 6.

An entity bean life cycle has three states: *Does Not Exist*, *Pooled*, and *Ready*. Figure 2–5 shows the life cycle diagram.

To transition from the *Does Not Exist* state to the *Pooled* state, the container creates a bean instance with Class.newInstance() and calls the setEntity-Context() method in the bean. This allows bean developers to access a bean's

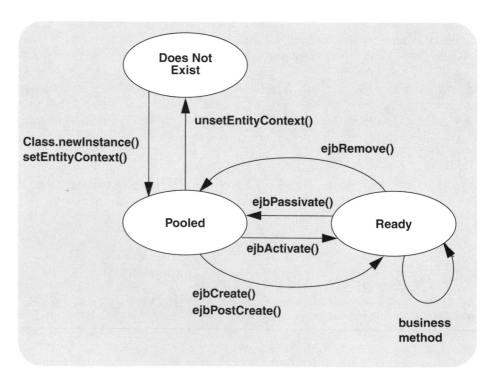

Figure 2–5 Entity Bean Life Cycle

context from the argument passed to `setEntityContext()`. In the *Pooled* State, all entity bean instances are identical.

Note that there are two paths for an entity bean to transition from the *Pooled* state to the *Ready* state. The client can invoke the entity bean's `create()` method and consequently insert *new data* into the underlying database. The client can alternatively invoke one of the bean's "finder" methods. This performs a select query on the underlying database, synchronizing the bean's persistent fields from the *data already in* the database.

If a client wants to insert data into the database, the client calls the `create()` method with arguments representing the data values. This makes the container call `ejbCreate()` to initialize the bean before calling `ejbPostCreate()`. In the *Ready* state, clients may invoke business methods in the entity bean.

If, on the other hand, a client reads data from the database, the client calls the `findByPrimaryKey()` method or another finder method. This makes the container deliver an entity bean instance directly to the client if its state is *Ready*. If the requested bean is in the *Pooled* state, the container activates the bean and calls the bean's `ejbActivate()` method. This changes the bean's state to *Ready*.

There are also two paths from the *Ready* state to the *Pooled* state. If a client wants to remove data from the database, the client calls `remove()`. This makes the container call the bean's `ejbRemove()` method. If the container needs to reclaim resources used by an entity bean, it can passivate the bean. To passivate an entity bean, the container calls `ejbPassivate()`. Both calls change the bean's state from *Ready* to *Pooled*.

At the end of the life cycle, the container removes the bean instance from the pool and calls the bean's `unsetEntityContext()` method. This changes the bean's state from *Pooled* to *Does Not Exist*.

When should you use entity beans? An entity bean is appropriate for any situation where data must be maintained (created, updated, selected, deleted) in persistent storage. Entity beans should represent business data rather than perform a task-related function.

Entity beans have two types of persistence: Bean-Managed Persistence (BMP) and Container-Managed Persistence (CMP). Let's take a look at each persistence type as it relates to a database.

Bean-Managed Persistence (BMP)

Entity beans with bean-managed persistence contain code that accesses a database. The beans' code contains SQL calls to read and write to the database. BMP gives developers more control over how an entity bean interacts with a database.

An entity bean with BMP can implement SQL code targeted for a specific database platform or it can use a Data Access Object (DAO) to hide the details of a particular database. A DAO encapsulates database operations into helper classes for a specific database. DAOs make entity beans with BMP more portable, although the bean developer still has to manipulate database access with Java methods and classes. We present the DAO pattern for BMP entity beans in Chapter 6 (see"DAO Pattern Implementation" on page 215).

Container-Managed Persistence (CMP)

Entity beans with container-managed persistence do not contain code for database access. The container generates the necessary database calls for you. This approach makes CMP entity beans more portable than BMP entity beans with DAOs. With the deployment descriptor set to specific attributes for CMP behavior, entity bean developers are spared from having to write SQL code for database access.

Entity Relationships

Entity beans, regardless of whether they use BMP or CMP for database access, can have relationships with other entity beans according to an *abstract persistence schema*. An entity bean's abstract schema defines a bean's persistent fields and its relationships with other entity beans. The persistent fields of an entity bean are stored in a database.

A bean's relationship to another bean is stored as a *relationship field*. Relationship fields must also be stored in the database. With BMP, the developer decides how relationship fields are represented in the underlying database (using foreign keys allows data in one table to relate to data in another table). With CMP, the container constructs the appropriate cross-reference tables based on the abstract schema description the bean developer provides. Chapter 7 explores entity relationships with CMP.

Message-Driven Beans

Message-driven beans allow J2EE applications to receive messages asynchronously. This means a client's thread does not block while waiting for an EJB's business method to complete. Instead of calling a business method directly in a bean, clients send messages to a server that stores them and returns control to the client right away. The EJB container has a pool of message bean instances that it uses to process messages. When the message is received, the message bean can access a database or call an EJB business method. This arrangement allows the invocation of lengthy business methods without making the client wait for the method to complete its job.

Using JMS

Message beans use the Java Message Service (JMS) to handle messaging. Figure 2–6 shows the approach. Clients use a JMS server to store messages in a

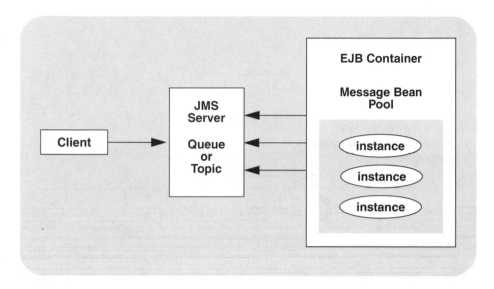

Figure 2–6 Message-Driven Bean, JMS, and EJB Container Architecture

queue or topic destination. In JMS, a topic is used for a one-to-many broadcast and a queue for a one-to-one communication. When a message arrives, the container calls the onMessage() method in the message bean to process the message. Using the JMS server as an intermediary *decouples* the client from the message bean. This is a key point with message beans.

The container uses a bean instance from a pool of message beans. The container also handles all the details of registering a message bean as a listener for queue or topic messages.

Another key point with message beans is that they are stateless. This makes message beans highly scalable, like stateless session beans. A message bean retains no conversational state and can handle messages from multiple clients. Message beans can connect to databases and call methods in other EJBs, too. This makes message beans a valuable component in enterprise designs that require asynchronous processing from clients.

Message beans also have a simple life cycle, as shown in Figure 2–7. There are only two states: *Does Not Exist* and *Ready.* To change from the *Does Not Exist* state to the *Ready* state, the container instantiates the message bean with Class.newInstance() and calls its setMessageDrivenContext() and ejb-Create() methods.

In the *Ready* state, a message bean may receive messages from the JMS server. When a message arrives, the container calls the onMessage() method in the message bean and passes the message to the method as an argument. Note that message processing does not make a message bean change state.

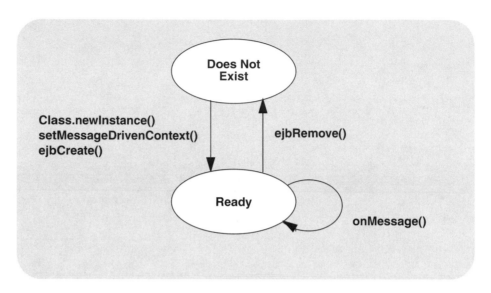

Figure 2–7 Message Bean Life Cycle

Like stateless session beans, the container never passivates a message bean because message beans do not contain client-specific data. The life cycle of a message bean ends when the container calls the `ejbRemove()` method. This makes the message bean's state change back to the *Does Not Exist* state.

When should you use message beans? In general, message beans are useful for receiving messages asynchronously (no waiting). You should consider using a message bean to decouple a client who cannot tolerate waiting for a lengthy business method to complete. A message bean that sends an e-mail confirmation to a large group of recipients is a good example.

The J2EE application server uses JMS to implement message-driven beans. A message bean is relatively easy to implement, since the container does most of the setup work that JMS requires.

Clients and Interfaces

A well-designed interface is important in enterprise programming because it represents the client's view of an enterprise bean. Clients invoke business methods in a session bean or an entity bean only through a bean's interface. This approach allows the EJB container to intercept client calls made through the EJB interface. The container can then perform any required system processing (such as transaction management) before forwarding the call to the method inside the EJB implementation class.

Two types of interfaces are possible with session and entity beans. Let's find out what they are and how you might use them. (Note that message-driven beans do not have client interfaces since access is only through the JMS server.)

Home and Remote Interfaces

Clients may access session and entity beans remotely (from a machine running a different JVM) or locally (within the same JVM). For remote access, session and entity beans have a *remote interface* and a *home interface*. These interfaces represent the client's view of an enterprise bean. The remote interface defines a bean's business methods and the home interface defines life cycle methods. The home interface also defines finder and home methods for entity beans. Figure 2–8 shows the home and remote interfaces for a Customer EJB entity bean that has remote access.

Remote clients can be web components, J2EE application clients, or other enterprise beans. Remote clients may execute on one machine, and the enterprise bean it uses may run on a different machine. You must create both a remote interface and a home interface for a client to have remote access to the bean.

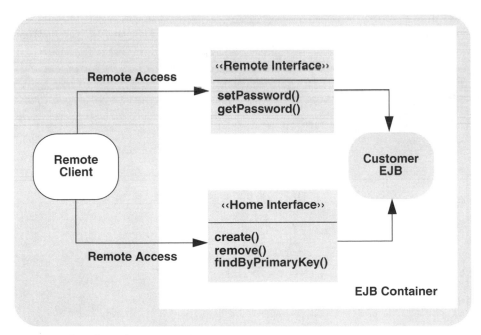

Figure 2–8 Interfaces for Remote Access

Local Home and Local Interfaces

Clients may also interact with session or entity beans locally. This means a local client executes on the same machine as the enterprise bean it uses. Local clients can be web components or other enterprise beans, but not J2EE client applications. A common use of local interfaces is among related entity beans (entity beans with relationship fields to other entity beans). Also, you can construct a business process session bean as a front end (a session facade) to one or more entity beans. The session bean would typically use local access to the entity beans. (See "Session Facade Pattern" on page 250 as well as "Session Facade Pattern" on page 329 for the description, motivation, and implementation of this important design pattern.)

To have local access, you must create a *local interface* with business methods and a local home interface with life cycle and finder methods. A local interface is also the *only way* to have entity beans communicate with other entity beans in container-managed relationships. In an abstract schema, any entity bean that is the target of a container-managed relationship field must have a local interface. Figure 2–9 shows the local home and local interfaces for a Customer EJB entity bean with local access.

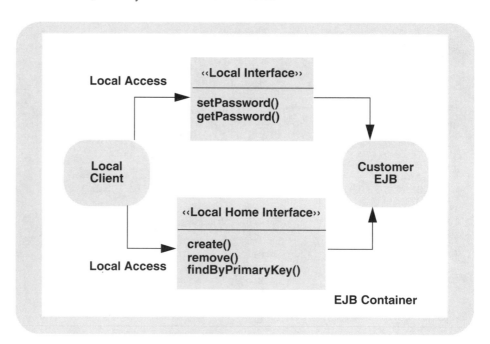

Figure 2–9 Interfaces for Local Access

The primary reason for using local interfaces is increased performance. With local access to session or entity beans, method calls execute faster than remote calls, since both client and bean execute under control of the same EJB container.

2.5 Key Point Summary

This chapter introduced the J2EE architecture, J2EE components, and presents an overview of enterprise beans. You learned the basic concepts behind enterprise beans and how the container manages different beans in the J2EE architecture. You also learned how an enterprise bean might be used in a distributed architecture.

Here are the key points from this chapter.

- The J2EE platform gives you a multitiered application model to develop distributed components.
- A three-tier architecture places web components and business components in the middle tier. The presentation tier contains client applications and the database tier contains database programs.
- The J2EE components consist of technologies like enterprise beans, servlets, and JSP. They also contain APIs that are valuable to EJBs, such as JNDI, JDBC, and JMS.
- Remote Method Invocation (RMI) provides support for network calls used by enterprise beans in the J2EE architecture.
- The J2EE application server has containers that provide services to enterprise beans and web components.
- A deployment descriptor is an XML file that describes how the container will configure an EJB to run on a J2EE application server.
- The containers in the J2EE architecture manage many services, such as EJB and servlet life cycles, database connection pooling, security, transaction management, and data persistence.
- Enterprise beans are server-side components that encapsulate business logic and business data.
- The EJB container provides system-level services to each bean deployed in a J2EE application server. These services include transaction management, resource pooling, security, and multithreading control.
- There are three types of enterprise beans: session beans, entity beans, and message-driven beans. Session beans may be stateless

or stateful, and entity beans may use bean-managed persistence or container-managed persistence.

- Stateless session beans do not store client-specific data in their instance variables. Stateless session beans are scalable and can be shared by many clients.
- Stateful session beans do store client-specific data in their instance variables. Stateless session beans store the conversational state between a client and a bean. The EJB container may passivate or activate stateful session beans by moving the bean between memory and secondary storage.
- Stateless session beans are appropriate for general tasks that do not apply to a specific client. Stateful session beans apply to situations where a bean must remember nonpersistent client information between method invocations.
- Entity beans are in-memory business objects that correspond to data in persistent storage.
- Entity beans with bean-managed persistence contain SQL calls to read and write to a database.
- Entity beans with container-managed persistence do not contain code for database access. The container generates the necessary database calls for you.
- An entity bean's abstract schema defines a bean's persistent fields and its relationships with other entity beans.
- A bean's relationship to another bean is stored as a relationship field. The container uses relationship fields to identify related beans.
- Message beans allow J2EE applications to receive messages asynchronously. Message beans use the Java Message Service (JMS) to handle messaging.
- Message beans are highly scalable, similar to stateless session beans.
- The home or local home interface of an enterprise bean defines life cycle methods. The local or remote interface contains the business methods.
- Local interfaces allow enterprise beans to call methods locally, which performs better than remote calls across a network.

STATELESS SESSION BEANS

Topics in This Chapter

- Introducing Stateless Session Beans
- The Structure of an Enterprise Bean
- The Value Object Pattern
- Compiling, Packaging, and Deploying an EJB
- A Stand-alone Java Application Client
- JSP Overview
- A Web Component Client

Chapter 3

Now that we've explored the J2EE architecture, we're ready to look at our first EJB example. We'll be creating a stateless session bean, the simplest kind of enterprise bean.

3.1 Introducing Stateless Session Beans

A stateless session bean allows multiple clients to share a single instance. Clients may issue multiple requests to a stateless bean, but the bean does not keep track of any client-specific data.

What sorts of tasks can a stateless session bean perform on a client's behalf? A session bean (stateful or stateless) generally implements a business process. A business process is a series of tasks that conforms to a set of rules for a business enterprise. The session bean's job is to fulfill these steps and to make sure the process conforms to the rules. For example, a session bean may access a database in a read-only mode to supply certain information, such as items in a catalog. Or, the session bean could read company archive data looking for sales trends, popular items, or effective sales managers. Given certain data, a session bean can also perform some sort of conversion on that data. A currency converter can look up current conversion rates. A translator session bean can translate text from one language to another. All of these processes manipulate data, but the results of the manipulation are transient: they're simply returned to the client.

Session beans can also create permanent data. In the enterprise world, we call permanent data a *business entity*. Examples of business entities are customers, orders, and transactions. In general, a session bean that manipulates a business entity will not do so directly; it will make a request of an *entity bean*, which in turn oversees the creation or modification of a business entity.

Our first EJB is an example of a business process that takes data and provides a transformation. The input data and the resultant transformation are returned to the client without being stored. Since there's no need to save state, we use a stateless session bean. This example is conceptually simple; however, throughout its presentation, we explore design issues that will help us create far more complicated enterprise applications later. We will point out these design issues as we go along.

Design Guideline

The main advantage of a stateless session bean is that the EJB container can make a single instance of the bean available to multiple clients. A stateful session bean, on the other hand, must maintain a single client's state. Consequently, the EJB container cannot allow multiple clients to access the same instance. Also, the EJB container might have to passivate a stateful session bean to free up resources and save the session bean's state to secondary storage. A stateless session bean, therefore, can be more efficient than a stateful session bean because it imposes fewer constraints on the container.

3.2   The Loan Enterprise Bean

Ok, interest rates have fallen and it's time to refinance that loan you've been thinking about. How much should you borrow and for how many years? What would your new monthly payment be?

Let's design a Loan enterprise bean that provides methods to calculate long-term fixed rate loans, such as home loans. Our Loan EJB will have three business methods. The first method returns the monthly payment (principal and interest) one must pay given the loan amount, annual interest rate, and term (the length of the loan in years). The second method produces an amortization table providing a month-by-month payment schedule of the loan. A third method produces a year-by-year payment schedule.

In presenting this example, we'll show you the structure and source code for the Loan EJB first and then examine two different ways to call its methods. This includes a Java stand-alone client application called `AmortClient` and a JSP web component called `payment` that can be called from your favorite browser. Figure 3–1 provides an architectural overview of these components, their containers, and their relationship to each other.

The EJB Container manages the Loan EJB and executes under the J2EE application server on the J2EE server machine. Our stand-alone `AmortClient` program runs within the application client container on the client machine and communicates with the Loan EJB with the services provided by the application server and the EJB container. The JSP web component (`payment`) runs within the web container under management of the application server. A client communicates with this JSP web component through a browser running on the client machine.

Before we show you the Java code for this enterprise bean, let's first examine the structure required of all enterprise session beans using our Loan EJB as an example.

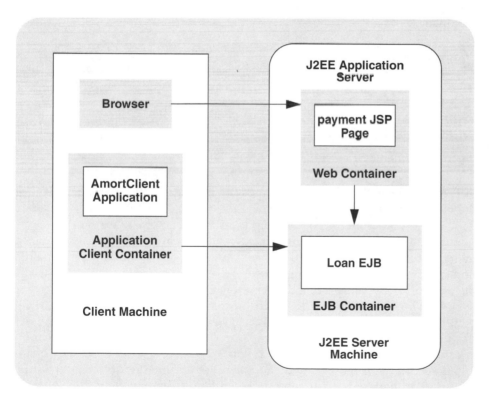

Figure 3–1 Architectural Overview of the Loan Amortization Enterprise Application

Enterprise Session Bean Structure

To build an enterprise session bean, we need to create at least one class and two interfaces: an interface that extends the EJBHome interface (the "home interface"), an interface that extends the EJBObject interface (the "remote interface"), and a class that implements the SessionBean interface (the "bean implementation" class). Each of these constructs plays a unique role in the EJB architecture and has constraints that a bean developer must follow. As we go through the structure of an enterprise bean, we will detail the role and constraints of each class and interface. In addition, an enterprise bean frequently makes use of other "helper" classes that encapsulate related data, methods, or both. We'll also explore the architectural role of these helper classes as we present our first EJB example.

Although there are no rules on what names a bean developer may choose, it's always a good idea and a common practice to follow a consistent naming strategy. Table 3.1 shows the naming conventions we use for our EJB class/interface names.

Table 3.1 Naming Conventions for EJB Class and Interface Names

EJB Class/Interface	Name	Example
Remote Interface	Bean Name	Loan
Home Interface	Bean Name + Home	LoanHome
Bean Implementation Class	Bean Name + Bean	LoanBean

Figure 3–2 shows a class diagram of the standard EJB interfaces as well as the classes and interfaces that we write to form the Loan EJB. Interface LoanHome is the home interface extending interface EJBHome. Interface Loan is the remote interface extending interface EJBObject and contains the business methods for our Loan EJB. And finally, class LoanBean is the bean implementation class which implements interface SessionBean. The ellipsis (. . .) after the methods in class LoanBean indicates there are other methods from the SessionBean interface that LoanBean must implement (but we do not show them). Note that you must provide ejbCreate() inside class LoanBean even though it does not appear in interface SessionBean. (Not all session beans have zero-argument ejbCreate() methods. When we discuss stateful session beans, you'll see that you must provide an ejbCreate() method for each create() method you define in the home interface.) During deployment, the container generates classes that implement the home and remote interfaces. These classes invoke methods in the ContainerProxy class, which forwards calls to methods in class LoanBean.

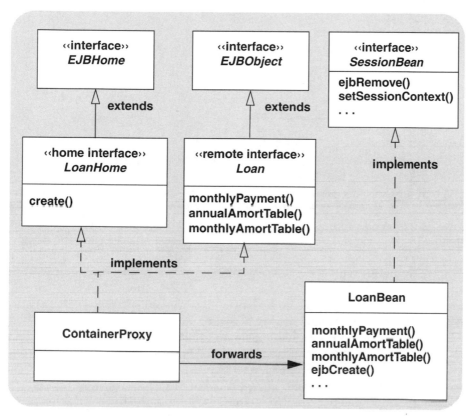

Figure 3–2 Class Diagram Showing the EJB Classes and Interfaces for a Session Bean.

Home Interface

In a session bean, the role of the home interface is to provide a `create()` method that the client calls to create the enterprise bean. A client uses the lookup and naming service provided by the application server to find a "handle" (reference) to the home interface. A client's call to the `create()` method of the object that implements the home interface makes the EJB container instantiate the EJB. In general, we need four Java statements to make all this happen, as well as some helper classes provided by the J2EE component API. Here is a code snippet that shows how a client might create our Loan EJB.

```
import javax.naming.Context;
import javax.naming.InitialContext;
import javax.rmi.PortableRemoteObject;
  . . .
```

```
try {
  Context initial = new InitialContext();
  Object objref = initial.lookup(
        "java:comp/env/ejb/MyLoan");
  LoanHome home =
        (LoanHome)PortableRemoteObject.narrow(objref,
            LoanHome.class);
  Loan loanEJB = home.create();

} catch (Exception ex) {...}
```

The imports are necessary to access all the classes we need. A try block must enclose all statements (otherwise, the compiler complains). When a client wants to reference a remote object such as an enterprise Java bean or a database resource, a coded name must be mapped to the target object inside the deployment descriptor. Here we specify the coded name "ejb/MyLoan" with the application server-dependent prefix "java:comp/env/". The lookup() method returns an object which we then pass to the narrow() method in PortableRemoteObject. This important step allows us to call create() with an instance of an object (home) that implements the home interface (LoanHome).

In a stateless session bean like our Loan EJB, the home interface provides a single create() method with no arguments. Note that create() returns an object that implements the remote interface (Loan). This is the object we will use to invoke the business methods specified in the remote interface.

Listing 3.1 contains the LoanHome interface found in **LoanHome.java**:

Listing 3.1 LoanHome.java

```
// LoanHome.java
import java.io.Serializable;
import java.rmi.RemoteException;
import javax.ejb.CreateException;
import javax.ejb.EJBHome;

public interface LoanHome extends EJBHome {

    Loan create() throws RemoteException, CreateException;
}
```

LoanHome is an interface extending from the EJBHome interface and therefore contains no implementation code. The create() method in a stateless session bean contains no arguments and returns the remote interface type of the enterprise bean (in this case, interface Loan). Both RemoteException and CreateException must appear in the throws clause of this method.

Where is the implementation for the `create()` method? Each `create()` method in the home interface has a corresponding `ejbCreate()` method in the bean implementation class. The client application invokes the `create()` method in the home interface. The EJB container, in turn, invokes the corresponding `ejbCreate()` method in the bean implementation class. We will examine the bean implementation class shortly.

Remote Interface

The business processes that an enterprise bean performs are called its *business methods*. Clients access the `create()` method through the home interface but call the business methods through the enterprise bean's remote interface. Our Loan EJB has three business methods that must appear in the remote interface. Method `monthlyPayment()` returns the monthly payment including principal and interest. The `monthlyAmortTable()` method produces a month-by-month payment table for the loan. Method `annualAmortTable()` produces a year-by-year payment schedule.

Listing 3.2 contains the source code in **Loan.java** for the `Loan` remote interface, which extends the `EJBObject` interface.

Listing 3.2 Loan.java

```
// Loan.java
import javax.ejb.EJBObject;
import java.rmi.RemoteException;
import java.util.*;

public interface Loan extends EJBObject {

    public double monthlyPayment(LoanVO loan)
        throws LoanObjectException, RemoteException;
    public ArrayList annualAmortTable(LoanVO loan)
        throws LoanObjectException, RemoteException;
    public ArrayList monthlyAmortTable(LoanVO loan)
        throws LoanObjectException, RemoteException;
}
```

All business methods in the remote interface must specify `RemoteException` in their `throws` clauses. If any method throws an application-specific exception, the name of the exception class must also appear in the `throws` clause. Here, the business methods all specify `LoanObjectException` in the `throws` clause. Like the home interface's `create()` method, each business method in the remote interface has a corresponding implementation method in the bean implementation class. The method in the remote interface should match its implementation method for all arguments and the return type. The arguments and return values must also be valid RMI types (built-in or serializable), since the J2EE server transmits and receives them remotely to and from the client.

LoanObjectException

LoanObjectException is an example of an *application exception*. Application exceptions are usually nonfatal errors produced by inconsistent user input or some other recoverable situation. The EJB container does not perform any special error handling during the processing of an application exception. The container simply propagates the exception back to the client.

By contrast, a *system exception* is generally a nonrecoverable condition, such as a failure to obtain a database connection, the inability to load a class, or a database query that fails. We discuss system exceptions in more detail in Chapter 4 (see "MusicDAOSysException" on page 126). Listing 3.3 shows the source for application exception LoanObjectException.

Listing 3.3 LoanObjectException.java

```
// LoanObjectException.java
// Application Exception
public class LoanObjectException extends Exception {

    public LoanObjectException() { }

    public LoanObjectException(String msg) {
        super(msg);
    }
}
```

Value Objects

In the Loan remote interface, monthlyPayment() returns a double, but annualAmortTable() and monthlyAmortTable() return ArrayList. The Java collection class ArrayList is serializable and holds any Object type. Our amortization methods return collections that hold monthly and annual payment schedules for the loan. Because this payment information is important, a helper class called PaymentVO is used to create *value objects* in the ArrayList collection. Similarly, our Loan EJB business methods make calculations regarding long-term fixed rate loans given certain data about the loan: its annual interest rate, amount, and term. The methods that produce an amortization table also require a start date. To make life easier for both the Loan EJB's clients and the EJB itself, we use another value object to encapsulate the values required to make these calculations. This LoanVO value object is an argument type in all business methods of our remote interface.

Design Guideline

A value object is a class that encapsulates useful data into a larger "coarse-grained" object. This avoids multiple remote calls on an EJB to store or receive information. Value objects do not implement any methods other than "setters" and "getters" to access encapsulated data. Here, our use of value objects is both convenient and efficient.

LoanVO Class

Let's look at our first value object, LoanVO, which describes the loan. This class stores the loan's annual interest rate, total amount borrowed, length of the loan in years, and the loan's start date. Listing 3.4 shows the code in **LoanVO.java**:

Listing 3.4 LoanVO.java

```java
// LoanVO.java
import java.util.*;
public class LoanVO implements java.io.Serializable
{
  private double amount;        // in dollars
  private double rate;          // percent
  private int years;
  private Calendar startDate;

  public LoanVO (
    double amount,
    double rate,
    int years,
    Calendar startDate) {
      setAmount(amount);
      setRate(rate);
      setYears(years);
      setStartDate(startDate);
  }
```

Listing 3.4 LoanVO.java *(continued)*

```
public LoanVO (
   double amount,
   double rate,
   int years) {
     setAmount(amount);
     setRate(rate);
     setYears(years);
     // use today since no date provided
     this.startDate = (GregorianCalendar)
            new GregorianCalendar();
}

// getters
public double getAmount() { return amount; }
public double getRate() { return rate; }
public int getYears() { return years; }
public Calendar getStartDate() {
     return (Calendar)startDate.clone(); }

// setters
public void setAmount(double a) { amount = a; }
public void setRate(double r) { rate = r; }
public void setYears(int y) { years = y; }
public void setStartDate(Calendar d) {
   startDate = (GregorianCalendar)new GregorianCalendar(
     d.get(Calendar.YEAR),
     d.get(Calendar.MONTH),
     d.get(Calendar.DATE)); }
} // LoanVO
```

An import of java.util allows LoanVO to use Calendar and Gregorian-Calendar. LoanVO also needs to implement java.io.Serializable, since all data that we transmit remotely must be serializable for network calls.

The LoanVO class has two constructors to handle an optional startDate argument. If the client does not provide a date, the second constructor uses today's date (an empty constructor for GregorianCalendar). The remaining methods are getters and setters for the instance variables. Method setStart-Date() changes a loan object's start date.

Here's an example of instantiating a LoanVO object with a start date of March 1, 2002, for a fifteen year $90,000 loan at 6.85%.

```
LoanVO myloan = new LoanVO(90000, 6.85, 15,
        new GregorianCalendar(2002, 2, 1));
```

Programming Tip

Rather than have `getStartDate()` *return a reference to the* `Calendar` *object from* `LoanVO`'s `startDate` *instance variable, we use* `clone()` *to return a copy of the* `Calendar` *object. Thus, we make sure that the* `Calendar` *object referred by a* `LoanVO` *object is not modified, except through its setter,* `setStartDate()`.

PaymentVO Class

Recall that in the `Loan` remote interface, business methods `annualAmortTable()` and `monthlyAmortTable()` return `ArrayList`. Both methods actually return an `ArrayList` collection of `PaymentVO` value objects that encapsulate payment data. Like value object `LoanVO`, `PaymentVO` is a convenient way to return the payment schedule within a collection. By returning all the data in a collection, we reduce the number of remote calls required to retrieve payment data. Listing 3.5 shows the source for value object `PaymentVO`.

The `PaymentVO` class consists of a constructor with an argument for each of its instance variables and getter methods for clients to access their values. Note that setter methods aren't necessary, since a `PaymentVO` object is always created by the Loan EJB and `PaymentVO`'s instance variables don't change once they're set. A `PaymentVO` object stores an integer payment number, the payment date, and the current balance.

For a 15-year loan the payment number is 0 through 180, where 0 is the state of the loan before any payments have been made. On the 0th payment, the balance is equal to the total amount of the loan and is decremented by the principal part of the payment each month. The next two instance variables are the current interest and current principal, which vary each month. The final two instance variables hold the accumulated interest and the accumulated principal. Got all that? On the last payment, the accumulated principal equals the total amount of money borrowed, and the accumulated interest is how much the customer paid in interest over the entire term of the loan (ouch!).

Listing 3.5 PaymentVO.java

```java
// PaymentVO.java
import java.util.*;

public class PaymentVO implements java.io.Serializable
{
  private int paymentNumber;
  private Calendar paymentDate;
  private double balance;

  private double currentInterest;
  private double currentPrincipal;
  private double accumInterest;
  private double accumPrincipal;

  public PaymentVO (
    int paymentNumber,
    Calendar paymentDate,
    double balance,
    double currentInterest,
    double currentPrincipal,
    double accumInterest,
    double accumPrincipal) {

      this.paymentNumber = paymentNumber;
      this.paymentDate = (GregorianCalendar)
          new GregorianCalendar(
        paymentDate.get(Calendar.YEAR),
        paymentDate.get(Calendar.MONTH),
        paymentDate.get(Calendar.DATE));

      this.balance = balance;
      this.currentInterest = currentInterest;
      this.currentPrincipal = currentPrincipal;
      this.accumInterest = accumInterest;
      this.accumPrincipal = accumPrincipal;
  }

  // getters
  public int getPaymentNumber()
      { return paymentNumber; }
  public Calendar getPaymentDate()
      { return (Calendar)paymentDate.clone(); }
```

Listing 3.5 PaymentVO.java *(continued)*

```
public double getBalance()
    { return balance; }
public double getCurrentInterest()
    { return currentInterest; }

public double getCurrentPrincipal()
    { return currentPrincipal; }
public double getAccumInterest()
    { return accumInterest; }
public double getAccumPrincipal()
    { return accumPrincipal; }

} // PaymentVO
```

Bean Implementation Class

Now we are ready to examine our bean implementation class. This is where we implement all the code in an EJB.

The bean implementation class for a **session** bean must implement the `SessionBean` interface. You also need to provide methods for `ejbCreate()`, `ejbRemove()`, `ejbActivate()`, `ejbPassivate()`, and `setSessionContext()`. Method `ejbCreate()` is the implementation of `create()` in the home interface. This method is typically empty since there are no instance variables to initialize. However, we can certainly add specialized code to `ejbCreate()` if we want to. For example, `System.out.println()` statements let us know when the EJB container creates our bean. You should also include code that you want to execute once at initialization time inside `ejbCreate()`. Likewise, the other `SessionBean` methods are usually empty, since no cleanup tasks are necessary when the EJB container destroys a stateless session bean. The EJB container also does not passivate or activate stateless session beans.

Regardless, the bean implementation class needs to implement the business methods defined in the remote interface. For our Loan EJB, this includes `monthlyPayment()`, `annualAmortTable()`, and `monthlyAmortTable()`. Listing 3.6 shows the `LoanBean` implementation class and the code for these methods.

Listing 3.6 LoanBean.java

```java
// LoanBean.java
import java.rmi.RemoteException;
import javax.ejb.SessionBean;
import javax.ejb.SessionContext;
import java.util.*;
import java.lang.Math;

public class LoanBean implements SessionBean {

  // Private helper methods

  // Private helper method checkLoanObject() makes
  // sure that the LoanVO argument is valid.
  // Valid means: interest rate is positive (> .001),
  // loan amount is positive (> $1),
  // and term is positive (> 1 year).
  // It throws LoanObjectException if there is
  // a problem.

  private void checkLoanObject(LoanVO loan)
          throws LoanObjectException {
    if (loan.getYears() < 1 || loan.getRate() < .001
        || loan.getAmount() < 1.0) {
      throw new LoanObjectException(
            "LoanBean: Bad LoanVO argument");
    }
  }

  // Private helper method getPayment calculates monthly
  // principal and interest payment based on the
  // annual interest rate, term, and loan amount.
  // Called by monthlyPayment() and doAmortTable().

  private double getPayment(LoanVO loan)
          throws LoanObjectException {
    checkLoanObject(loan);
    double monthly_interest = loan.getRate() / (1200);
    int months = loan.getYears() * 12;
    return loan.getAmount() *
      (monthly_interest /
      (1 - Math.pow(1+monthly_interest,-1*months))) ;
  }
```

Listing 3.6 LoanBean.java *(continued)*

```java
// Private helper method produces an ArrayList
// of PaymentVO objects based on
// values stored in LoanVO argument and the
// requested time period.
// Called by business methods annualAmortTable() and
// monthlyAmortTable().

private ArrayList doAmortTable(LoanVO loan,
        int time_period) throws LoanObjectException {
  ArrayList table = new ArrayList();
  // this output appears on the J2EE server console
  System.out.println("table size = " + table.size());

  // Initialize all calculations to 0
  double currentInterest = 0.;
  double currentPrincipal = 0.;
  double accumInterest = 0.;
  double accumPrincipal = 0.;

  // Obtain values from LoanVO argument
  double currentBalance = loan.getAmount();
  double monthly_interest = loan.getRate() / (1200);
  int months = loan.getYears() * 12;
  // Use helper function to calculate payment
  double monthly_payment = getPayment(loan);
  Calendar curdate = loan.getStartDate();

  // Calculate payment breakdown for each
  // month for the term of the loan
  for (int i = 0; i <= months; i++) {
    if (i % time_period == 0) {
      // create a PaymentVO object
      // depending on time_period
      // and add to ArrayList

      PaymentVO p = new PaymentVO(i, curdate,
        currentBalance,
        currentInterest,
        currentPrincipal,
        accumInterest,
        accumPrincipal);
      table.add(p);
    }
```

Listing 3.6 LoanBean.java *(continued)*

```
        // Update all of the calculation
        // variables
        currentInterest = currentBalance * monthly_interest;
        currentPrincipal = monthly_payment -
              currentInterest;
        currentBalance -= currentPrincipal;
        accumInterest += currentInterest;
        accumPrincipal += currentPrincipal;
        curdate.add(Calendar.MONTH, 1);
    }

    // Output appears on J2EE console;
    // shows new ArrayList size.
    // This number depends on term and
    // whether client requested annual
    // or monthly amortization table.
    System.out.println("table size = " + table.size());
    return table;
  }

// Business Methods

// Amortization tables. Annual table specifies
// time period 12 (every 12 months) and
// monthly table specifies 1 (every month).
 public ArrayList annualAmortTable(LoanVO loan)
        throws LoanObjectException {
  return doAmortTable(loan, 12);
 }

 public ArrayList monthlyAmortTable(LoanVO loan)
        throws LoanObjectException {
  return doAmortTable(loan, 1);
 }

// Business method monthlyPayment; calls helper
// method getPayment().
 public double monthlyPayment(LoanVO loan)
        throws LoanObjectException {
  return getPayment(loan);
 }
```

Listing 3.6 LoanBean.java *(continued)*

```
// EJB Methods
public LoanBean() {}
public void ejbCreate() {}
public void ejbRemove() {}
public void ejbActivate() {}
public void ejbPassivate() {}
public void setSessionContext(SessionContext sc) {}

} // LoanBean
```

The `getPayment()` method contains the math to do payment calculations for `LoanVo` objects. Both `monthlyAmortTable()` and `annualAmortTable()` call private method `doAmortTable()` with the `LoanVO` object and the `time_period` as arguments. The `doAmortTable()` method builds an `ArrayList` of `PaymentVO` objects within a loop based on the number of payments in the life of the loan. Depending on the value of integer `time_period`, this method creates a new `PaymentVO` instance based on the calculations for the data and adds this payment object to the `ArrayList` collection. In each iteration, we decrement the balance by the principal, add the current interest to the accumulated interest, add the current principal to the accumulated principal, and add one month to the current date. This is true business logic in action, hidden inside the EJB.

Compiling, Packaging, and Deployment

Now that you've seen the Loan EJB design, let's show you how to compile, package, and deploy our stateless EJB. Although the steps are dependent on your J2EE application server and the tools you are using, we'll discuss each step separately. You can follow along even if the details of your development system differ somewhat. Figure 3–3 is an activity diagram showing the relationship of these three steps. Figure 3–4 and Figure 3–5 expand the packaging and deployment steps.

Compiling

First, we must build **.class** files from the Java programs. In any large-scale application, some sort of makefile tool, such as the public domain `ant` utility can be handy. Here, we simply use `javac` to compile our source files on the command line. The `-classpath` argument (`$CPATH`) specifies **j2ee.jar**, the J2EE JAR file that contains the EJB support classes.

```
$ javac -classpath "$CPATH" LoanVO.java Loan.java
LoanBean.java LoanHome.java PaymentVO.java LoanVO.java
```

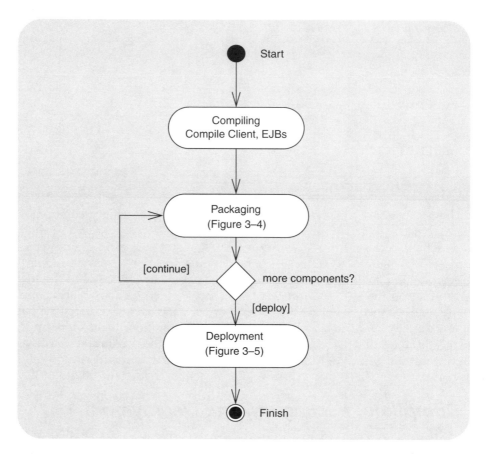

Figure 3–3 Activity Diagram Showing the Steps to Compile, Package, and Deploy an Enterprise Application

This compilation step produces all the **.class** files we need for our Loan EJB example, including the helper classes PaymentVO and LoanVO.

Packaging

Packaging an EJB involves not only placing the required **.class** files into a JAR file, but you must also package the JAR file into an enterprise application EAR (Enterprise ARchive) file. For any type of J2EE component, you must first create a J2EE application (or add a component to an existing J2EE application). An enterprise application may contain one or more EJBs, web components (such as a JSP component or a servlet), and an application client.

Sun Microsystems provides a reference implementation that includes a deployment tool called **deploytool**. This tool allows bean developers to perform the steps necessary to package an enterprise bean within a J2EE applica-

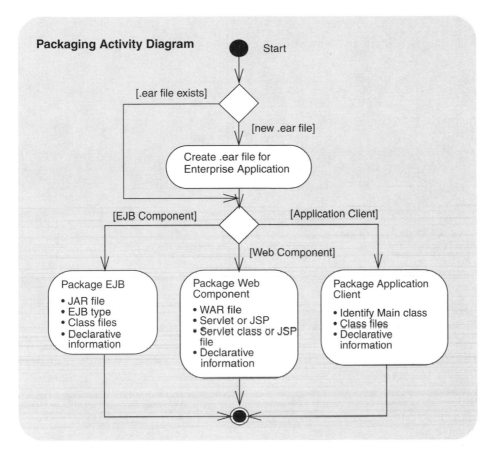

Figure 3–4 Activity Diagram Showing the Steps to Package an Enterprise Component Within an Enterprise Application **.ear** File

tion. As you package the components, the deployment tool steps you through the appropriate screens. The deployment tool generates each component's deployment descriptor for you from the declaration information you provide.

The deployment descriptor describes a component's deployment settings for the application server. An enterprise bean's deployment settings include the names of the home interface, the remote interface, and the bean implementation class. The deployment descriptor also specifies bean type (session or entity), and stateful or stateless for session beans.

The deployment descriptor is implemented in an XML file. Extensible Markup Language (XML) is a portable, text-based specification language for defining text-based data. Any program or tool that uses the XML API (JAXP) can read the data, making deployment descriptors portable among many application servers. Furthermore, an administrator who is in charge of deploy-

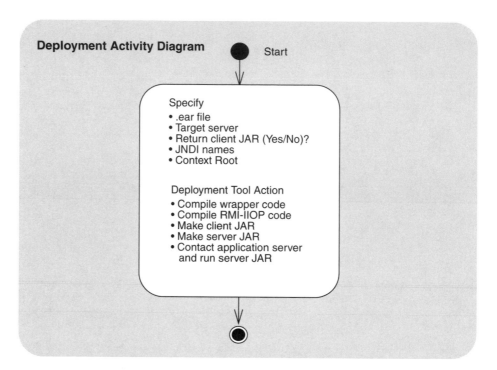

Deployment Activity Diagram   Start

Specify
• .ear file
• Target server
• Return client JAR (Yes/No)?
• JNDI names
• Context Root

Deployment Tool Action
• Compile wrapper code
• Compile RMI-IIOP code
• Make client JAR
• Make server JAR
• Contact application server
  and run server JAR

Figure 3–5 Activity Diagram Showing the Steps to Deploy an Enterprise Application

ing applications can change deployment settings without modifying a bean's source code.

Listing 3.7 is the deployment descriptor created by Sun's **deploytool** for our Loan EJB. We show the tag values in **bold** to enhance readability.

Listing 3.7 Deployment Descriptor for Loan EJB

```
<ejb-jar>
 <display-name>LoanJAR</display-name>
 <enterprise-beans>

   <session>
      <display-name>LoanEJB</display-name>
      <ejb-name>LoanEJB</ejb-name>
      <home>LoanHome</home>
      <remote>Loan</remote>
      <ejb-class>LoanBean</ejb-class>
```

Listing 3.7 Deployment Descriptor for Loan EJB *(continued)*

```
        <session-type>Stateless</session-type>
        <transaction-type>Bean</transaction-type>

        <security-identity>
          <description></description>
          <use-caller-identity></use-caller-identity>
        </security-identity>

      </session>
    </enterprise-beans>
  </ejb-jar>
```

XML encloses each tag in brackets (`<tag>`) then terminates the definition with `</tag>`. The deployment tool uses `<display-name>` and `<ejb-name>` to access the name of our bean (`LoanEJB`). We specify the `Session` bean classes and interfaces with tags `<home>` (home interface `LoanHome`), `<remote>` (remote interface `Loan`) and `<ejb-class>` (bean implementation class `LoanBean`). The tag `<session-type>` flags our `LoanEJB` as a stateless session bean. The `<transaction-type>` tag specifies `Bean` because our EJB does not have methods that require transaction control. This tells the EJB container not to generate any transaction-control code for our methods. Definitions for `<security-identity>` are empty.

Deployment

Before deployment, a J2EE application server must be running. The deployment tool's job is to prepare all components of an enterprise application for the J2EE server. For an EJB component, the deployment tool compiles the "stub" classes, loads the EJB JAR files, and binds coded names to the JNDI names. Although the deployment process loads the JAR file for the EJB container, the EJB does not truly exist until a remote client calls `create()` through the home interface.

3.3 Stand-alone Java Application Client

Well, we've certainly done a lot of work to create and deploy our EJB. Now let's show you a client that uses it.

Our first example is a stand-alone Java application that runs on a client machine. We use a command-line interface to keep the client simple. The program accesses our Loan EJB running in the business tier, possibly on a different machine.

The client program hard-codes loan values and invokes methods in the Loan remote interface. We create a Loan Value Object (LoanVO) with $90,000 for the loan amount, 6.85 % for the interest rate, and 15 years for the term. Because we don't provide a start date, the LoanVO constructor uses today's date.

The first part of the client program calls monthly_payment() to generate monthly payment information for the input values. Next, we call monthlyAmortTable() to generate a monthly amortization table. Finally, we call annualAmortTable() to generate an annual amortization table. Listing 3.8 shows the code for our client program in **AmortClient.java**.

Listing 3.8 AmortClient.java

```
// AmortClient.java
import javax.naming.Context;
import javax.naming.InitialContext;
import javax.rmi.PortableRemoteObject;
import java.util.*;
import java.text.*;

public class AmortClient {

   public static void main(String[] args) {
     try {
       // Format monetary values with 2 places to right
       // of decimal point, use $ sign and comma separator
       DecimalFormat money = new
                 DecimalFormat("$###,###.00");
       // Format percentage values with 3 places
       // to right of decimal point
       DecimalFormat percent = new DecimalFormat("##.000");

       // Format dates using 3 letter month and 4 digit year
       SimpleDateFormat date =
         new SimpleDateFormat("MMM yyyy");

       // Get initial context and lookup coded
       // name for Loan EJB
       Context initial = new InitialContext();
       Object objref = initial.lookup(
               "java:comp/env/ejb/MyLoan");
```

Listing 3.8 AmortClient.java *(continued)*

```java
// Get a handle to the home interface
LoanHome home = (LoanHome)
        PortableRemoteObject.narrow
        (objref,LoanHome.class);
// Instantiate the Loan EJB
Loan loanEJB = home.create();

// Create a Loan Value Object, loan amount = $90,000
// interest rate = 6.85 %, and term = 15 years
LoanVO myloan = new LoanVO(90000, 6.85, 15);

// Invoke business method to find out monthly payment
double monthly_payment =
        loanEJB.monthlyPayment(myloan);

// Display the monthly payment information
System.out.println("Loan Amount\t"
    + money.format(myloan.getAmount()));
System.out.println("Interest Rate\t"
    + percent.format(myloan.getRate()) + "%");
System.out.println("Loan Term\t" + myloan.getYears()
    + " Years");
System.out.println("Monthly P&I\t"
    + money.format(monthly_payment));

// Get a monthly amortization table
ArrayList table = loanEJB.monthlyAmortTable(myloan);
System.out.println("Pay #\tMonth\tBalance" +
    "\tInterest\tPrincipal\tInterest\tPrincipal");

// Use Iterator to loop through ArrayList table
Iterator i = table.iterator();
while (i.hasNext()) {
  PaymentVO p = (PaymentVO)i.next();

  // Display payment information
  // for each PaymentVO object
  System.out.print(p.getPaymentNumber() + "\t");

  System.out.print(
    date.format(p.getPaymentDate().getTime())
    + "\t");
  System.out.print(money.format(p.getBalance())
    + "\t");
```

Listing 3.8 AmortClient.java *(continued)*

```
        System.out.print(money.format(
            p.getCurrentInterest()) + "\t");
        System.out.print(money.format(
            p.getCurrentPrincipal()) + "\t");
        System.out.print(money.format(
            p.getAccumInterest()) + "\t");
        System.out.print(money.format(
            p.getAccumPrincipal()) + "\n");
    } // end while loop

    // Get an annual amortization table:
    table = loanEJB.annualAmortTable(myloan);
    System.out.println("Pay #\tMonth\tBalance" +
        "\tInterest\tPrincipal\tInterest\tPrincipal");

    // Use Iterator to loop through ArrayList table
    i = table.iterator();
    while (i.hasNext()) {
      PaymentVO p = (PaymentVO)i.next();

      // Display payment information
      // for each PaymentVO object
      System.out.print(p.getPaymentNumber() + "\t");
      System.out.print(date.format(
        p.getPaymentDate().getTime()) + "\t");
      System.out.print(money.format(
          p.getBalance()) + "\t");

      System.out.print(money.format(
          p.getCurrentInterest()) + "\t");
      System.out.print(money.format(
          p.getCurrentPrincipal()) + "\t");
      System.out.print(money.format(
          p.getAccumInterest()) + "\t");
      System.out.print(money.format(
          p.getAccumPrincipal()) + "\n");
    } // end while loop

    // Create a bad Loan Value Object
    // to generate an exception
    myloan = new LoanVO(1000, 6.85, 0);
    // Invoke business method to find out monthly payment
    monthly_payment = loanEJB.monthlyPayment(myloan);
```

Listing 3.8 AmortClient.java *(continued)*

```
    } catch (LoanObjectException ex) {
      System.err.println(ex.getMessage());
    } catch (Exception ex) {
      System.err.println(
          "Caught an unexpected exception!");
    } finally {
      System.exit(0);
    }
  }
} // AmortClient
```

Any code that accesses an EJB must import the J2EE classes `Context`, `InitialContext`, and `PortableRemoteObject` from the Java packages shown. Client code uses these classes to find the EJB's home interface from the context and coded names.

Our client uses `Iterator` and `ArrayList` from the `java.util` package to manage the payment data collection. `DecimalFormat` and `SimpleDateFormat` (from package `java.text`) help with formatting decimal numbers and dates. To deal with money values, we create a `DecimalFormat` object (money) that specifies two digits to the right of the decimal point, a comma separator for thousands and millions, and a preceding dollar sign. Percent values use another `DecimalFormat` object (percent) that requires three digits to the right of the decimal point. We don't need a separator for thousands since we expect percent values to be in the range of 0 to 99.999.

We also want a simple way to display dates. For loan payments we are only concerned with the month and year. A `SimpleDateFormat` object called date that specifies the month as a three-letter abbreviation and four-digit year does the job.

Here's the output from the first part of our client application, showing the monthly payment for the specified loan.

```
Loan Amount      $90,000.00
Interest Rate    6.850%
Loan Term        15 Years
Monthly P&I      $801.42
```

Next, the client displays monthly amortizations.

Pay #	Month	Balance	Interest	Principal	Interest	Principal
0	Oct 2001	$90,000.00	$.00	$.00	$.00	$.00
1	Nov 2001	$89,712.33	$513.75	$287.67	$513.75	$287.67
2	Dec 2001	$89,423.02	$512.11	$289.31	$1,025.86	$576.98
3	Jan 2002	$89,132.06	$510.46	$290.96	$1,536.31	$867.94
4	Feb 2002	$88,839.44	$508.80	$292.62	$2,045.11	$1,160.56
5	Mar 2002	$88,545.15	$507.13	$294.29	$2,552.24	$1,454.85
	. . .					
177	Jul 2016	$2,377.06	$18.04	$783.38	$54,227.82	$87,622.94
178	Aug 2016	$1,589.21	$13.57	$787.85	$54,241.39	$88,410.79
179	Sep 2016	$796.87	$9.07	$792.34	$54,250.46	$89,203.13
180	Oct 2016	$.00	$4.55	$796.87	$54,255.01	$90,000.00

The last part of the client program displays yearly amortizations for the life of the loan.

Pay #	Month	Balance	Interest	Principal	Interest	Principal
0	Oct 2001	$90,000.00	$.00	$.00	$.00	$.00
12	Oct 2002	$86,437.53	$495.16	$306.25	$6,054.53	$3,562.47
	. . .					
180	Oct 2016	$.00	$4.55	$796.87	$54,255.01	$90,000.00

Design Guideline

Why does the client contain the code to format money and dates? Why don't we provide formatting inside our enterprise bean? In large-scale enterprise applications we want to keep the business methods that represent business processes in the EJB tier. Formatting and display issues do not belong in the EJB tier. In our application, the business processes manipulate money and date values. How we display these values in client code, however, belongs in the presentation tier. Since our example is simplistic, we provide the formatting inside our client application. In a large-scale application, you might use a JSP tag library to create formatting objects, similar to the DecimalFormat *and* SimpleDateFormat *objects we show here.*

Code Development Tip

In writing and testing client applications that use Java classes not in EJB code, write separate programs to test and debug this non-EJB code. The edit-compile-run cycle is much faster when you are not accessing remote objects and redeploying. For example, to experiment with different formats for decimal number and date values, there is no need to use the data generated by the Loan EJB. Once the formatting strings are to your liking, you can import the code into your EJB client application.

Compiling and Packaging the Client Application

Compiling

To compile the client on the command line, we run the `javac` command with the `-classpath` option. The `$CPATH` environment variable contains the full pathname of the JAR file required to compile programs with EJB components. In our development environment (the Sun reference implementation), the JAR file is **j2ee.jar** and resides in the `lib` subdirectory containing the J2EE software. Our application source file is **AmortClient.java**. Here's how we compile the application on our system using `ksh` (Korn shell) on the command line.

```
$ javac -classpath "$CPATH" AmortClient.java
```

Packaging

You must package your client into an application client JAR file. This JAR file contains the deployment descriptor and the **.class** files for the client. An application client container manages the execution of the client component for a given J2EE application. The application client container and any client components execute on the client machine.

Listing 3.9 shows the deployment descriptor that our deployment tool creates for the `AmortClient` application.

Listing 3.9 Deployment Descriptor for AmortClient Application

```
<application-client>
  <display-name>AmortClient</display-name>
  <ejb-ref>
     <ejb-ref-name>ejb/MyLoan</ejb-ref-name>
     <ejb-ref-type>Session</ejb-ref-type>

     <home>LoanHome</home>
     <remote>Loan</remote>
  </ejb-ref>
</application-client>
```

Note that the deployment descriptor specifies a reference to the Loan EJB under the <ejb-ref> tag. This includes the coded name (ejb/MyLoan), the fact that Loan EJB is a Session bean, its home interface (LoanHome), and its remote interface (Loan).

Running the Stand-alone Java Client Application

Once we've created the enterprise application EAR file and packaged both the EJB and application client into JAR files, we're ready to run the client application. Remember that even though you may develop your enterprise application on the same machine as the application server, the client and the EJBs typically interact across a network from different machines.

Starting the J2EE Application Server

Regardless of whether you're running Sun's J2EE research implementation or an application server from another vendor, you must start a J2EE application server before running any clients. In Sun's implementation, the following command fires up a J2EE server in verbose mode (suggested).

```
$ j2ee -verbose
```

After the server completes its initialization, you'll see the message

```
J2EE server startup complete.
```

Deployment

With a vendor-provided deployment tool, you can deploy the enterprise application once the J2EE application server is running. The deployment process compiles any "stubs" required by EJB components and loads the EJB JAR files in the EJB container.

Running the J2EE Application Client

You must specify three files to run an application client: the J2EE application EAR file (**LoanApp.ear**), the name of the client class (AmortClient), and the application JAR file (**AmortAppClient.jar**). If you are running the client on a different machine than the application server, you'll need to specify the name of the host that's running the J2EE server, too.

Sun's reference implementation provides a runclient command that bundles arguments for application clients. The commands we use to start up our stand-alone Java client (with the J2EE server running as localhost) is

```
$ APPCPATH=LoanAppClient.jar; export APPCPATH
$ runclient -client LoanApp.ear -name AmortClient
```

If you're a C shell user, the syntax for initializing environment variable APPCPATH is slightly different.

```
% setenv APPCPATH LoanAppClient.jar
% runclient -client LoanApp.ear -name AmortClient
```

There's a lot of output from this client program, so it's perhaps best to redirect it to a file. Otherwise you will see the result in all its glory, including monthly payment information, a monthly amortization schedule (181 lines plus headers) and an annual amortization schedule (16 lines plus headers). This should be more than enough to help you analyze your refinancing.

3.4 Web Component Client (JSP Client)

A stand-alone Java application is appropriate when the client performs an administrative function on a specific machine with a limited user base. A web component client, on the other hand, can run on any machine with a web browser as long as it is connected to a J2EE application server (either directly or across the Internet). In this section, we'll create a JSP component that is a typical browser-based procedure. This JSP program will be a web-enabled version of the Loan EJB client that we showed you in the previous section.

Introducing Servlets and JSP

If you are already familiar with JSP and servlets, you can skip this section. JSP is really just a front end for servlets, so let's provide an overview of the Java servlet architecture first. Readers wishing a more in-depth treatment can read the Prentice Hall text *Core Servlets and JavaServer Pages™* by Marty Hall.

A servlet is a server-side Java software component that allows two-way interaction between a client and server. Servlets execute on a Java-enabled web server and are an efficient and effective way to produce dynamic page content for web-based applications. The web server loads servlets once but each request spawns a new thread rather than a new process. Because the Java Virtual Machine (JVM) executes servlet bytecode, the server is protected from poorly written or malicious servlets. Furthermore, Java provides strong type checking and exception handling to help servlet designers write robust code. Servlets provide support for HTTP protocol, although servlet technology is not specifically limited to HTTP.

HttpServlet Class

The `HttpServlet` class is abstract so you can subclass and create your own HTTP servlet. To do this, you must override one or more methods. The two most important methods are `doGet()` and `doPost()`. The server calls `doGet()` to handle HTTP GET requests and `doPost()` to handle HTTP POST requests.

The `HttpServlet` class defines several useful objects. `HttpServletRequest` encapsulates client request information and `HttpServletResponse` contains information returned to the client. The `HttpSession` object also provides `putValue()` and `getValue()` methods, which store and retrieve session data associated by string names.

JSP Engine

Java Server Pages (JSP) provide dynamic content for web pages. With JSP, you can embed Java source code within HTML source files. When a client requests a JSP's URL, the JSP engine (running within the web server) generates Java source code that uses the Servlet API. The web container compiles the servlet code and instantiates a Java thread to execute the servlet. By writing Java code within our JSP source file, we can access other components within the J2EE architecture, such as enterprise Java beans. JSP programs are simpler to write than servlets because the JSP engine generates servlet code for you.

JSP has several types of programming elements: declarations, scriptlets, expressions, directives, implicit objects, and comments. During initialization, the server invokes the `jspInit()` method if you provide one. The server also places scriptlets and expressions inside the generated `_jspService()` method, and calls `jspDestroy()` (if provided) during shutdown. The `jspInit()` routine is a good spot to place one-time initializations.

Let's examine these JSP elements now.

JSP Comments

The JSP tags `<%--` and `--%>` surround comments, which do not appear in the generated HTML source file. Here's an example of a JSP comment that documents the name of our JSP program.

```
<%--
   paymentGet.jsp
--%>
```

Declarations

A JSP declaration starts with `<%!` and terminates with `%>`. We use JSP declarations to define class-wide variables and methods. Variables declared within JSP declarations appear *outside* the `_jspService()` method. These class-wide variables are initialized when the JSP page is created and have class scope. Here's an example.

```
<%!
   private Loan loanEJB = null;
   DecimalFormat money = new DecimalFormat("$###,###.00");
   DecimalFormat percent = new DecimalFormat("##.000");
%>
```

Scriptlets

A scriptlet is a block of Java code executed at request-processing time. The JSP engine compiles scriptlet code in the order that it appears in your program and places it *inside* the `_jspService()` method of the generated servlet. Scriptlets appear within the JSP tags `<%` and `%>`. The following scriptlet instantiates a Java `Date` object and writes it to the servlet response stream (`out`), along with some HTML formatting tags.

```
<%
  out.println("<h1>Example using scriptlet</h1>");
  out.println("<h2>Hello, today is " +
        new java.util.Date() + "</h2>");
%>
```

Expressions

An expression is a shorthand notation for a scriptlet that outputs a value in the servlet response stream. Like scriptlets, the generated code appears *inside* the servlet's _jspService() method. During request processing, the Java VM evaluates the expression and converts it to a Java string. JSP expressions are extremely convenient for writing HTML code without those tedious out.println() statements. Use JSP tags <%= and %> to embed expressions. The following HTML code contains embedded expressions and is arguably more readable than its equivalent scriptlet presented above.

```
<h1>Example using expressions</h1>
<h2>Hello, today is <%= new java.util.Date() %></h2>
```

Implicit Objects

A JSP program instantiates several implicit objects through the automatically generated servlet code. These implicit objects simplify JSP authoring because you do not need to declare or instantiate them. Implicit objects are *not* available inside JSP declarations, but they are available inside scriptlets and expressions. The following table lists several of the most commonly used implicit objects.

Table 3.2 Commonly Used Implicit Objects

Object	Scope	Use
request	Request scope	Encapsulates the request; passed as a parameter to _jspService()
response	Page scope	Encapsulates the response; returned as a parameter to _jspService()
out	Page scope	Sends output to client
session	Session scope	Encapsulates session state
exception	Page scope	Refers to runtime exception that resulted in error page being invoked; only available in error page

One of the important implicit objects is the `request` object, which is an instance of `javax.servlet.ServletRequest`. This object is passed to the JSP by the web container as a parameter to the automatically generated `_jspService()` method. The `request` object has "request scope," which means that it is available to all pages processing the same request. A useful `ServletRequest` method is `getRequestURI()`, which saves the URL of the current page for later navigation.

The implicit `session` object is an instance of `javax.servlet.http.HttpSession`. This object has "session scope," which means that the same user may share multiple requests. Session objects are convenient for saving and restoring session state in applications where the size of the data is small and easily managed. This is done with the session object's `putValue()` and `getValue()` methods.

JSP Directives

The JSP tags `<%@` and `%>` surround JSP directives. Directives are messages to the JSP engine from the JSP file. They do not produce any output to the client. JSP directives have page scope (the results of the directives are available to actions and scriptlets within one page). In the following example, we use a page directive to import Java classes for our Loan EJB. (Without the correct classes named in the import directive, a compilation error occurs when the JSP engine compiles the generated Java servlet code.)

```
<%@ page import="LoanVO,Loan,LoanHome,javax.ejb.*,
javax.naming.*, javax.rmi.PortableRemoteObject,
java.rmi.RemoteException, java.util.*, java.text.*" %>
```

The JSP payment Client

Our JSP `payment` program presents an HTML form entitled "Monthly Payment Calculator" which prompts a user for a loan amount, annual interest rate, and term. Figure 3–6 shows the initial screen for this JSP program. After providing input values, the user clicks the "Calculate" button. Figure 3–7 shows the result of this calculation. The program displays the Monthly Payment (Principal and Interest) for the loan values that the user provided. To recalculate, the user clicks "Calculate with Different Parameters" which returns to the original page and saves the most recent input values.

If you're shopping for a home loan or refinancing, this is a handy program to run from your browser.

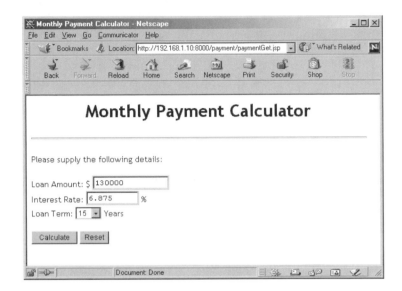

Figure 3–6 Initial Screen for the Monthly Payment Calculator

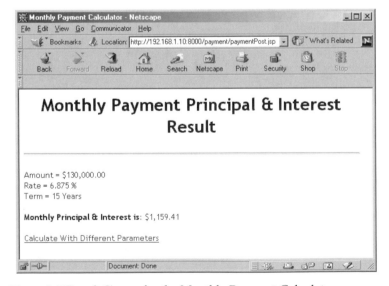

Figure 3–7 Result Screen for the Monthly Payment Calculator

paymentGet.jsp

The payment web component consists of two JSP files. The first program, **paymentGet.jsp**, collects user input, encapsulates data in a request object, and invokes the second program (**paymentPost.jsp**) to perform the monthly payment calculation. We store user request input in the HttpSession object (in program **paymentPost.jsp**). With this approach, the user doesn't have to provide all the data fields each time.

Listing 3.10 is the source code for **paymentGet.jsp** with comments to help explain the JSP tags.

Listing 3.10 paymentGet.jsp

```
<%--
  paymentGet.jsp
--%>

<%--
  The following scriptlet assigns the current URL to String
  requestURI and then stores this object into the implicit
  session object.
  We then attempt to assign to variables
  s_amount, s_rate, and s_term values stored previously
  in the session object.

  Obviously, the first time the user executes this page,
  these values will be null.
  To avoid null String runtime errors, we assign
  the empty String "" to them if they're indeed null.

  We use this mechanism to save the user's input data.
  Then the user only has to provide input
  for those parameters he or she wants to
  change for subsequent calculation requests.
--%>

<%
  String requestURI = request.getRequestURI();
  session.putValue("url", requestURI);
  String s_amount = (String)session.getValue("amount");
  String s_rate = (String)session.getValue("rate");
  String s_term = (String)session.getValue("term");
```

Listing 3.10 paymentGet.jsp *(continued)*

```
    if (s_amount == null) s_amount = "";
    if (s_rate == null) s_rate = "";
    if (s_term == null) s_term = "";
%>

<html>
<head>
    <title>Monthly Payment Calculator</title>
</head>

<body bgcolor=white>
<h1><b><center>
Monthly Payment Calculator
</center></b></h1>

<hr>
<p>
Please supply the following details:
<p>

<%--
  The HTML tag <form> allows us to request user input
  and provide this data to the URL named in the
  action argument: paymentPost.jsp.

  The form's elements include textual input
  to specify the loan amount,
  textual input to specify the rate,
  and a select element that requests
  one of three term lengths, 15, 20, or 30 years.
  We use expressions to provide default values
  for the amount and rate form input elements.
--%>

<form method="post" action="paymentPost.jsp">
Loan Amount: $
<input type="text" name="amount" value="<%= s_amount %>"
size="15">
<br>

Interest Rate:
<input type="text" name="rate" value="<%= s_rate %>"
size="10"> %
<br>
```

Listing 3.10 paymentGet.jsp *(continued)*

```
Loan Term:
<select name="term">

<%--
  The following scriptlet checks the value of s_term
  to determine the default value for the select element.
--%>

<%
    if (s_term.equals("30"))
      out.println("<option selected value=\"30\">30");
    else
      out.println("<option value=\"30\">30");
    if (s_term.equals("20"))
      out.println("<option selected value=\"20\">20");
    else
      out.println("<option value=\"20\">20");

    if (s_term.equals("15"))
      out.println("<option selected value=\"15\">15");
    else
      out.println("<option value=\"15\">15");
%>

</select> Years
<p>

<%--
  The user clicks "Calculate"
  to submit the input data to the JSP named
  in the form tag action argument.
  Clicking "Reset" returns
  the input values to their default settings.
--%>

<input type="submit" value="Calculate">
<input type="reset" value="Reset">
</form>
</body>
</html>
```

Design Guideline

Our application is very simple, so we store session data inside the implicit session *object. In large-scale J2EE applications, it is preferable to save session state inside an EJB component. If the session state represents persistent data, use an entity bean to save the data to permanent storage (a database). If the session state represents conversational state (data relevant throughout the session), use a stateful session bean.*

paymentPost.jsp

Now let's examine the second JSP program of our payment web component. File **paymentPost.jsp** in Listing 3.11 illustrates a few more features of JSP programming and shows the true power and ease of using JSP to interface with EJB components. This program parses user input and creates instances of our Loan EJB and LoanVO objects. The program also invokes the Loan EJB's monthlyPayment() method, displays the results of the calculation, and saves the values submitted by the user in a session object for subsequent calculations.

Listing 3.11 paymentPost.jsp

```
<%--
  paymentPost.jsp
--%>

<%--
  The following page directive tells the JSP engine to
  import the named classes and packages when compiling
  the generated servlet code.
--%>

<%@ page import="LoanVO,Loan,LoanHome,
LoanObjectException,javax.ejb.*,
javax.naming.*,javax.rmi.PortableRemoteObject,
java.rmi.RemoteException, java.text.*" %>

<%--
  The following declaration defines class-wide variables
  and methods jspInit() and jspDestroy().
  Recall that these declarations have class scope.
  We must place any method declarations inside a JSP
  declaration.
```

Listing 3.11 paymentPost.jsp *(continued)*

```
We declare a Loan remote interface object and
initialize it to null.

We also declare two DecimalFormat objects
(money and percent)
to format money values and percent values.

The web server invokes jspInit() during initialization
and jspDestroy() during shutdown.
We put our EJB lookup() and create() calls in jspInit(),
making this a one-time initialization.
--%>

<%!
  private Loan loanEJB = null;
  DecimalFormat money = new DecimalFormat("$###,###.00");
  DecimalFormat percent = new DecimalFormat("##.000");

  public void jspInit() {
      try {
          InitialContext ic = new InitialContext();
          Object objRef = ic.lookup(
                "java:comp/env/ejb/TheLoan");
          LoanHome home =
                (LoanHome)PortableRemoteObject.narrow(
                objRef, LoanHome.class);
          loanEJB = home.create();

      } catch (Exception ex) {
        System.out.println("Unexpected Exception: "
                + ex.getMessage());
      }
  }

  public void jspDestroy() {
        loanEJB = null;
  }
%>
```

Listing 3.11 paymentPost.jsp *(continued)*

```jsp
<%--
  The following scriptlet accesses the implicit
  session object to obtain the URL of the
  request page.
  It then accesses the implicit request object
  to obtain the user input values for the loan
  amount, rate, and term.

  It stores these values into the session object
  to use as the new default values
  in the request page.
--%>

<%
  String requestURI = (String)session.getValue("url");
  String s_amount =
            (String)request.getParameter("amount");

  String s_rate = (String)request.getParameter("rate");
  String s_term = (String)request.getParameter("term");

  session.putValue("amount", s_amount);
  session.putValue("rate", s_rate);
  session.putValue("term", s_term);
%>

<html>
<head>
    <title>Monthly Payment Calculator</title>
</head>

<body bgcolor=white>
<h1><b><center>
Monthly Payment Principal & Interest Result
</center></b></h1>
<hr>

<%
  Double d_amount;
  Double d_rate;
  int i_term;
  String errorString = null;
```

Listing 3.11 paymentPost.jsp *(continued)*

```
// We make sure all parameters have valid values by
// placing the Double constructor call and Integer's
// parseInt() call in a try block.
// These routines generate a NumberFormatException
// if the user input contains non-numerical characters
// or other formatting anomalies.

try {
  d_amount = new Double (s_amount);
  d_rate = new Double (s_rate);
  i_term = Integer.parseInt(s_term);

  // We create a LoanVO object with the user supplied
  // values and invoke our Loan EJB's business method
  // monthlyPayment().

  LoanVO myloan = new LoanVO(d_amount.doubleValue(),
       d_rate.doubleValue(),i_term);

  double monthly_payment =
       loanEJB.monthlyPayment(myloan);
%>

  <p>
  Amount = <%= money.format(d_amount.doubleValue()) %>
  <br>
  Rate = <%= percent.format(d_rate.doubleValue()) %> %
  <br>
  Term = <%= s_term %> Years
  <br>
  <p>
  <b>Monthly Principal & Interest is: </b>
  <%= money.format(monthly_payment) %>
  <p>

<%
  } catch (NumberFormatException ex) {
  // This is the catch handler for bad user input.
    errorString = "You have left a field empty or " +
      "specified an incorrect value for a number.<br>" +
      "Make sure there are no special characters, " +
      "commas, or symbols embedded in the numbers.";
```

Listing 3.11 paymentPost.jsp *(continued)*

```
    } catch (LoanObjectException ex) {
    // This is the catch handler for
    // bad LoanVO object values.
        errorString = "Loan amount must be at least 1 " +
            "<br>and rate cannot be zero.";
    }
    if (errorString != null) {

    // We use html formatting tags to create an error box
    // to display errorString
    // with red lettering so that it will stand out.
%>

<p STYLE="background:#e0e0e0;color:red;
font-weight:bold;border:double thin;padding:10">
<%= errorString %>
</font>
</center>

<%
    } // end if
%>

<%--
   We use an expression inside the html href tag to provide
   a dynamic link to the previous request page.
--%>

<p><a href="<%= requestURI %>">
Calculate With Different Parameters</a>
</body>
</html>
```

The Role of a JSP Client

What is the role of a JSP within a J2EE application and what are the benefits of using JSP? Since JSP is a web component, it is easily accessible to any client with a browser and an Internet connection. JSP components are simpler to write than servlets because the JSP engine automatically generates servlet code for you. Furthermore, JSP components are really just HTML files with Java code interspersed, so they look more like HTML than Java. The ability to use Java, however, allows developers to provide dynamic content. With JSP, developers can write code to interface with servlets, EJBs, and JavaBeans. Hence, JSP is best used for the "View" or "Presentation" portion of a J2EE application.

In our example, we use JSP to prompt for user input and invoke a business method in our Loan EJB. Once we have the calculation results, simple HTML code within the JSP formats output for the user.

After examining the code in our Loan EJB, you may wonder why we don't just put the monthly payment calculation directly inside the JSP? After all, we could easily write a `monthlyPayment()` method and place it in a JSP declaration.

The answer is that keeping `monthlyPayment()` as a business method of the Loan EJB provides more flexibility. Inside the JSP, `monthlyPayment()` would only be available to that specific JSP. As part of the remote interface of an enterprise Java bean, however, we can access `monthlyPayment()` from other enterprise Java beans, a Java application client (such as application client `AmortClient` shown earlier), a servlet, or even another JSP.

Our Loan EJB is meant to provide a well-defined business process that can be invoked from many different clients. In general, JSP programs should not provide business processes.

Packaging the Web Component

You will most likely use a deployment tool to package the JSP web component. Web components belong in Web Archive (WAR) files which have the same format as JAR files, but with a **.war** extension. JSP pages go directly into the WAR file; the web designer does not "compile" them. At request processing time, the JSP engine (a part of the J2EE application server) transforms the JSP source files into servlet Java source. The Java compiler creates **.class** files which are executed within a new thread instantiated by the application server.

During the packaging process, you specify any EJB references (in this case, our JSP references the Loan EJB). You will also specify a Context Root (which is like a home directory for "finding" web components) and an alias for naming the initial JSP page. In our example, the Context Root is `payment` and the alias is `paymentGet`.

The deployment tool creates a deployment descriptor for the JSP component. Our deployment tool creates the deployment descriptor in Listing 3.12 for the `payment` web component.

Listing 3.12 Deployment Descriptor for JSP

```
<web-app>
 <display-name>PaymentWAR</display-name>
 <servlet>
    <servlet-name>PaymentWAR</servlet-name>
    <display-name>PaymentWAR</display-name>
    <jsp-file>/paymentGet.jsp</jsp-file>
 </servlet>

 <servlet-mapping>
    <servlet-name>PaymentWAR</servlet-name>
    <url-pattern>/paymentGet</url-pattern>
 </servlet-mapping>

 <session-config>
    <session-timeout>30</session-timeout>
 </session-config>

 <ejb-ref>
    <ejb-ref-name>ejb/TheLoan</ejb-ref-name>
    <ejb-ref-type>Session</ejb-ref-type>
    <home>LoanHome</home>
    <remote>Loan</remote>
 </ejb-ref>
</web-app>
```

Note that the deployment descriptor includes the EJB reference information, including its coded name (ejb/TheLoan), type (Session), and the names of the home and remote interfaces (LoanHome and Loan).

Running the Web Client

To run the JSP web component from a browser, you need to specify the URL of the J2EE server machine, the Context Root, and an alias. Here's an example.

http://manny:8000/payment/paymentGet

On port 8000 of machine manny, the Context Root is payment and the alias is paymentGet. If the browser is running on the same machine as the J2EE server, use localhost for the machine name.

3.5   Design Guidelines and Patterns

Even though the Loan EJB is a simple example, it adheres to basic design guidelines common to all enterprise applications. Most importantly, the business methods of an enterprise Java bean are encapsulated into a reusable, distributed component. The business methods perform tasks to accomplish one or more business processes. These business methods are devoid of any formatting or presentation information.

We showed you the Loan EJB's reusability by presenting two different clients: a stand-alone Java application with a simple command-line interface and a JSP client using a browser with HTML. Both clients call EJB business methods and perform the formatting and presentation aspects of the application.

To further explore common J2EE application design guidelines, let's define several terms that were used in our design. We'll introduce more terms in subsequent chapters.

Business Object

A *Business Object* is an object that implements a business process or business data. We typically implement a business process with a Session Bean and business data with an Entity Bean. In a multitier J2EE application, a business object should be part of the business tier. In our Loan EJB example, the Loan Session Bean is a business object.

Controller

A complex J2EE application needs to efficiently handle user input requests and invoke the correct business process as a result of that request. Applications typically use a *Controller* object to perform this function. In web-based clients, a servlet usually acts as a Controller. The Controller is the interface between the *View* (what the client sees) and the *Model* (the data). In our Loan EJB example, the role of the Controller is diminished because both client applications (the JSP client and the stand-alone Java client) are simplistic. The Controller is one part of the triad that implements the Model-View-Controller Pattern.

Enterprise Bean

An *Enterprise Bean* refers to an Enterprise Java Bean component, a component that is accessed remotely within the J2EE architectural specifications. Enterprise Bean objects execute within EJB containers under the supervision of a J2EE application server. Enterprise Bean objects are usually Business Objects and may be either Session Beans, Entity Beans, or Message-Driven Beans. Our Loan EJB is a Session Bean.

Model

The *Model* is the underlying representation of a system. The Model includes objects that represent the data and the business processes. In our Loan J2EE application, the Loan EJB and the LoanVO and PaymentVO value objects are all part of the Model.

The Model is one part of the triad that implements the Model-View-Controller Pattern.

Session Bean

A *Session Bean* is an Enterprise Bean component that typically performs a business process. It may be stateless or stateful. Our Loan EJB is a stateless Session Bean because it does not store client-specific data. A Session Bean is part of the business tier and is an implementation of the Model (along with the LoanVO and PaymentVO objects).

Value Object

A *Value Object* is a Java component that encapsulates data for communicating between an EJB and a remote client. Encapsulating data in value objects is convenient for programming clients and EJB components. Perhaps more importantly, value objects reduce the number of remote calls to an EJB to obtain data with multiple access methods. In our Loan EJB, business method monthlyAmortTable() returns a collection of PaymentVO objects. A single remote call returns all the payment information. If we didn't encapsulate the data inside a PaymentVO object, we would have to make multiple remote calls to an expanded list of business methods that return interest amounts, balances, and so on. As the number of remote calls increases, the performance degrades with increased network overhead.

The Value Object Pattern helps keep network traffic minimized to avoid performance penalties. The Value Object Pattern is easy to implement and is a common design pattern in J2EE applications.

View

Another name for *View* is *Presentation*. View is also one part of the triad that implements the Model-View-Controller Pattern.

A client can look at the same data in more than one way. For example, we present the output of our monthlyAmortTable() business method as a table of monthly payments on separate lines. Another program might present a graph with different colors representing the interest and principal amounts. This program could display the numbers on a horizontal chart with payment dates representing the horizontal axis. The chart would look like an X, with the interest amount starting out high and gradually lowering towards zero. Meanwhile, the principal amount begins low and increases as more of the interest is paid off. Although this presentation is quite different from the first one, the two "views" represent the same underlying data (or model).

An object that is responsible for presenting data to the user is a View object. View objects should be in the Presentation tier of a J2EE application. In an application that might be more complicated than our Loan application, helper objects could perform specialized formatting of the data. These helper objects may be JavaBean components or JSP tag library components.

Although the Loan EJB example is simplistic, we adhere to the separation of Model and View by keeping only Model-related code and data in the EJB and confining the formatting tasks to the client. We collapse the View and Controller parts (again, because our example is simple).

3.6   Key Point Summary

Our first EJB is a stateless session bean with several business processes to calculate monthly payments for long-term, fixed rate loans. We show you how to design and code a stateless session bean and how to write different clients that call its methods. We use the common Value Object pattern to enhance performance and programming convenience. We also describe the steps required to compile the source programs, package the components, and generate the deployment descriptors for the J2EE application server.

As we present the example, we want to explore the design of a J2EE application. We also want to apply design patterns where appropriate. Here are the key points from the chapter.

- Use a session bean to fulfill a business process.
- Use a stateless session bean if the communication between the client and the bean does not require saving state.
- Provide a list of business methods to implement the tasks of a business process. Keep the business methods well defined and avoid including any formatting or presentation code in an EJB.
- List the business methods in the remote interface.
- There is only one `create()` method in the home interface of a stateless session bean.
- Implement the business methods in the bean implementation class.
- Class `LoanObjectException` is an example of an application exception, which represents nonfatal, recoverable errors. The EJB container propagates application exceptions to the remote client. Application exceptions should subclass `Exception`.

- Value objects help encapsulate useful data into a single object, providing performance enhancements and convenient packaging.
- Put business methods in the business tier. Place presentation and formatting code in the presentation tier.
- Package EJB components and helper classes (such as value objects) in an EJB JAR file. You must also include a deployment descriptor in the JAR file.
- A deployment tool will typically generate the deployment descriptor for you. The deployment descriptor includes declarative information about the Enterprise Bean (such as the bean type, the names of the home and remote interfaces, the name of the bean implementation class, and any EJB references or database resources that the bean uses).
- The deployment descriptor is an XML file and can be read by programming tools and J2EE components using the XML API.
- You must deploy an EJB before a client can use it. A deployment tool generates the Java "stubs" required for remote access and makes the EJB available through its coded name. The J2EE application server manages the life cycle of the EJB within the EJB container.

SESSION BEANS WITH JDBC

Topics in This Chapter

- Relational Databases and EJB
- Introducing Java Database Connectivity (JDBC)
- Session Beans as Database Readers
- A Java Swing Application Client
- A JSP Client
- The Data Access Object (DAO) Pattern
- Customizing EJBs with Deployment Descriptors

Chapter 4

Enterprise applications frequently need to access data stored permanently in a database. Depending on the application, it may be necessary to create records, search for records, or manipulate records by performing an update operation to a database. Consider, for instance, a web application allowing customers to purchase products online. This program might need to access a database to read catalog information, find or create customer records, and build purchase orders with line items from the catalog. The application must also store and retrieve purchase order information to fulfill orders, check order status, and assist customers with problems.

This chapter explores Java DataBase Connectivity (JDBC) for database access with EJB applications. Although JDBC is not a part of the Enterprise Bean API, database access is a vital component of the J2EE architecture. In this chapter, we'll show you how to read a database by integrating JDBC into stateless session beans.

4.1 Session Beans and JDBC

Suppose a record store wants to provide users with a way to display recordings from their Music Collection database. If the database is accessible from an EJB, recordings could be available on the web and from computers in the store. The Music EJB will be similar to our Loan EJB from the previous chapter. Using the J2EE architecture, Figure 4–1 shows the design approach.

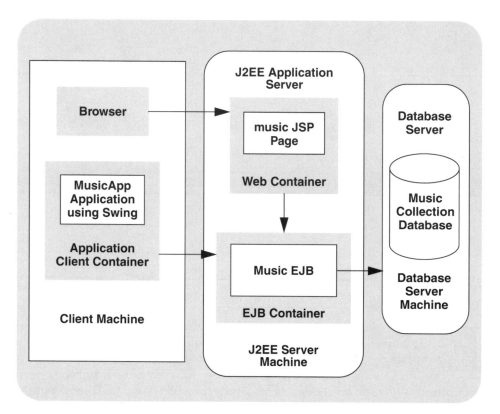

Figure 4–1 Architectural Overview of the Music Collection Enterprise Application

On the database server machine, the Music EJB accesses the Music Collection database in *read-only* mode. Music EJB is a stateless session bean because it does not perform any tasks whose results needs to be saved to persistent storage. This implies multiple clients may share the same instance of the Music EJB with no contention problems.

The Music Collection database has a specific format, which we'll describe shortly. Clients use the Music EJB to access recordings from the database and fetch tracks from a specific recording. To provide this information to the client, the bean implementation class must provide JDBC statements to access the music database and build objects that manage data requested by the client.

Two clients will use the Music EJB: a JSP web component and a stand-alone application with a Java Swing graphical user interface. The application client runs on a client machine, the web and EJB components run on a J2EE server machine, and the database runs on a database server machine.

Because the Music EJB is a stateless session bean, much of its structure should be familiar to you. However, by adding JDBC capability, we create a distributed, multitiered enterprise application that is the foundation for developing larger and more powerful enterprise applications.

Frequently, enterprise developers must create applications that use a preexisting database. A new application might only access a portion of the stored data, or it may create composite objects from data stored in different parts of the database.

Database Fundamentals

Let's begin with an overview of databases and JDBC. We'll discuss database tables and how to use JDBC to access the data. If you're already familiar with these subjects, you can skip to the next section.

A relational database consists of one or more tables, where each row in a table represents a database record and each column represents a field. Within each table, a record must have a unique key. This key, called a *primary key*, enables a database to distinguish one record from another. Database software prevents you from creating records with duplicate primary keys. A field within a table is either a primary key, a *foreign key* (used by the database to reference another table), or just plain data.

A very simple database will consist of a single table. However, many database schemata require multiple tables to efficiently represent related data. For example, in our Music Collection database, we centralize the information about each recording artist in one table, then cross reference a RecordingArtist-ID field in a different table that stores data about the recording itself. Thus, if a recording artist has more than one recording, you don't have to duplicate the recording artist information.

To achieve cross referencing and not duplicate data, a field in a database table may be marked as a foreign key. A foreign key in one table will match either a primary or foreign key in another table. By matching foreign keys to keys in other tables, we "relate" two or more tables.

Music Collection Database

The Music Collection database consists of four related tables. The database stores information about music recordings, a generic term we apply to music CDs and older LPs (long-playing records). Figure 4–2 shows the four tables, the fields in each table, and how they relate to each other through the foreign keys.

The Recordings table contains the bulk of the information about a recording. Its primary key (denoted PK) is the field RecordingID. It has two foreign key fields (denoted FK): RecordingArtistID and MusicCategoryID. These foreign key fields refer to records in the Recording Artists table and the Music Categories table, respectively. For each row in the Music Categories table, there may be multiple rows in the Recordings table. (We indicate this relationship by placing the word **Many** next to the Recordings table and a **1** next to the Music Cate-

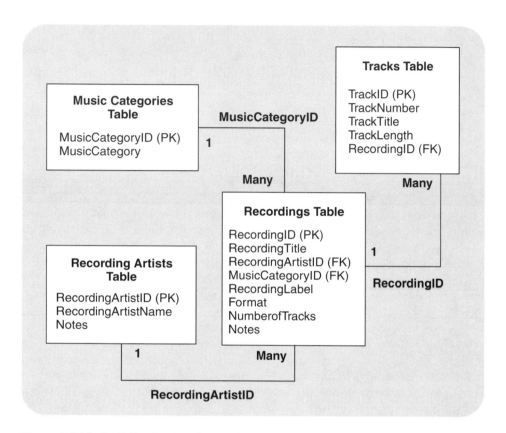

Figure 4–2 Music Collection Database Schema

gories table.) Similarly, for each row in the Recording Artists table, there may be multiple rows in the Recordings table. In the diagram, we show foreign key field names on the arrow lines that relate two tables.

The Tracks table contains the information about each track belonging to a recording. To determine which recording a track belongs to, we include the RecordingID as a foreign key in the Tracks table. Thus, for each row in the Recordings table, there are multiple rows in the Tracks table.

Introducing JDBC

To communicate with a database using the JDBC API, you must obtain a database connection. In the J2EE environment, access to a database resource is done the same way as an Enterprise Java Bean reference. First, you obtain the context and then use the JNDI API to perform a lookup. A successful lookup returns a `DataSource` object, which you use to obtain a connection. Here's an example.

```
// get context and perform a lookup of the coded name
InitialContext ic = new InitialContext();
DataSource ds =
    (DataSource) ic.lookup("java:comp/env/jdbc/MusicDB");
// Obtain a Connection from the DataSource
Connection con = ds.getConnection();
```

To communicate with various database vendors, JDBC provides a Java Driver Manager mechanism to handle the different JDBC drivers. Theoretically, the JDBC API provides access to relational databases from any vendor. The Sun Microsystems reference implementation includes the Cloudscape relational database server with the JDBC driver automatically configured.

(The key word here is *theoretically*. We have found minor differences in SQL punctuation, use of quotation marks, and other special characters among different database vendors. We'll discuss how to cope with these database portability issues later on with the J2EE Data Access Object pattern. See "Data Access Object Pattern" on page 119 of this chapter.)

Design Guideline

When the JDBC software detects a problem, it throws an SQLException. Therefore, you must either place SQL code inside a try block or within a method that includes SQLException in its throws *clause.*

Statement Object

Once you have a connection, the next step is to create an SQL `Statement` object and execute it. The SQL `Select` command lets you search a database for certain records that satisfy some criteria. Calling the `Statement` object's `execute-Query()` method with a `Select` command as a `String` argument makes the database server return the data in a JDBC `ResultSet` object. Here's an example.

```
// con is a Connection object
Statement stmt = con.createStatement();
ResultSet rs = stmt.executeQuery(
  "Select RecordingTitle,RecordingLabel From Recordings");
```

SQL also has `Insert`, `Update`, and `Delete` commands that modify a database. With these commands, you would use the `executeUpdate()` method, which does not return data.

ResultSet Object

JDBC's ResultSet object provides access to the data generated by the SQL Select command. Unfortunately, the ResultSet is a somewhat clumsy object to work with. Basically, it's a table that consists of columns and rows. A cursor points to the current row, where you can extract data from the columns as fields. (You'd better know what data type is in these fields or you'll get gibberish!) Initially, the cursor is positioned before the first row, so you'll have to increment it before grabbing any data. The JDBC 2.0 specification includes ResultSet methods to manipulate the cursor position, but for maximum portability, you should not read the data more than once. (If this is necessary, clone() the ResultSet before reading it.) Accessing the data in a ResultSet object is normally done in a loop, until the ResultSet indicates that there is no more data to read.

A ResultSet object provides a set of getter methods to extract data. The method you use depends on a field's data type. For example, getString(arg) is used for strings and getInt(arg) for longs or shorts. The argument to these methods is an integer representing the ResultSet's column number (starting at column 1) or a field name in the database table. Here's an example.

```
// ResultSet rs is set from previous executeQuery() call
while (rs.next()) {
  String title = rs.getString(1);      // get column 1
  String label = rs.getString(2);      // get column 2
  // do something with title and label
}
```

The ResultSet object provides a next() method to access the data row by row. For each row, we get the first and second fields and store them into strings. The database will return the fields in the order they appear in the query.

Getter methods with field name arguments are not as efficient as integer arguments but may be more maintainable and readable. Looking ahead, the strategy we use is to step through a ResultSet in a loop, instantiate appropriate value objects with data from the ResultSet, and place these objects in a collection (such as ArrayList).

Design Guideline

Recall that since the EJB container oversees thread issues, ArrayList *is a more efficient data collection object than* Vector, *for example. Although both collections grow automatically and are serializable, the fetch and store methods are not synchronized with ArrayList (as they are with* Vector). *So with ArrayList, you do not pay twice for synchronization. And, you can easily manipulate elements with* Iterator *objects.*

PreparedStatement Object

The PreparedStatement object extends Statement and allows precompiled SQL statements, which are more efficient. When you instantiate a Prepared-Statement with the prepareStatement() method of the Connection object, the SQL string is sent to the database and compiled. Any statement that is valid with executeQuery() may be precompiled in a PreparedStatement object.

PreparedStatement objects also provide positional input parameters. Positional parameters (there can be more than one) appear in an SQL string with ? (question mark). Typically, you assign values to positional parameters with PreparedStatement setter methods and then invoke executeQuery() to run the SQL command. Here's an example.

```
// create a PreparedStatement from Connection con
PreparedStatement trackStmt = con.prepareStatement(
    "Select * From Tracks Where RecordingID = ?");
trackStmt.setInt(1, 6);       // set parameter 1 to value 6
// execute statement, return results in rs
ResultSet rs = trackStmt.executeQuery();
```

The Select statement accesses all columns (fields) from the Tracks table whose RecordingID is set at run time via a positional parameter. The setInt() method assigns value 6 (a RecordingID) to the first positional parameter. A call to executeQuery() with the PreparedStatement object fetches the data from the database.

JDBC Code Sample

Now let's look at several snippets of code in a J2EE environment that access an SQL database using the JDBC API. First, we look up the datasource from the initial context and obtain a Connection. Getting a connection from a datasource is efficient, since the EJB container maintains a pool of database connections. All JDBC related statements should be placed in try blocks to handle exceptions.

Design Guideline

After connecting, make sure you release the connection as soon as you're done with the database operation. This technique makes the connection resource available to other clients, since the EJB container maintains a pool of database connections.

```
// dbName contains the coded name of the database source
String dbName = "java:comp/env/jdbc/MusicDB";
Connection con = null;
PreparedStatement trackStmt = null;
ResultSet rs = null;

try {
  // get context and perform a lookup of the coded name
  InitialContext ic = new InitialContext();
  DataSource ds = (DataSource) ic.lookup(dbName);
  // Obtain a Connection from the DataSource
  con = ds.getConnection();
```

Next, we'll create a `Select` statement to access the Tracks table and initialize a `PreparedStatement` with the connection object. This `Select` statement has a positional parameter which finds a record with a specific RecordingID and orders the track numbers from lowest to highest.

```
// SQL query that selects all rows from the Tracks table
// where the RecordingID is equal to the input parameter
// Sort the records by the TrackNumber field

String selectQuery = "Select * From Tracks " +
     "Where RecordingID = ? Order By TrackNumber";
// Create a PreparedStatement with the above SQL query
trackStmt = con.prepareStatement(selectQuery);

// Set the first input parameter to 5
// This makes the SQL query read:
// "Select all records from the Tracks table
// where the RecordingID field is 5.
// Order the records by field TrackNumber."
trackStmt.setInt(1, 5);
```

A call to executeQuery() executes our SQL Select statement and returns the data in a ResultSet. Now we can build an ArrayList collection of Widget value objects with the data in the ResultSet.

```
// execute the query
// store results into object ResultSet rs
rs = trackStmt.executeQuery();
// Put Widgets into ArrayList collection
ArrayList tList = new ArrayList();

while (rs.next())
{
  // create Widget object and add to tList ArrayList
    tList.add(new Widget(
    rs.getInt(2),            // Track Number
    rs.getString(3),         // Track Title
    rs.getString(4)));       // Track Length
}
```

How do you determine what numbers and which ResultSet getter methods to use? Recall that the database returns fields in the order they appear in the query. When you use * in a Select statement (indicating all fields in the table), the database builds a ResultSet with fields in the same order as the database table. The Tracks table contains five fields listed in Figure 4–2 on page 88. Field 2 is the Track Number (integer), field 3 is the Track Title (string) and field 4 is the Track Length (string).

When we exit the loop, we close the ResultSet, PreparedStatement, and Connection objects in a finally block.

```
} catch (Exception ex) {
    throw new EJBException("Unexpected error: " +
      ex.getMessage());

} finally {
  if (rs != null) rs.close(); // close ResultSet
  if (trackStmt) != null)
      trackStmt.close();       // close Prepared Statement
  if (con != null)
      con.close();             // close connection
}
```

The catch handler throws an EJBException for any exceptions generated by methods called in the try block. This includes SQLException objects, which can be thrown from JDBC calls.

Design Guideline

It's a good idea to close database connections in a `finally` *block. This technique ensures that we always close the connection, even if a thrown exception makes us exit the try block early. Closing a connection returns it to the container's pool of database connections.*

4.2 Music Stateless Session Bean

Because read-only access is all we need with the Music Collection database, it makes sense to perform this task with a session bean. And because we do not need to keep track of client-specific data, a stateless session bean will suffice. Let's examine the code for the Music EJB now.

Home Interface

Listing 4.1 is the home interface (`MusicHome`) for the Music EJB. Since this is a stateless session bean, we need only a single `create()` method with no arguments. Note that this method returns the remote interface object, `Music`.

Listing 4.1 MusicHome.java

```
// MusicHome.java
import java.io.Serializable;
import java.rmi.RemoteException;
import javax.ejb.CreateException;
import javax.ejb.EJBHome;

public interface MusicHome extends EJBHome {

    Music create() throws RemoteException, CreateException;
}
```

Remote Interface

The remote interface in Listing 4.2 contains the Music EJB's business methods. The `getMusicList()` method returns an `ArrayList` collection of recordings from the Music Collection database. Method `getTrackList()` accepts a `RecordingVO` object as an argument and returns an `ArrayList` collection of tracks for the specified recording. Both methods have the required `RemoteException` in their `throws` clauses. The `getTrackList()` method throws a user-defined `NoTrackListException` if a track list does not exist for a recording. This is used as a consistency check of the database.

Listing 4.2 Music.java

```
// Music.java
import javax.ejb.EJBObject;
import java.rmi.RemoteException;
import java.util.*;

public interface Music extends EJBObject {

    public ArrayList getMusicList() throws RemoteException;
    public ArrayList getTrackList(RecordingVO rec)
            throws NoTrackListException, RemoteException;
}
```

`NoTrackListException` is an example of an *application exception*. Recall that application exceptions are usually nonfatal errors produced by inconsistent user input or some other recoverable situation. The EJB container propagates the exception back to the client. While it's true that a recording without a track list may seem surprising to a client, the application could continue executing if the user selects a different recording.

NoTrackListException

Listing 4.3 shows the class definition for `NoTrackListException`. Since `NoTrackListException` extends `Exception`, we can catch this exception in any catch handler with an `Exception` signature. However, depending on the application, we might want to check for this specific exception type independently of other exceptions. We'll discuss this further when we present the application client later in the chapter.

Listing 4.3 NoTrackListException.java

```
// NoTrackListException.java
// Application Exception
public class NoTrackListException extends Exception {

  public NoTrackListException() { }
  public NoTrackListException(String msg) {
    super(msg);
  }
}
```

RecordingVO Class

In the previous chapter, our Loan EJB example used value objects LoanVO and PaymentVO to encapsulate data transmitted back and forth between a client and the Loan EJB. This handy J2EE design pattern can be applied here as well. We'll use two value objects: RecordingVO to encapsulate data associated with a recording, and TrackVO to encapsulate data associated with a track. Both classes implement the java.io.Serializable interface, since they'll be transmitted in remote calls to and from the Music EJB.

Listing 4.4 shows the code for the RecordingVO class, which defines only a constructor and getter methods to access the data. The class also implements an equals() method. This allows Java collection classes to compare two RecordingVO objects for equality by comparing recordID fields.

Listing 4.4 RecordingVO.java

```java
// RecordingVO.java
public class RecordingVO implements java.io.Serializable
{
  private int recordID;
  private String title;
  private String artistName;
  private String musicCategory;
  private String label;
  private int numberOfTracks;

  public RecordingVO(int recordID, String title,
      String artistName, String musicCategory,
      String label, int numberOfTracks)
  {
    this.recordID = recordID;
    this.title = title;
    this.artistName = artistName;
    this.musicCategory = musicCategory;
    this.label = label;
    this.numberOfTracks = numberOfTracks;
  }

  public int getRecordID() { return recordID; }
  public String getTitle() { return title; }
  public String getArtistName() { return artistName; }
  public String getMusicCategory()
        { return musicCategory; }
  public String getLabel() { return label; }
  public int getNumberOfTracks() { return numberOfTracks; }
```

Listing 4.4 RecordingVO.java *(continued)*

```
      // Implement equals; convenient way to determine if
      // 2 RecordingVO objects represent the same recording.
      // Used by Java Collection classes to indicate
      // successful removal from Collection.
      public boolean equals(Object rec) {
            return (recordID == ((RecordingVO)rec).recordID);
      }
}
```

If you return to Figure 4–2 on page 88, you'll note that our RecordingVO object does not appear in the diagram. That's because it's an abstraction of a class that selects data from three different tables. By encapsulating data from disparate sources into a single object, we group component information that belongs together. This abstraction hides the underlying database representation and creates a special kind of value object called a *Composite Object*.

Design Guideline

Composite objects make the Music EJB interface very simple and reduce the number of remote calls required to fetch data. The Music EJB returns all the recordings in one call, and a single call returns the track data associated with a specific recording.

TrackVO Class

The TrackVO class in Listing 4.5 has a constructor to store track information and getter methods to access the data.

Listing 4.5 TrackVO.java

```
// TrackVO.java
public class TrackVO implements java.io.Serializable
{
    private int trackNumber;
    private String title;
    private String trackLength;
```

Listing 4.5 TrackVO.java *(continued)*

```
public TrackVO(int trackNumber, String title,
    String trackLength) {
        this.trackNumber = trackNumber;
        this.title = title;
        this.trackLength = trackLength;
    }

    public String getTitle() { return title; }
    public String getTrackLength() { return trackLength; }
    public int getTrackNumber() { return trackNumber; }
}
```

Bean Implementation Class

Now let's look at the heart of the Music Collection design, the implementation of the Music EJB. The MusicBean implementation in Listing 4.6 is divided into three sections. The first section contains the implementation of the getMusic-List() and getTrackList() business methods. Both methods make calls to private helper functions that obtain connections to the database. By moving the database SQL code out of the business methods into private methods, we isolate database-dependent code. Furthermore, if we create a Data Access Object (DAO) to further isolate database access, there will be minimal impact to our bean implementation code. (We implement the DAO pattern later in this chapter; see "Data Access Object Pattern" on page 119.)

The second section of our bean implementation class contains the EJB methods, most of which are empty. The ejbCreate() method, however, performs the database name lookup and DataSource instantiation. Note that we save the DataSource instantiation in private instance variable ds for access in other methods. Doesn't this imply that our stateless session bean is maintaining state information? It's perfectly all right for stateless session beans to store state information as long as the data does not contain any client-specific information. A stateless session bean, therefore, *can* store client independent data if the information doesn't change. Furthermore, the EJB container may create copies of the data when instantiating multiple bean instances and this operation must be acceptable. Since we should always perform the lookup and instantiation once within the life cycle of an EJB, the ejbCreate() method is a good spot to perform these "once-only" initialization tasks.

The third section of the MusicBean class contains the private helper methods. We have one method to connect to the database and a second one to disconnect. We also have two database access methods, dbLoadMusicList() and dbLoadTrackList(). Each method connects to the database, defines an SQL PreparedStatement object, uses the JDBC API to read data from the database, builds the appropriate value object, and adds the value object to the `ArrayList` collection. Note that although we instantiate the `DataSource` just once, we wait and acquire the database connection inside the method that actually accesses the database. When we finish reading from the database, we release the database connection and close the open JDBC objects in `finally` blocks. We therefore keep the connection open only as long as we need it.

Listing 4.6 MusicBean.java

```java
// MusicBean.java
import java.sql.*;
import javax.sql.*;
import java.util.*;
import javax.ejb.*;
import javax.naming.*;
import java.rmi.RemoteException;

public class MusicBean implements SessionBean {

  // Business methods

  public ArrayList getMusicList()
  {
    try {
      // Encapsulate database calls in separate method
      return (dbLoadMusicList());
    } catch (Exception ex) {
      throw new EJBException("getMusicList: " +
          ex.getMessage());
    }
  }

  public ArrayList getTrackList(RecordingVO rec)
    throws NoTrackListException {

    ArrayList trackList;
    try {
      // Encapsulate database calls in separate method
      trackList = dbLoadTrackList(rec);
    } catch (Exception ex) {
      throw new EJBException("getTrackList: " +
        ex.getMessage());
    }
```

Listing 4.6 MusicBean.java *(continued)*

```java
    if (trackList.size() == 0) {
      throw new NoTrackListException(
        "No Track List found for RecordingID " +
        rec.getRecordID());
    }
    return trackList;
  }

  // JDBC Database Connection
  private Connection con = null;
  private DataSource ds;              // DataSource

  // EJB methods

  // Do the DataSource lookup just once
  // (put the lookup in ejbCreate() method)
  public void ejbCreate() {
    String dbName = "java:comp/env/jdbc/MusicDB";
    try {
      InitialContext ic = new InitialContext();
      ds = (DataSource) ic.lookup(dbName);

    } catch (Exception ex) {
      throw new EJBException("Cannot find DataSource: " +
        ex.getMessage());
    }
  }

  public MusicBean() {}
  public void ejbRemove() {}
  public void ejbActivate() {}
  public void ejbPassivate() {}
  public void setSessionContext(SessionContext sc) {}

  // Database methods

  // Obtain a JDBC Database connection
  private void getConnection()
  {
    try {
      con = ds.getConnection();
```

Listing 4.6 MusicBean.java *(continued)*

```java
    } catch (Exception ex) {
      throw new EJBException(
        "Cannot connect to database: " + ex.getMessage());
    }
}

// Release JDBC Database connection
private void disConnect()
{
  try {
    if (con != null) con.close();
  } catch (SQLException ex) {
    throw new EJBException("disConnect: " +
      ex.getMessage());
  }
}

private ArrayList dbLoadMusicList() throws SQLException
{
  ArrayList mList = new ArrayList();

  // Objects needed for the JDBC API SQL calls:
  PreparedStatement musicStmt = null;
  ResultSet rs = null;

  // The following query searches 3 tables in
  // the Music Collection database to create a composite
  // RecordingVO object.
  // We select all fields in the Recordings table,
  // the RecordingArtistName field in the
  // Recording Artists table, and the MusicCategory
  // field from the Music Categories table.
  // The Where clause matches the correct records from
  // the Recording Artists and Music Categories tables.
```

Listing 4.6 MusicBean.java *(continued)*

```
String selectQuery = "Select Recordings.*, " +
  "\"Recording Artists\".RecordingArtistName, " +
  "\"Music Categories\".MusicCategory " +
  "From Recordings, \"Recording Artists\", " +
  " \"Music Categories\" " +
  "Where Recordings.RecordingArtistID = " +
  "\"Recording Artists\".RecordingArtistID and " +
  "Recordings.MusicCategoryID = " +
  "\"Music Categories\".MusicCategoryID ";

try {
  // Obtain a database connection
  getConnection();
  musicStmt = con.prepareStatement(selectQuery);

  // Execute the query; results are in ResultSet rs
  rs = musicStmt.executeQuery();

  // Loop through ResultSet and create RecordingVO
  // object for each row
  while (rs.next())
  {
    // Create RecordingVO object and
    // add to mList ArrayList
    // Use getInt() and getString() to pull data from
    // ResultSet rs.
    // The parameter numbers match the order of the
    // field names in the query statement.

    mList.add(new RecordingVO(
      rs.getInt(1),       // RecordingID
      rs.getString(2),    // RecordingTitle
      rs.getString(9),    // RecordingArtistName
      rs.getString(10),   // MusicCategory
      rs.getString(5),    // RecordingLabel
      rs.getInt(7)));     // NumberofTracks
  }

} catch (SQLException ex) {
  throw new EJBException(
    "SQLException reading recording data:\n" +
    ex.getMessage());
```

Listing 4.6 MusicBean.java *(continued)*

```
  } finally {
    // Close the ResultSet and the
    // PreparedStatement objects
    if (rs != null) rs.close();
    if (musicStmt != null) musicStmt.close();
    // Release the database connection
    disConnect();
  }
  return mList;
}

private ArrayList dbLoadTrackList(RecordingVO rec)
      throws SQLException
{
  ArrayList tList = new ArrayList();
  // Objects needed for the JDBC API SQL calls:
  PreparedStatement trackStmt = null;
  ResultSet rs = null;

  // Select all records from Tracks table
  // where RecordingID is the same as the In parameter
  // Order the records by TrackNumber field
  String selectQuery = "Select * From Tracks " +
    "Where RecordingID = ? Order By TrackNumber";

  try {
    // Obtain a database connection
    getConnection();
    // Get a PreparedStatement with query
    trackStmt = con.prepareStatement(selectQuery);
    // Set In parameter to RecordingID argument
    trackStmt.setInt(1, rec.getRecordID());
    // Execute query; return in ResultSet rs
    rs = trackStmt.executeQuery();

    while (rs.next())
    {
      // Loop through ResultSet, create TrackVO object
      // and add to tList ArrayList
```

Listing 4.6 MusicBean.java *(continued)*

```
        tList.add(new TrackVO(
        rs.getInt(2),          // trackNumber
        rs.getString(3),       // title
        rs.getString(4)));     // trackLength
      }

    } catch (SQLException ex) {
      throw new EJBException(
        "SQLException reading track data:\n" +
        ex.getMessage());

    } finally {
      if (rs != null) rs.close();
      if (trackStmt != null) trackStmt.close();
      // Release the database connection
      disConnect();
    }
    return tList;
  }
} // MusicBean
```

Design Guideline

You should always access a database by obtaining a connection from the EJB container's DataSource. *This allows the container to efficiently assign connections from a connection pool. Because obtaining the connection doesn't cost much, we acquire it just before accessing the database. After we're finished reading or writing the database, we release the connection. Note that the code to release our database connection and the JDBC objects is inside a* finally *block. This ensures that the connection resources are always released, even if the system throws exceptions.*

Design Guideline

Whenever possible use the JDBC PreparedStatement instead of Statement. This allows the database to cache the "compiled" statement internally, avoiding multiple recompilations when the text of the query is unchanged. This provides increased performance when a database has a large number of client requests.

Deployment Descriptor

Since we've added database access to this enterprise bean, let's examine the effects on the deployment descriptor. Listing 4.7 shows the deployment descriptor for the Music EJB. The information describing the database is included within the tags <resource-ref> and </resource-ref>. (We show the tag values in **bold**.) The resource name is jdbc/MusicDB, its type is javax.sql.DataSource, and the EJB container provides authorization. The resource is shareable.

Listing 4.7 Deployment Descriptor for MusicEJB

```
<ejb-jar>
  <display-name>MusicSessionJAR</display-name>
  <enterprise-beans>

    <session>
      <display-name>MusicEJB</display-name>
      <ejb-name>MusicEJB</ejb-name>
      <home>MusicHome</home>
      <remote>Music</remote>
      <ejb-class>MusicBean</ejb-class>
      <session-type>Stateless</session-type>
      <transaction-type>Bean</transaction-type>

      <security-identity>
        <description></description>
        <use-caller-identity></use-caller-identity>
      </security-identity>

      <resource-ref>
        <res-ref-name>jdbc/MusicDB</res-ref-name>
        <res-type>javax.sql.DataSource</res-type>
        <res-auth>Container</res-auth>
        <res-sharing-scope>Shareable</res-sharing-scope>
      </resource-ref>
    </session>
  </enterprise-beans>
</ejb-jar>
```

4.3   A Java Swing Application Client

Our first client for the Music EJB is a stand-alone application with a Java Swing graphical user interface.

Information Source

The Java Swing API is outside the scope of this text. For more information, consult Sun's Java web site at http://java.sun.com/.

This program includes Swing components to control screen layout with multiple panels. It reads the Music Collection database and places recording titles into a Swing JList component for viewing and selection by the user. The program also uses a JTextArea Swing component. When the user selects the "View Tracks" button, the textarea component shows additional information about the recording and the track list. A JTextField component displays status and error messages. Figure 4–3 shows the program after the user selects the recording "Graceland."

Appendix A contains the complete source code for the Swing client application, **MusicApp.java**. We'll just show you snippets of the code here. Here's the MusicApp constructor, which performs the setup work for the application.

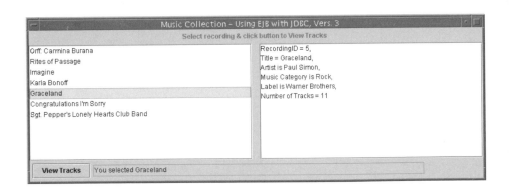

Figure 4–3 Music Client Application After Selecting Recording "Graceland"

```java
public MusicApp() {
  // set up Swing components
  . . .
  try {
    // Create Music EJB
    Context initial = new InitialContext();
    Object objref = initial.lookup(
            "java:comp/env/ejb/MyMusic");
    musicHome = (MusicHome)PortableRemoteObject.narrow(
            objref, MusicHome.class);
    mymusic = musicHome.create();

  } catch (Exception ex) {
    System.out.println("Unexpected Exception: " +
        ex.getMessage());
    ex.printStackTrace();
  }
  // Access the EJB to read the Music Collection database
  // and put the title names in the JList swing component
  getRecordings();
  status.setText("There are " + albums.size() +
      " recordings");
  . . .
}
```

After setting up the Swing components and creating the Music EJB, the constructor calls getRecordings(). This private method reads the Music Collection database with the Music EJB business method getMusicList() and returns a collection of recordings. The getRecordings() method also puts the recording titles into the JList Swing component for the user to select.

The Java Swing event handler mechanism invokes valuechanged() and actionPerformed() to process user input. It calls valuechanged() when a user changes a title selection in the JList component.

```
public void valueChanged(ListSelectionEvent e) {

   // Event handler for ListSelectionEvent
   // (user changes selection in musicTitle
   // JList component)

   if (!e.getValueIsAdjusting()) {
      . . .

      // Access the RecordingVO object at the index
      // of the selected music title.
      // Method getSelectedIndex() returns the index of
      // the selected list item,
      // which corresponds to the same
      // index value in the albums ArrayList collection.
      RecordingVO r =
          (RecordingVO)albums.get(
              musicTitle.getSelectedIndex());
      . . .
   }
}
```

This method fetches a `RecordingVO` object from the recording collection indicated by the selected title and displays the recording information in the `JText-Area` component.

The event handler invokes `actionPerformed()` when the user selects the "View Tracks" `JButton`.

```
public void actionPerformed(ActionEvent e) {

   // Event handler for ActionEvent
   // (user clicks "View Tracks" button)
   . . .

   data.setText("Track information for " +
      musicTitle.getSelectedValue());
```

```
// getTracks() calls Music EJB
// business method getTrackList()
// getTracks() puts track info into the
// JTextArea component
getTracks(
  (RecordingVO)albums.get(
    musicTitle.getSelectedIndex()));
    . . .
}
```

For a selected title, this method gets the recording tracks by calling getTracks(). The private getTracks() method invokes the Music EJB business method getTrackList(), which in turn reads the Music Collection database. Method getTracks() also displays recording track information in the JTextArea Swing component. Figure 4–4 shows the result after the user clicks the "View Tracks" button for recording selection "Graceland."

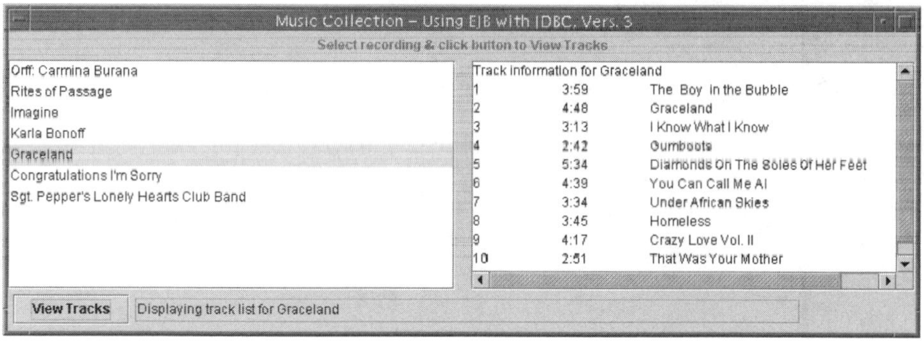

Figure 4–4 Music Client Application After Selecting "View Tracks" for Recording "Graceland"

4.4   JSP Web Component Client

The Music EJB can interact with web clients, too. In this section, we'll show you how a JSP client can access the Music Collection database using the same EJB component.

The web component client uses three JSP programs. The first one, **musicGet.jsp**, displays recording titles and collects user input. Figure 4–5 shows a screen shot of this page.

The second JSP program, **musicPost.jsp**, displays track information for a recording title. Figure 4–6 shows a screen shot after the user selects "Graceland" and clicks the "View Tracks" button.

The web container invokes the third JSP program, **error.jsp**, only when a runtime exception is thrown.

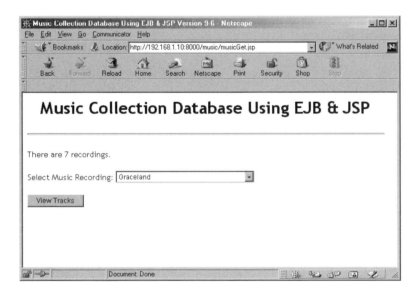

Figure 4–5 Screen Shot of Initial JSP Web Client Program for the Music EJB

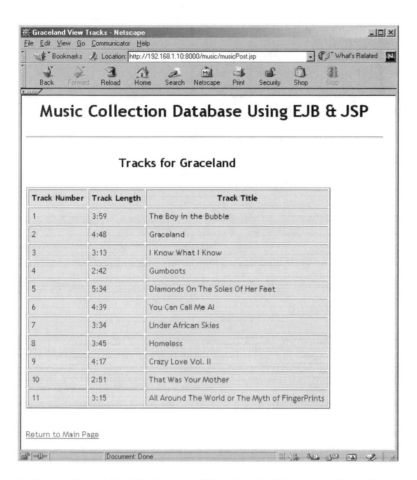

Figure 4–6 Screen Shot After Clicking the "View Tracks" Button for Recording "Graceland"

musicGet.jsp

This JSP program in Listing 4.8 accesses the Music EJB to read recordings from the Music Collection database. It creates a Music EJB in method jspInit(), which the web container invokes once during JSP initialization. This method also invokes Music EJB business method getMusicList() to read the recording titles. A HttpSession object saves the Music EJB and the ArrayList of RecordingVO objects. The web container invokes JSP **musicPost.jsp** with the user's recording title selection stored in the request object. The JSP page remembers the selected title by getting it from the session object (it will be null the first time).

Both **musicGet.jsp** and **musicPost.jsp** designate **error.jsp** as the error page in the JSP page directive `errorPage`. If a runtime exception occurs, the web container invokes the JSP's error page and makes the implicit object `exception` available within the error page.

Listing 4.8 musicGet.jsp

```
<%--
  musicGet.jsp
--%>

<%--
  JSP web component to read the Music Collection Database
  using the Music EJB stateless session bean.
  Place recording titles inside an HTML select component.
  When user clicks the "View Tracks" button,
  invoke musicPost.jsp to display the track information.
--%>

<%--
  The following page directive tells the JSP engine to
  import the named classes and packages when compiling
  the generated servlet code and to use "error.jsp"
  for an errorPage.
--%>

<%@ page import="Music,MusicHome,RecordingVO,java.util.*,
javax.naming.Context, javax.naming.InitialContext,
javax.rmi.PortableRemoteObject" errorPage="error.jsp" %>

<%--
  The following 3 variables appear in a JSP declaration.
  They appear outside the generated _jspService() method,
  which gives them class scope.

  Since we want to initialize our Music EJB object once
  and read the Music Collection database to get the
  recording titles once, we place this code inside
  method jspInit().
  The EJB business method getMusicList()
  returns a collection of RecordingVO objects which we
  store in ArrayList albums.
--%>
```

Listing 4.8 musicGet.jsp *(continued)*

```
<%!
  MusicHome musicHome;
  Music mymusic;
  ArrayList albums;

  public void jspInit() {
    try {
      Context initial = new InitialContext();
      Object objref = initial.lookup(
                  "java:comp/env/ejb/EJBMusic");
      musicHome = (MusicHome)PortableRemoteObject.narrow(
          objref, MusicHome.class);
      mymusic = musicHome.create();
      albums = mymusic.getMusicList();

    } catch (Exception ex) {
      System.out.println("Unexpected Exception: " +
          ex.getMessage());
      ex.printStackTrace();
    }
  }
%>

<%--
  The following scriptlet accesses the implicit
  request object to obtain the current URL and
  saves it to the session object for later retrieval.
  It also saves variable mymusic, so we can
  make remote calls to our Music EJB, and the collection of
  RecordingVO objects. These variables will all be
  available to other pages within the session.
--%>

<%
  String requestURI = request.getRequestURI();
  session.putValue("url", requestURI);
  session.putValue("mymusic", mymusic);
  session.putValue("albums", albums);
%>
```

Listing 4.8 musicGet.jsp *(continued)*

```
<%--
  The following html code sets up the page to display
  the recording titles in a select element and invokes
  page musicPost.jsp with the selected user input.
--%>

<html>
<head>
<title>Music Collection Database Using EJB & JSP</title>
</head>
<body bgcolor=white>
<h1><b><center>Music Collection Database Using EJB & JSP</
center></b></h1>
<hr>
<p>
There are <%= albums.size() %> recordings.

<form method="post" action="musicPost.jsp">
<p>
Select Music Recording:
<select name="TITLE">

<%
  // Generate html <option> elements with the recording
  // titles stored in each RecordingVO element.
  // Obtain the current title from the session object
  // (this will be null the first time).

  String title;
  String currentTitle =
        (String)session.getValue("curTitle");
  if (currentTitle == null) currentTitle = "";
  RecordingVO r;
  Iterator i = albums.iterator();

  while (i.hasNext()) {
    r = (RecordingVO)i.next();
    title = r.getTitle();

    if (title.equals(currentTitle)) {
      out.println("<option selected>" + title
            + "</option>");
    }
```

Listing 4.8 musicGet.jsp *(continued)*

```
      else {
         out.println("<option>" + title + "</option>");
      }
   }
%>
</select><p><p>

<%--
   Provide a "View Tracks" button to submit
   the requested title to page musicPost.jsp
--%>

<input TYPE="submit" NAME="View" VALUE="View Tracks">
</form>
</body>
</html>
```

---

musicPost.jsp

The web container invokes **musicPost.jsp** when a user submits a recording title request. The title comes from the `request` object and the `session` object contains the Music EJB and the `ArrayList` of `RecordingVO` objects. Listing 4.9 shows the code.

In this program we'll search the `ArrayList` collection in a loop looking for the `RecordingVO` object with a matching title. When we find it, a call to `getTrackList()` from the Music EJB obtains the track list for that recording. Now we can display track information in an HTML table with three columns: the track number, the track length, and the track title.

Listing 4.9 musicPost.jsp

```
<%--
   musicPost.jsp
--%>

<%--
   JSP web component to display the track information
   for the selected recording passed in the session object.
   We obtain the track information by calling the
   Music EJB's getTrackList() business method.
--%>
```

Listing 4.9 musicPost.jsp *(continued)*

```jsp
<%--
  Use a page directive to import needed classes and
  packages for compilation.
  Specify "error.jsp" as the page's errorPage.
--%>

<%@ page import="Music,MusicHome,
RecordingVO,TrackVO,java.util.*, javax.naming.Context,
javax.naming.InitialContext,
javax.rmi.PortableRemoteObject" errorPage="error.jsp" %>

<%--
  Declare the class variables.
--%>

<%!
  Music mymusic;
  ArrayList albums;
%>

<%--
  The following scriptlet accesses the session
  object to assign values to requestURI, mymusic,
  and albums. It obtains the user selected title
  from the request object and stores it into the
  session object to be used by the request page
  as the new default.
--%>

<%
  ArrayList tracks;
  String requestURI = (String)session.getValue("url");
  mymusic = (Music)session.getValue("mymusic");
  albums = (ArrayList)session.getValue("albums");
  String currentTitle = request.getParameter("TITLE");
  session.putValue("curTitle", currentTitle);
%>

<html>
<head>
<title><%= currentTitle %> View Tracks</title>
</head>
```

Listing 4.9 musicPost.jsp *(continued)*

```
<body bgcolor=white>
<h1><b><center>Music Collection Database Using EJB & JSP</
center></b></h1>
<hr><p>

<%
  // Access the albums ArrayList to find the RecordingVO
  // object with the selected title.
  RecordingVO r = null;
  Iterator i = albums.iterator();
  boolean found = false;

  while (i.hasNext()) {
    r = (RecordingVO)i.next();
    if (r.getTitle().equals(currentTitle)) {
      found = true;
      break;
    }
  }

  if (found) {              // found title
    // Access the MusicEJB to read the Music Collection
    // database and get the track list for the
    // selected recording
    tracks = mymusic.getTrackList(r);
%>

<%--
  Set up an html table to hold the data.
--%>

    <table bgcolor=#e0e0e0 border=2 cellpadding=5>
    <caption><h2>
    <%= "Tracks for " + currentTitle %>
    </h2></caption>
    <tr>
    <th>Track Number</th>
    <th>Track Length</th>
    <th>Track Title</th>
    </tr>
```

Listing 4.9 musicPost.jsp *(continued)*

```
<%
    // Use a combination of scriptlet code,
    // html and JSP expressions to build the table
    TrackVO t;
    i = tracks.iterator();
    while (i.hasNext()) {
      t = (TrackVO)i.next();
%>

    <tr>
    <td> <%= t.getTrackNumber() %></td>
    <td> <%= t.getTrackLength() %></td>
    <td> <%= t.getTitle() %></td>
    </tr>

<%
    }
    out.println("</table>");
  }
  else {
    out.println("No tracks for " + currentTitle
          + " found.<br>");
  }
%>

<%--
  Provide a dynamic link to the request page so
  the user can request another track list to display.
--%>

<br><br><a href="<%= requestURI %>">Return to Main Page</a>
</body>
</html>
```

error.jsp

The JSP engine can recognize a JSP file as an error page. When an exception is thrown, the web container invokes the error page. A JSP file is an error page if the JSP page directive isErrorPage is set to true.

The implicit exception object (an instance of class java.lang.Throwable) is available only in error pages. This object refers to the runtime exception that caused the error page to be invoked. In Listing 4.10 for **error.jsp**, we call the printStackTrace() method with class exception to display the exception object's stack trace in an HTML table. The <pre> and </pre> tags maintain formatting of the stack trace.

Listing 4.10 error.jsp

```
<%--
  error.jsp
--%>

<%@ page isErrorPage="true" import="java.io.*" %>

<html>
<head>
<title>Error Page</title>
</head>
<body>
<h1>You Have Encountered an Error</h1>

<table border="1">
  <tr>
    <td><b><font size="+1">Stack Trace</font></b></td>
  </tr>
  <tr>
    <td><pre>

<%
  StringWriter sw = new StringWriter();
  PrintWriter pw = new PrintWriter(sw);
  exception.printStackTrace(pw);
  out.println(sw);
%>

    </pre></td>
  </tr>
</table>
</body>
</html>
```

4.5 Data Access Object Pattern

The Music EJB shown in this chapter accesses a database using the JDBC's SQL interface. It works fine with Cloudscape's reference implementation of SQL (provided by Sun's J2EE reference implementation) but what happens if we change databases? How would this affect our code? Unfortunately, porting the current version of the Music EJB to a different database is not as smooth as one would like. Specifically, changes may be necessary to the bean implementation class, **MusicBean.java**. Although we isolated database access to separate private methods in the Music EJB, the EJB code must still be recompiled and redeployed.

The **Data Access Object** (DAO) pattern introduces a deeper level of abstraction for any EJB that accesses databases. Figure 4–7 shows you how this pattern might be applied to the Music EJB. First, we create an interface (MusicDAO) that defines the methods necessary for database access. Second, we define a Factory class (MusicDAOFactory) with a static method that instantiates an implementation of our abstract interface. This Factory class performs a lookup to get the actual name of the implementation class. Because the class name appears in the EJB's deployment descriptor, it's possible to change implementation classes without recompiling any code. This is the obvious benefit of the DAO approach. Third, we create at least one implementation class (MusicDAOCloudscape) with the code to access a database (in this case, Cloud-

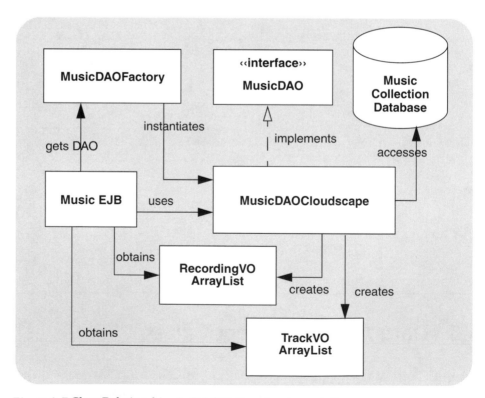

Figure 4–7 Class Relationships in DAO Pattern Implementation

scape). In our application, the `MusicDAOCloudscape` class creates the `Record-ingVO` and `TrackVO` value objects and sends them back to the EJB client.

DAO Pattern Implementation

Now we're ready to show you how to implement the DAO Pattern for the Music EJB. The Swing client (**MusicApp.java**) and the web component client (**musicGet.jsp**, **musicPost.jsp**, and **error.jsp**) do not require changes. Likewise, the home and remote interfaces (`MusicHome` and `Music`) are also unchanged. The bean implementation class, **MusicBean.java**, does change, since we now access the database differently. In fact, the bean implementation code shrinks quite a bit with the DAO approach.

Figure 4–8 is a sequence diagram showing the interactions between the DAO client, Music EJB, and the other objects required to implement the DAO

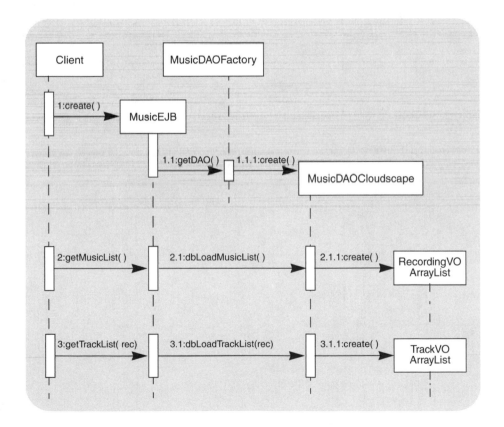

Figure 4–8 Sequence Diagram Showing Interactions Among Objects in DAO Pattern

pattern. You might find it helpful to consult this diagram while reading through the implementation code.

MusicBean

Listing 4.11 is the altered source for **MusicBean.java**, which uses the DAO pattern for database access. The code is similar to what we had before, except for several changes. Inside `ejbCreate()`, where we previously performed the database name lookup and `DataSource` instantiation, we now call `MusicDAO-Factory.getDAO()` to obtain a single instance of a `MusicDAO` object (dao). This change allows our two business methods (`getMusicList()` and `getTrack-List()`) to invoke methods with a `dao` reference from the `MusicDAO` interface (`dbLoadMusicList()` and `dbLoadTrackList()`, respectively). Hence, the bean implementation class becomes simpler with this approach, since we have extracted all of the SQL code. This use of the DAO pattern is significant, because it decouples our business methods from the database they access.

Listing 4.11 MusicBean.java Using DAO Pattern

```
// MusicBean.java
import java.util.*;
import javax.ejb.*;
import javax.naming.*;
import java.rmi.RemoteException;

public class MusicBean implements SessionBean {

    // class-wide MusicDAO object to access the data
    // MusicDAO object is instantiated in ejbCreate()
    // and provides implementation of the MusicDAO interface
    // for the particular database we're using
    private MusicDAO dao;

    // Business methods

    public ArrayList getMusicList()
    {
      try {
        // Encapsulate database calls in MusicDAO
        return(dao.dbLoadMusicList());
```

Listing 4.11 MusicBean.java Using DAO Pattern *(continued)*

```java
      } catch (MusicDAOSysException ex) {
        throw new EJBException("getMusicList: " +
              ex.getMessage());
      }
  }

  public ArrayList getTrackList(RecordingVO rec)
            throws NoTrackListException {
    ArrayList trackList;
    try {
      // Encapsulate database calls in MusicDAO
      trackList = dao.dbLoadTrackList(rec);

    } catch (MusicDAOSysException ex) {
      throw new EJBException("getTrackList: " +
          ex.getMessage());
    }

    if (trackList.size() == 0) {
      throw new NoTrackListException(
          "No Track List found for RecordingID " +
                rec.getRecordID());
    }
    return trackList;
  }

  // EJB methods

  public void ejbCreate() {
    try {
      // The MusicDAOFactory class returns
      // an implementation of the MusicDAO interface
      dao = MusicDAOFactory.getDAO();
    }

    catch (MusicDAOSysException ex) {
      throw new EJBException(ex.getMessage());
    }
  }
```

Listing 4.11 MusicBean.java Using DAO Pattern *(continued)*

```
public MusicBean() {}
public void ejbRemove() {}
public void ejbActivate() {}
public void ejbPassivate() {}
public void setSessionContext(SessionContext sc) {}

} // MusicBean
```

Naming Environment Entry

The MusicDAOFactory class is responsible for instantiating the appropriate MusicDAO class. Remember, MusicDAO is an interface and cannot be instantiated. It exists solely to provide the method signatures our Music EJB calls to access the database.

How do we tell the MusicDAOFactory which implementation class to instantiate? By specifying a *naming environment entry* in the Music EJB deployment descriptor, we can customize a component during deployment without changing the component's source code. The EJB container oversees the naming environment and provides access through the JNDI naming context. Class InitialContext provides a single point of access to naming services.

A deployment tool lets you specify such an environment entry. Here's what the entry in a deployment descriptor might look like.

```
<env-entry>
  <env-entry-name>MusicDAOClass</env-entry-name>
  <env-entry-type>java.lang.String</env-entry-type>
  <env-entry-value>MusicDAOCloudscape</env-entry-value>
</env-entry>
```

The <env-entry> tag specifies a naming environment entry consisting of a name (MusicDAOClass), type (java.lang.String), and value (MusicDAOCloudscape). The MusicDAOFactory uses class name MusicDAOCloudscape to create the correct instance.

MusicDAOFactory

Listing 4.12 is the code for class MusicDAOFactory consisting of a single getDAO() static method. First, this method instantiates InitialContext to perform a lookup of java:comp/env/MusicDAOClass in the naming environment entry of the deployment descriptor. To create the correct instance, getDAO() reads MusicDAOCloudscape from the corresponding naming environment entry and uses it as a String argument to an invocation of Class.for-

Name().newInstance(). The return type from this call is an implementation of a MusicDAO object, which is then returned from the static method.

Listing 4.12 MusicDAOFactory.java

```java
// MusicDAOFactory.java
import javax.naming.NamingException;
import javax.naming.InitialContext;
import MusicDAOSysException;

public class MusicDAOFactory {

  // Instantiate a subclass that implements the
  // MusicDAO interface.
  // Obtain subclass name from the deployment descriptor

  public static MusicDAO getDAO()
          throws MusicDAOSysException {

    MusicDAO musicDAO = null;
    String musicDAOClass = "java:comp/env/MusicDAOClass";
    String className = null;

    try {
      InitialContext ic = new InitialContext();

      // Lookup value of environment entry
      // for DAO classname
      // Value is set in deployment descriptor
      className = (String) ic.lookup(musicDAOClass);

      // Instantiate class, which will provide
      // implementation for the MusicDAO interface
      musicDAO = (MusicDAO) Class.forName(
                className).newInstance();

    } catch (Exception ex) {
      throw new MusicDAOSysException(
          "MusicDAOFactory.getDAO: " +
          "NamingException for <" + className +
          "> DAO class : \n" + ex.getMessage());
    }
    return musicDAO;
  }
}
```

MusicDAO

Interface `MusicDAO` in Listing 4.13 provides the methods for accessing the Music Collection database. This interface has the same functionality as the methods we wrote in the first version of the Music EJB implementation. The two methods, `dbLoadMusicList()` and `dbLoadTrackList()`, both return `ArrayList` and have the same signatures as before. Note that the `throws` clauses for both methods include `MusicDAOSysException`. This user-defined exception allows client EJB code to discriminate exceptions generated in the `MusicDAO` object from other runtime exceptions.

Listing 4.13 MusicDAO.java

```
// MusicDAO.java
import java.util.ArrayList;
import MusicDAOSysException;
import RecordingVO;

// Interface for Music Data Access Object

public interface MusicDAO {
  public ArrayList dbLoadMusicList()
      throws MusicDAOSysException;
  public ArrayList dbLoadTrackList(RecordingVO rec)
      throws MusicDAOSysException;
}
```

MusicDAOSysException

Listing 4.14 is the class definition for `MusicDAOSysException`. Note that this exception class extends from `RuntimeException`, making it a *system exception*. The EJB container catches system exceptions and typically wraps them in `RemoteException` to send back to the client. However, the container may instead perform some sort of error handling to address the problem.

Listing 4.14 MusicDAOSysException.java

```
// MusicDAOSysException.java
// System Exception
import java.lang.RuntimeException;

public class MusicDAOSysException extends RuntimeException
{
```

Listing 4.14 MusicDAOSysException.java *(continued)*

```
// MusicDAOSysException extends standard RuntimeException.
// Thrown by MusicDAO subclasses when there is an
// unrecoverable system error (typically SQLException)

  public MusicDAOSysException(String msg) {
    super(msg);
  }
  public MusicDAOSysException() {
    super();
  }
}
```

MusicDAOCloudscape

The MusicDAOCloudscape class implements the MusicDAO interface specifically for the Cloudscape database. Using a database from another vendor, such as Oracle or Sybase, would require a different implementation. To use an alternative implementation, all you have to do is change the environment entry value for MusicDAOCloudscape to a different value in the EJB's deployment descriptor. No recompilation of any code is required (other than compiling the new implementation class). Listing 4.15 shows the code for **MusicDAOCloudscape.java**.

The constructor performs a lookup of the DataSource name to instantiate a DataSource object. We have private methods to make a connection, release the connection, and close the prepared statements and result sets. These private methods make it easier to connect for each database operation and close the resources from within a finally block when we're done.

The workhorse methods, dbLoadMusicList() and dbLoadTrackList(), are almost identical to the methods in the first version of the Music EJB. One important difference is the changes to all the catch handlers. Each catch handler now has an SQLException signature and throws a MusicDAOSysException in its catch block. In a large application it is always helpful to know the source of an exception. Only a subclass of MusicDAO will generate the MusicDAO-SysException.

Listing 4.15 MusicDAOCloudscape.java

```java
// MusicDAOCloudscape.java
import java.util.ArrayList;
import javax.ejb.*;
import javax.naming.*;
import javax.sql.DataSource;
import java.sql.*;
import MusicDAOSysException;

// Implements MusicDAO for Cloudscape database.
public class MusicDAOCloudscape implements MusicDAO {

  private Connection con = null;
  private DataSource datasource = null;

  public MusicDAOCloudscape()
             throws MusicDAOSysException {
    String dbName = "java:comp/env/jdbc/MusicDB";
    try {
      InitialContext ic = new InitialContext();
      datasource = (DataSource) ic.lookup(dbName);
    } catch (NamingException ex) {
      throw new MusicDAOSysException(
          "Exception during datasource lookup: " +
            dbName + ":\n" + ex.getMessage());
    }
  }

  // Obtain a JDBC Database connection
  private void getConnection() throws MusicDAOSysException
  {
    try {
      con = datasource.getConnection();

    } catch (SQLException ex) {
      throw new MusicDAOSysException(
        "SQLException during DB Connection:\n" +
        ex.getMessage());
    }
  }
```

Listing 4.15 MusicDAOCloudscape.java *(continued)*

```java
// Release JDBC Database connection
private void disConnect() throws MusicDAOSysException
{
  try {
    if (con != null) con.close();
  } catch (SQLException ex) {
    throw new MusicDAOSysException(
      "SQLException during DB close connection:\n" +
      ex.getMessage());
  }
}

private void closeStatement(PreparedStatement s)
        throws MusicDAOSysException {
  try {
    if (s != null) s.close();
  } catch (SQLException ex) {
    throw new MusicDAOSysException(
      "SQL Exception during statement close\n"
      + ex.getMessage());
  }
}

private void closeResultSet(ResultSet rs)
        throws MusicDAOSysException {
  try {
    if (rs != null) rs.close();
  } catch (SQLException ex) {
    throw new MusicDAOSysException(
      "SQL Exception during result set close\n"
      + ex.getMessage());
  }
}

public ArrayList dbLoadMusicList()
      throws MusicDAOSysException {

  ArrayList mList = new ArrayList();

  // The following query searches 3 tables in
  // the Music Collection database to create a composite
  // RecordingVO objcct.
```

Listing 4.15 MusicDAOCloudscape.java *(continued)*

```
// We select all fields in the Recordings table,
// the RecordingArtistName field in the
// Recording Artists table, and the MusicCategory field
// from the Music Categories table.
// The Where clause matches the correct records from
// the Recording Artists and Music Categories tables.

String selectQuery = "Select Recordings.*, " +
  "\"Recording Artists\".RecordingArtistName, " +
  "\"Music Categories\".MusicCategory " +
  "From Recordings, \"Recording Artists\", " +
  "\"Music Categories\" " +
  "Where Recordings.RecordingArtistID = " +
  "\"Recording Artists\".RecordingArtistID and " +
  "Recordings.MusicCategoryID = " +
  "\"Music Categories\".MusicCategoryID ";

PreparedStatement musicStmt = null;
ResultSet rs = null;
try {
  // Obtain a database connection
  getConnection();
  musicStmt = con.prepareStatement(selectQuery);

  // Execute the query; results are in ResultSet rs
  rs = musicStmt.executeQuery();

  // Loop through ResultSet and create RecordingVO
  // object for each row

  while (rs.next())
  {
    // Create RecordingVO object and add to mList
    // Use getInt() and getString() to pull data from
    // ResultSet rs.

    // The parameter numbers match the order of the
    // field names in the query statement.
```

Listing 4.15 MusicDAOCloudscape.java *(continued)*

```
        mList.add(new RecordingVO(
          rs.getInt(1),         // RecordingID
          rs.getString(2),      // RecordingTitle
          rs.getString(9),      // RecordingArtistName
          rs.getString(10),     // MusicCategory
          rs.getString(5),      // RecordingLabel
          rs.getInt(7)));       // NumberofTracks
      }

    } catch(SQLException ex) {
      throw new MusicDAOSysException(
        "SQLException reading recording data:\n" +
        ex.getMessage());

    } finally {
      closeResultSet(rs);
      closeStatement(musicStmt);

      // Release the database connection
      disConnect();
    }
    return mList;
}

public ArrayList dbLoadTrackList(RecordingVO rec)
      throws MusicDAOSysException {

  ArrayList tList = new ArrayList();

  // Select all records from Tracks table
  // where the RecordingID is the same as the
  // In parameter
  // Order the records by TrackNumber field

  String selectQuery = "Select * From Tracks " +
    "Where RecordingID = ? Order By TrackNumber";

  PreparedStatement trackStmt = null;
  ResultSet rs = null;
```

Listing 4.15 MusicDAOCloudscape.java *(continued)*

```java
try {
  // Obtain a database connection
  getConnection();

  trackStmt = con.prepareStatement(selectQuery);

  // Set In parameter to RecordingID in
  // RecordingVO argument
  trackStmt.setInt(1, rec.getRecordID());

  // Execute query; return in ResultSet rs
  rs = trackStmt.executeQuery();

  while (rs.next())
  {
    // Loop through ResultSet and create TrackVO
    // Add to tList ArrayList
    tList.add(new TrackVO(
    rs.getInt(2),              // trackNumber
    rs.getString(3),        // title
    rs.getString(4)));      // trackLength
  }

} catch (SQLException ex) {
  throw new MusicDAOSysException(
    "SQLException while reading track data:\n"
    + ex.getMessage());

} finally {
  closeResultSet(rs);
  closeStatement(trackStmt);
  // Release the database connection
  disConnect();
}
  return tList;
}
} // MusicDAOCloudscape
```

4.6   Design Guidelines and Patterns

We have added a level of complexity to the example in this chapter by including an Enterprise Java Bean that accesses a database. The Music EJB can be a stateless session bean because it accesses the database in a read-only capacity.

DAO Pattern

Our first implementation keeps things as simple as possible by implementing database calls as private methods inside the bean implementation code. The trade-off between simplicity and lack of flexibility means that our code is "hard wired" to access a particular vendor's database. The second version uses the Data Access Object (DAO) Pattern to solve this lack of flexibility. Our approach is to create an interface that the bean implementation code invokes, and to write at least one implementation class for a particular database vendor. A factory class instantiates the implementation object based on the declarative information inserted into the DAO client's deployment descriptor. The EJB container reads the deployment descriptor and makes this information available to EJB components through the JNDI naming service.

Factory Pattern

The DAO Pattern uses the *Factory* Pattern for part of its implementation. A factory is responsible for creating objects or families of objects. A factory can also reuse existing objects, if possible. The strategy is that you place the logic for what gets created and how it gets created inside a factory class. The client (who wants to use one of these objects) makes a request to the factory object for instantiation. Our example shows the factory class using the JNDI naming service to acquire the name of the class that it instantiates.

Connection Pooling

One of the services provided by the EJB container is to manage a pool of database connections. Connections are made by invoking the `getConnection()` method of class `javax.sql.DataSource`. By acquiring a database connection through the `DataSource` object, you allow the EJB container to optimize connection pooling and management. It's also a good idea to acquire, use, and release connections before returning to the client. You should hold on to a connection only for as long as you need it.

The Role of finally

Make sure you release all database connections within `finally` blocks. This ensures that the connection will always be released, even when an exception is thrown. Furthermore, you should release the database connection *after* closing any JDBC statements and result sets.

Using Exceptions with EJBs

The J2EE architecture provides for the detection and handling of exceptions. There are two kinds of exceptions: system exceptions and application exceptions. Application exceptions indicate recoverable-type problems (for example, bad user input or a requested purchase item being unavailable). The EJB container propagates application exceptions to the remote client, who presumably will have a catch handler in place to correct the problem (if possible) or take evasive action. The NoTrackListException shown in Listing 4.3 on page 95 is an example of an application exception. Application exceptions should be subclasses of Exception.

System exceptions indicate nonrecoverable errors, such as a lost database connection or some fatal system resource error. Enterprise beans are responsible for catching system exceptions and converting them to EJBException. The EJB container will either handle the exception itself (it may be a resource problem that the application server controls and can correct), or it will wrap the exception in a RemoteException and send it back to the client.

System exceptions should be subclasses of RuntimeException. The MusicDAOSysException shown in Listing 4.14 on page 126 is an example of a user-defined system exception.

4.7   Key Point Summary

The Music EJB accesses a database through the JDBC API. Because this access is read only, we implement our business process with a session bean. A stateless session bean is appropriate because keeping track of client-specific state is not necessary.

The Music EJB uses the Value Object pattern introduced in the previous chapter. In addition, we introduce the Data Access Object pattern, which abstracts persistence operations into a separate helper class. Using an interface for vendor-independent database access helps implement classes that work with a particular vendor's SQL implementation. A factory instantiates the correct implementation class by looking up the class name in the naming context environment entry.

Here are the key points from the chapter.

- The Java Database Connectivity (JDBC) API provides a portable way to access a relational database using SQL.
- The JDBC API provides a way to instantiate Statements and PreparedStatements, which consists of SQL query, update,

create, or delete commands. In general, `PreparedStatements` are more efficient than `Statements`, because the database can cache a compiled statement and not recompile it with each access.

- Be careful to close statements and result sets properly. This frees up database resources and makes a difference with high-volume database hits. Closing database resources within a `finally` block guarantees that it's closed even if an exception is thrown.
- The `Statement` method `executeQuery()` requests SQL execution, returning the query data in an object called a `ResultSet`. Method `executeUpdate()` performs other SQL operations, such as updates, deletions, removals, and insertions.
- The Music Collection Database consists of four related tables, as diagrammed in Figure 4–2 on page 88. Relational databases use foreign keys to relate records from one table to records of another.
- The Music EJB provides read-only business methods to access the Music Collection Database.
- The bean implementation class (`MusicBean`) contains a non-empty `ejbCreate()` method that we use to perform initializations of instance variables. These variables are not client-specific, so we are able to use a stateless session bean.
- Class `NoTrackListException` is an example of an application exception, which represents nonfatal, recoverable errors. The EJB container propagates application exceptions to the remote client. Application exceptions should subclass `Exception`.
- Class `MusicDAOSysException` is an example of a system exception, which represents nonrecoverable system errors. Enterprise bean code should catch all system exceptions and throw an `EJBException` back to the EJB container. The container can then decide what to do. Frequently, the container wraps a system exception in a `RemoteException` and sends it to the remote client. System exceptions should subclass `RuntimeException`.
- Classes `RecordingVO` and `TrackVO` implement the Value Object pattern and encapsulate related data into coarse-grained objects. This reduces the number of remote calls needed to access the encapsulated data.
- The Data Access Object (DAO) pattern improves database access flexibility and encapsulates all database access into separate helper classes. Use the Factory pattern to instantiate the specific DAO class by performing a naming service lookup.
- The Music EJB is client independent. In this chapter, we've used both a Java Swing application client and a web-based JSP program to access the Music EJB.

STATEFUL SESSION BEANS

Topics in This Chapter

- Introducing Stateful Session Beans
- Implications of Stateful vs. Stateless EJBs
- Leveraging your EJB Components
- Extending Multiple Interfaces
- Value List Iterator Pattern
- Example with a JSP Client
- Local Interfaces

Chapter 5

In the previous two chapters, we explored the design of stateless session beans. The most important characteristic of a stateless session bean is that it does not retain client-specific data. Thus, multiple clients can share stateless session beans, providing performance benefits. Stateless session beans also provide important business processes, but the results are transient, even during a session. Although a method of a stateless session bean could keep track of client-specific data, the bean does not retain the data when the method returns. Hence, the EJB container is free to assign the same instance of a stateless session bean to another client. All instances of a stateless session bean are therefore identical.

In contrast, stateful session beans *do* keep track of client-specific data. Multiple clients cannot share stateful session beans because the EJB container assigns a specific instance to each client. Stateful session beans have the advantage of being tightly coupled with clients, but there is more overhead involved. It's important, therefore, to understand how to properly design applications with stateful session beans so that performance does not suffer.

In this chapter, we'll look closely at stateful session beans and show you their benefits and costs over stateless session beans. We'll also discuss how the EJB container manages stateful session beans in a J2EE environment.

5.1 Introducing Stateful Session Beans

A *stateful* session bean keeps track of client-specific data over the course of a session. The client-related data is stored in instance variables of the stateful session bean. The lifetime of the bean corresponds to one client's session and its state reflects the work performed throughout the session. The session bean keeps track of the ***conversational state*** between the client and the bean. Throughout its lifetime, the EJB container assigns an instance of a stateful session bean to a *single* client. The state of any given instance is dependent on how the client creates the bean and the invocation of its business methods. When the session terminates, the bean's state is released and the bean's instance no longer exists.

Stateful Session Passivation and Activation

In a J2EE environment, a running application uses many system resources. The EJB container, which controls the life cycle and activation state of its enterprise beans, may need to reacquire resources used by a stateful session bean. These resources include system memory, socket connections, and database connections. When resources must be reclaimed, the container serializes a bean's state and copies it to secondary storage. This process is called ***passivation***. When it's time to restore a bean to its active state, the container reads the bean's state from secondary storage and de-serializes the objects. This process is called ***activation***. In general, the EJB container performs this work quietly and transparently.

It's not always possible for the EJB container to serialize all state information in a session bean. If an instance variable, for example, does not implement the `Serializable` interface, the container cannot save and restore the data. In this case (and in other scenarios which might require special attention), the bean developer provides code to reinitialize the bean properly.

The session bean interface provides the `ejbPassivate()` and `ejbActivate()` methods, which allow bean developers to control the passivation and activation tasks for a session bean. The container invokes `ejbPassivate()` just *before* it passivates the instance and `ejbActivate()` just *after* it activates the instance. The bean developer places the code for these methods in the session bean implementation class.

Let's look at an example. Suppose a stateful session bean contains an instance variable (`ds`) which is a reference to a `DataSource` object. To properly passivate this instance, we must assign null to the `ds` reference in `ejbPassivate()`, since a reference to an object cannot be serialized. To activate the

instance, we provide the code to reinitialize the ds reference in ejbActivate().
The following code snippets show how to do this.

```
// example ejbPassivate() inside bean implementation class
public void ejbPassivate() {
  // DataSource ds is an instance variable
  ds = null;
}

// example ejbActivate() inside bean implementation class
public void ejbActivate() {
    String dbName = "java:comp/env/jdbc/MusicDB";
    try {
      InitialContext ic = new InitialContext();
      // DataSource ds is an instance variable
      ds = (DataSource) ic.lookup(dbName);
    } catch (Exception ex) {
      throw new EJBException("Cannot find DataSource: " +
        ex.getMessage());
    }
}
```

Design Guideline

In general, you should design an ejbPassivate() *method to "undo" (or
release) any actions (or resources) performed (or acquired) by the*
ejbActivate() *method. For example, close a database connection in*
ejbPassivate() *if you acquire it in* ejbActivate().

The astute reader will recognize part of this code from our Music EJB session
bean in Chapter 4, specifically the ejbCreate() method found in the Music-
Bean implementation class (see its source on page 100). Why didn't we need
ejbPassivate() and ejbActivate() methods for the Music EJB session bean?
Recall that Music EJB is a *stateless session bean*. The EJB container never needs to
passivate it. Once a client returns from a method invocation, the container may
assign the instance to another client. This sharing means that expensive
resources are more easily distributed among various clients. Furthermore, if
the container needs to recover resources, it simply destroys the instance. There
is no "conversational state" to save. Thus, there is no need to save and restore
state through passivation and activation.

Design Guideline

When you're choosing between a stateful or stateless session bean to implement a business process, it helps to understand how the EJB container manages different session beans. A knowledge of each bean's life cycle is one way to gauge the performance impact to your enterprise application.

How does the EJB container decide which stateful bean to passivate? Usually, a container uses heuristics based on how recently a client has accessed a bean (typically the container will passivate the bean that has been called the least recently). Furthermore, if the bean is in the middle of a method call or involved in a transaction, the container cannot passivate it. (A transaction defines the boundaries of uninterruptible database operations. We discuss transactions in Chapter 6.)

This chapter will demonstrate two stateful session beans by building on previous designs from earlier chapters. Our first example, a MusicCart EJB, implements the (now traditional) online shopping paradigm. A client creates a shopping cart of music recordings, adds or removes recordings from the cart, and displays the cart's contents.

Our second stateful session bean implements the Value List Iterator Pattern. This pattern is extremely useful for managing large lists of data. We'll modify our stateless session Music EJB slightly and reuse the MusicDAO from the previous chapter to access the Music Collection database. You will see that our implementation takes advantage of the performance differences between stateful and stateless session beans, leveraging the different benefits of each one to fit our application.

5.2 MusicCart Stateful Session Bean

The MusicCart EJB is a stateful session bean that allows clients to create a shopping cart and add and remove recordings (read from the Music Collection database). Before we show you the code, we'll describe a general, architectural view of the major components of our example enterprise application.

The Big Picture

Figure 5-1 presents an architectural overview of our design using J2EE components. A client becomes the "customer" which we encapsulate in the value object CustomerVO (not shown). The stateful session bean MusicCart (denoted SFSB) manipulates RecordingVO objects (see Listing 4.4 on page 96) which

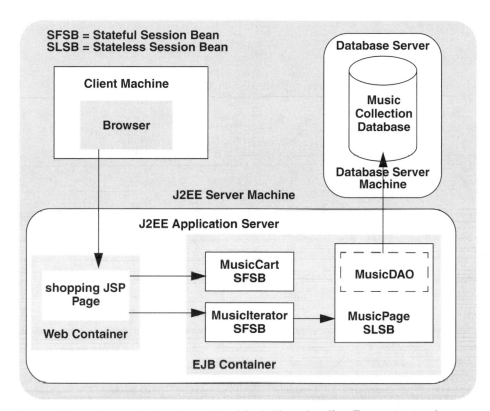

Figure 5-1 Architectural Overview of the Music Shopping Cart Enterprise Application

originate from the database store we presented in the previous chapter. To keep database access vendor independent, we use the MusicDAO implementation from Chapter 4 (see "DAO Pattern Implementation" on page 121). A new, stateful MusicIterator session bean (denoted SFSB) implements the **Value List Iterator Pattern**. The Value List Iterator Pattern allows a client to request data in small, manageable chunks instead of all at once. In addition, the *stateful* MusicIterator EJB accesses the *stateless* session bean MusicPage (denoted SLSB) to read the data. Finally, the user interacts with all these components through a JSP web component that manages the user input and presentation aspects of the application.

Figure 5-2 is a sequence diagram that shows the interactions between the client and the MusicCart EJB. The diagram shows the creation of the MusicCart EJB, which in turn creates a CustomerVO and shopping ArrayList object. It also depicts the MusicCart EJB's business methods.

As we present each component, we'll discuss the design issues that motivate our choice of stateful versus stateless session bean implementation.

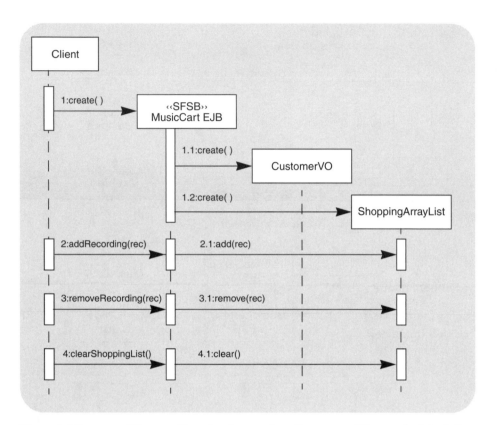

Figure 5-2 Sequence Diagram Showing Interactions Between a Client and a MusicCart EJB

CustomerVO

Listing 5.1 shows the class definition for value object CustomerVO, which holds a String name (name), a String password (password), and a String e-mail address (email). Its constructor takes three String arguments, and the class provides the typical getter and setter methods of a value object.

Note that CustomerVO implements the java.io.Serializable interface. There are two reasons for this. One, CustomerVO must be serializable because we use it in remote EJB calls as an argument. Two, the MusicCart EJB will use a CustomerVO instance variable to hold state information for a specific customer. This field must be serializable for possible activation and passivation in the MusicCart EJB stateful session bean. Remember that fields declared as instance variables in stateful session beans must either be serializable or specifically passivated and activated.

Listing 5.1 CustomerVO.java

```
// CustomerVO.java
public class CustomerVO implements java.io.Serializable
{
  private String name;
  private String password;
  private String email;

  public CustomerVO(String name, String password,
        String email) {
    setName(name);
    setPassword(password);
    setEmail(email);
  }

  // getters
  public String getPassword() { return password; }
  public String getName() { return name; }
  public String getEmail() { return email; }

  // setters
  public void setPassword(String password) {
        this.password = password; }
  public void setName(String name) { this.name = name; }
  public void setEmail(String email) {
        this.email = email; }
}
```

Home Interface

A stateful session bean has the following: a home interface containing one or more create() methods, a remote interface with business methods, and a bean implementation class with the code for the methods in both interfaces. Let's look at the home interface of our MusicCart EJB first.

Because the MusicCart EJB is stateful, there may be multiple ways to create the bean and initialize its state. In Listing 5.2, you will find two create() methods in the home interface of the MusicCart EJB. The first one accepts only a customer name, whereas the second one creates the bean from a CustomerVO object. Note that both create() methods return an object of the bean's remote interface type (MusicCart). And, as we've seen in previous examples, each create() method must specify RemoteException and CreateException in its throws clause. The home interface always extends EJBHome.

Listing 5.2 MusicCartHome.java

```
// MusicCartHome.java
import java.io.Serializable;
import java.rmi.RemoteException;
import javax.ejb.CreateException;
import javax.ejb.EJBHome;

public interface MusicCartHome extends EJBHome {

  MusicCart create(String person) throws RemoteException,
      CreateException;
  MusicCart create(CustomerVO customer) throws
      RemoteException, CreateException;
}
```

Remote Interface

The MusicCart EJB remote interface in Listing 5.3 contains the bean's business methods. We have methods for adding and removing recordings to the shopping cart, obtaining the current shopping list, and querying customer information.

Listing 5.3 MusicCart.java

```
// MusicCart.java
import javax.ejb.EJBObject;
import java.rmi.RemoteException;
import java.util.*;

public interface MusicCart extends EJBObject {

  public void addRecording(RecordingVO album)
        throws RemoteException;
  public void removeRecording(RecordingVO album)
        throws ShoppingException, RemoteException;

  public void clearShoppingList() throws RemoteException;
  public ArrayList getShoppingList()
        throws RemoteException;
  public CustomerVO getCustomer() throws RemoteException;
}
```

The `addRecording()` and `removeRecording()` methods both accept `RecordingVO` value objects as arguments. Method `getShoppingList()` returns an `ArrayList` collection of recordings and method `clearShoppingList()` removes all objects from the shopping list. The `removeRecording()` method also specifies `ShoppingException` in its `throws` clause. This application exception indicates that the client requested removal of a recording that was not in the shopping cart.

Note that `addRecording()`, `clearShoppingList()`, and `removeRecording()` update the `MusicCart`'s state, whereas `getShoppingList()` and `getCustomer()` are getter methods that return portions of the bean's state.

Bean Implementation

The bean implementation class for the MusicCart EJB is shown in Listing 5.4. Because this session bean is stateful, it must have instance variables that maintain state information. For our MusicCart EJB, this state consists of a `CustomerVO` value object (`customer`) and an `ArrayList` of recordings in the shopping cart (`shoppingList`). Because both of these variables are serializable, we do not need to write implementation code for methods `ejbPassivate()` and `ejbActivate()`. The bean class also contains the implementations of the home and remote interface methods.

Each `create()` method in the home interface has a corresponding `ejbCreate()` method in the bean implementation class with matching arguments. Note that `create()` always returns a remote interface type but `ejbCreate()` has `void` for the return type.

The job of `ejbCreate()` is to make sure that the EJB container instantiates the MusicCart EJB object correctly. Both `ejbCreate()` methods check for valid initialization parameters before they initialize the `shoppingList` and `customer` instance variables. If either `ejbCreate()` method finds inconsistencies in the input parameters, it throws a `CreateException`.

The `ArrayList` collection is serializable and stores recordings in the shopping cart. Its methods `add()`, `contains()`, `clear()`, and `remove()` manipulate the collection of recordings.

Implementation Factoid

`ArrayList` *method* `contains()` *returns true if the collection contains the specified object.* `ArrayList` *uses the Java* `Object`*'s* `equals()` *method to determine equality. This is why we implement method* `equals()` *in class* **RecordingVO.java** *(see Listing 4.4 on page 96).*

Note that `removeRecording()` checks to see if the recording to be removed is actually in the collection. If it isn't, the method throws a `ShoppingExcep-`

tion. A client of the MusicCart EJB should check for this exception separately from a more drastic system exception.

Listing 5.4 MusicCartBean.java

```java
// MusicCartBean.java
import javax.ejb.*;
import javax.naming.*;
import java.rmi.RemoteException;
import java.util.*;

public class MusicCartBean implements SessionBean {

  // EJB instance variables
  CustomerVO customer;
  ArrayList shoppingList;

  // create() methods implementation
  // from the EJBHome interface
  // Methods ejbCreate() should initialize the
  // instance variables

  public void ejbCreate(String person)
        throws CreateException {
    if (person == null || person.equals("")) {
      throw new CreateException(
          "Name cannot be null or empty.");
    }
    else {
      customer = new
          CustomerVO(person, "NoPassword", "NoEmail");
    }
    shoppingList = new ArrayList();
  }

  // Implementation for create(CustomerVO cust)
  public void ejbCreate(CustomerVO cust)
        throws CreateException {
    if (cust.getName() == null) {
      throw new CreateException("Name cannot be null.");
    }
```

Listing 5.4 MusicCartBean.java *(continued)*

```java
    if (cust.getPassword() == null ||
            cust.getPassword().equals("")) {
      throw new CreateException(
          "Password cannot be null or empty.");
    }

    if (cust.getEmail() == null ||
            cust.getEmail().equals("")) {
      throw new CreateException(
          "Email cannot be null or empty.");
    }
    customer = cust;
    shoppingList = new ArrayList();
  }

  // Business methods implementation

  public CustomerVO getCustomer() {
    return customer;
  }

  public void addRecording(RecordingVO album) {
    shoppingList.add(album);
  }

  // ShoppingException is an application exception
  public void removeRecording(RecordingVO album)
      throws ShoppingException
  {
    if (shoppingList.contains(album)) {
      shoppingList.remove(shoppingList.indexOf(album));
    }
    else {
      throw new ShoppingException(
            album.getTitle() + " not in cart.");
    }
  }

  // clear the shopping list
  public void clearShoppingList() {
    shoppingList.clear();
  }
```

Listing 5.4 MusicCartBean.java *(continued)*

```
public ArrayList getShoppingList() {
    return shoppingList;
}

// EJB Methods
public MusicCartBean() {}
public void ejbRemove() {}
public void ejbActivate() {}
public void ejbPassivate() {}
public void setSessionContext(SessionContext sc) {}

} // MusicCartBean
```

Deployment Descriptor

Listing 5.5 shows the deployment descriptor for the MusicCart EJB. Here, we indicate that it is a stateful session bean, its home interface is `MusicCartHome`, its remote interface is `MusicCart`, and its bean implementation class is `Music-CartBean`. We show tag values in **bold**.

Listing 5.5 MusicCart EJB Deployment Descriptor

```
<ejb-jar>
  <display-name>MusicCartJAR</display-name>
 <enterprise-beans>
    <session>

      <display-name>MusicCartBean</display-name>
      <ejb-name>MusicCartBean</ejb-name>
      <home>MusicCartHome</home>
      <remote>MusicCart</remote>
      <ejb-class>MusicCartBean</ejb-class>
      <session-type>Stateful</session-type>
      <transaction-type>Bean</transaction-type>
      <security-identity>
        <description></description>
        <use-caller-identity></use-caller-identity>
      </security-identity>
    </session>
 </enterprise-beans>
</ejb-jar>
```

Before we examine the other EJBs in our MusicCart design, let's learn about the Value List Iterator Pattern. This important pattern helps you understand the advantages of both stateless and stateful session bean properties.

5.3 Value List Iterator Pattern

The client programs in the previous chapter read in all the recordings from the Music Collection database by invoking the `getMusicList()` method in the Music EJB. These clients use Swing components and HTML `Option` tags to display the recording list on the user's display screen. This works just fine if we have a short list, say something under 25 items. What happens if our database contains 100 items, 1,000 items, or even 10,000 items?

For a client application to effectively deal with a list that big presents logistic problems. No user wants to page through a 1,000-item list. In fact, a user machine with a browser and a large list may not be able to run the application at all, due to limited resources and memory constraints. Furthermore, a user may not be interested in seeing the entire list of items, resulting in wasted resources and time required to transmit all the list items.

The Value List Iterator Pattern can help with large lists of data. This pattern allows clients to request data a page at a time. A Value List Iterator applies to many common situations. For example, it applies when a user wants to access only portions of a list, or if the list doesn't fit in memory or on the user's display. A Value List Iterator can also be handy if transmitting the entire list takes too much time or if a client application has no idea how large the list is.

There are several consequences to implementing a Value List Iterator. First of all, the client controls how much data to transmit. By breaking up a list into multiple remote calls for retrieval, the client makes more requests on the server, thereby increasing network traffic. Also, the Value List Iterator should be applied to *read-only* lists, since concurrent updates to mutable lists could possibly invalidate the data.

There are several strategies for implementing the Value List Iterator Pattern.

- *Stateful session bean.* The bean implementation keeps track of the client's current page and desired page size. This presents a clean and simple interface to the client, because a client can request the next page, grab the previous page, or ask if there are more elements to read (either forward or in reverse). The downside is that a stateful session bean must be tied to a single client. This can be a strain on the server's resources when many clients make simultaneous requests. Most alarmingly, the server must cache multiple copies of the data.

- *Stateless session bean*. The bean implementation does not keep track of client-specific data. This means more bookkeeping tasks for the client, who is now responsible for the current page, page size, and any other variables needed to effectively manage the list. However, the EJB container can reuse a stateless session bean easily, requiring far fewer copies of the data in the server's memory.
- *Stateless session bean/stateful session bean combination*. This strategy uses a stateless session bean to access the data and a stateful session bean to manage the iteration of the list. A stateful session bean presents a clean interface to a client and keeps track of all the client-specific data. The stateful session bean also translates client-specific parameters into calls to the stateless bean, which holds the data. This approach provides the best features of both of the previous implementation strategies.

Design Guideline

The combination approach unburdens clients by encapsulating client-specific data into a stateful bean. Moreover, the stateless bean requires less server-side resources because the EJB container can easily switch instances among clients. This is the strategy we use to implement our Value List Iterator Pattern.

Now we are ready to show you the implementations for the MusicIterator EJB and the MusicPage EJB. Figure 5-3 shows a class diagram of the Value List Iterator Pattern participants. You can see how these EJB components interact to implement this pattern. The MusicIterator EJB is a *stateful* session bean that keeps track of client-specific data and provides methods to page through the recording data forward and backward. The MusicPage EJB is a *stateless* session bean that uses the MusicDAO to read and hold the recording data from the Music Collection database. (Note that the box labeled MusicDAO is an *implementation* of the MusicDAO interface.) Although the MusicPage EJB does not track any client-specific data, it provides a method to get a page of recording data for the MusicIterator EJB.

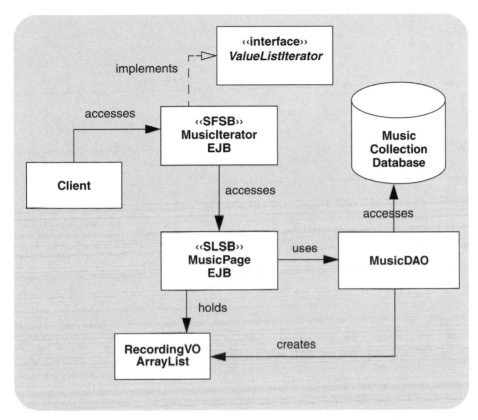

Figure 5-3 Class Diagram Showing the Participants of the Value List Iterator Pattern

Figure 5-4 is a sequence diagram showing the method invocations (messages) sent between client, MusicIterator EJB, MusicPage EJB, and the MusicDAO implementation object. This interaction diagram shows the messages required to create the data (the ArrayList of RecordingVOs) and read a page (using MusicIterator method nextpage()).

Let's look at the MusicPage stateless session bean first.

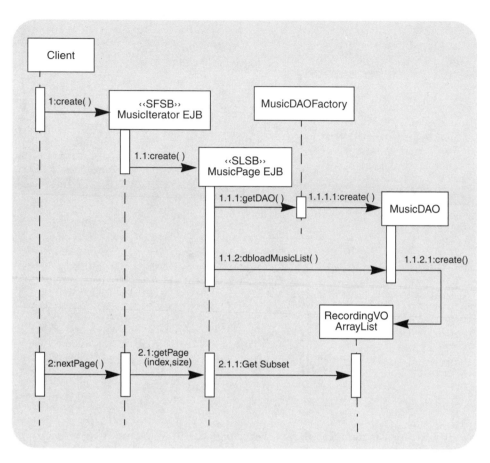

Figure 5-4 Sequence Diagram Showing the Interactions for Reading a Page of Data from the MusicDAO Object

MusicPage Stateless Session Bean

The MusicPage EJB is similar to the Music EJB from Chapter 4. Listing 5.6 shows the home interface for the MusicPage EJB. Since this is a stateless session bean, it has only one create() method.

Listing 5.6 MusicPageHome.java

```
// MusicPageHome.java
import java.rmi.RemoteException;
import javax.ejb.CreateException;
import javax.ejb.EJBHome;

public interface MusicPageHome extends EJBHome {

    MusicPage create() throws CreateException,
            RemoteException;
}
```

Listing 5.7 shows the remote interface for the MusicPage EJB, consisting of three business methods. The getSize() method returns the number of recordings in the Music Collection database and getPage() returns a single page of data. Method getTrackList() reads the track list from a specific recording.

Listing 5.7 MusicPage.java

```
// MusicPage.java
import java.rmi.RemoteException;
import javax.ejb.EJBObject;
import java.util.*;

public interface MusicPage extends EJBObject {

  public ArrayList getTrackList(RecordingVO rec)
      throws NoTrackListException, RemoteException;
  public int getSize() throws RemoteException;
  public ArrayList getPage(int currentIndex,
      int pageSize) throws RemoteException;
}
```

The MusicPage EJB implementation class is shown in Listing 5.8. To access the Music Collection database, we use a MusicDAO object to encapsulate the vendor-dependent details. This is the same DAO pattern technique we used with the Music EJB in Chapter 4 (see "DAO Pattern Implementation" on page 121).

The getPage() method is responsible for returning a page of recordings from the recording list. To do this, the method builds an ArrayList with the page of data. As you will soon see, the MusicIterator EJB calls this method with a page index (currentIndex) and a page size (pageSize). Inside the getpage()

method, we do some sanity checks on the arguments before creating the page as an `ArrayList`.

Since MusicPage EJB is a stateless session bean, the EJB container is free to assign the same instance to a new client as soon as the current client returns from a method call. This allows one instance to be shared among many clients.

Listing 5.8 MusicPageBean.java

```java
// MusicPageBean.java
import java.util.*;
import javax.ejb.*;
import javax.naming.*;

public class MusicPageBean implements SessionBean {

  // Instance variable MusicDAO object
  // to access database.
  // MusicDAO object is instantiated in ejbCreate()
  // and provides implementation of the MusicDAO interface
  // for the particular database we're using.
  private MusicDAO dao;

  // Instance variable ArrayList that holds all recordings
  private ArrayList musicList;

  // Business methods

  public int getSize() { return musicList.size(); }

  public ArrayList getPage(int currentIndex, int pageSize)
  {
    // perform a sanity check on the arguments
    if (currentIndex > musicList.size())
      currentIndex = musicList.size();
    else if (currentIndex < 0)
      currentIndex = 0;
    if (pageSize <= 0) pageSize = 1;
    else if (pageSize > musicList.size())
      pageSize = musicList.size();
```

Listing 5.8 MusicPageBean.java *(continued)*

```java
    // create the sublist
    ArrayList page = new ArrayList();

    // initialize an iterator to point to
    // the requested element
    ListIterator current =
          musicList.listIterator(currentIndex);

    // grab the elements for the desired page size
    for (int i = 0;
         current.hasNext() && i < pageSize; i++)
      page.add(current.next());
    return page;
  }

  public ArrayList getTrackList(RecordingVO rec)
              throws NoTrackListException {
    ArrayList trackList;
    try {
      // Encapsulate database calls in MusicDAO
      trackList = dao.dbLoadTrackList(rec);
    } catch (MusicDAOSysException ex) {
      throw new EJBException("getTrackList: " +
              ex.getMessage());
    }

    if (trackList.size() == 0) {
      throw new NoTrackListException(
            "No Track List found for RecordingID " +
            rec.getRecordID());
    }
    return trackList;
  }

  // EJB methods

  public void ejbCreate() {
    try {
      // The MusicDAOFactory class returns an
      // implementation of the MusicDAO interface
      dao = MusicDAOFactory.getDAO();
```

Listing 5.8 MusicPageBean.java *(continued)*

```
        // initialize the shared music ArrayList
        musicList = dao.dbLoadMusicList();
        System.out.println("MusicPageBean:ejbCreate():" +
            "initialized musicList from DAO object");
    }
    catch (MusicDAOSysException ex) {
      throw new EJBException(ex.getMessage());
    }
  }

  public MusicPageBean() {}
  public void ejbRemove() {}
  public void ejbActivate() {}
  public void ejbPassivate() {}
  public void setSessionContext(SessionContext sc) {}

} // MusicPageBean
```

Deployment Descriptor

Listing 5.9 contains the deployment descriptor for the MusicPage EJB. It is similar to the one for the Music EJB, shown previously in Listing 4.7 on page 105. We'll include it here, since this descriptor also includes the environment entry for specifying the DAO class. Note that MusicPageBean is stateless.

Listing 5.9 MusicPage EJB Deployment Descriptor

```
<ejb-jar>
 <display-name>MusicPageJAR</display-name>
 <enterprise-beans>
    <session>
      <display-name>MusicPageBean</display-name>
      <ejb-name>MusicPageBean</ejb-name>
      <home>MusicPageHome</home>
      <remote>MusicPage</remote>
      <ejb-class>MusicPageBean</ejb-class>
      <session-type>Stateless</session-type>
      <transaction-type>Bean</transaction-type>
```

Listing 5.9 MusicPage EJB Deployment Descriptor *(continued)*

```xml
  <env-entry>
    <env-entry-name>MusicDAOClass</env-entry-name>
    <env-entry-type>java.lang.String</env-entry-type>
    <env-entry-value>MusicDAOCloudscape</env-entry-value>
  </env-entry>

      <security-identity>
        <description></description>
        <use-caller-identity></use-caller-identity>
      </security-identity>

      <resource-ref>
        <res-ref-name>jdbc/MusicDB</res-ref-name>
        <res-type>javax.sql.DataSource</res-type>
        <res-auth>Container</res-auth>
        <res-sharing-scope>Shareable</res-sharing-scope>
      </resource-ref>

    </session>
  </enterprise-beans>
</ejb-jar>
```

MusicIterator Stateful Session Bean

We're now ready to examine the MusicIterator EJB. This stateful session bean keeps track of the client's page size and current position in the recording list. Here is the home interface, found in Listing 5.10. Note that even though Music-Iterator EJB is a stateful session bean, its home interface contains only a single `create()` method.

Listing 5.10 MusicIteratorHome.java

```java
// MusicIteratorHome.java
import java.io.Serializable;
import java.rmi.RemoteException;
import javax.ejb.CreateException;
import javax.ejb.EJBHome;

public interface MusicIteratorHome extends EJBHome {
    MusicIterator create() throws RemoteException,
            CreateException;
}
```

We'll look at the remote interface for the MusicIterator EJB in a moment. Before we do, let's define a set of useful operations that apply to all Value List Iterator objects. To do this formally, we'll create an interface called Value-ListIterator and define methods for the operations. Then we can extend our MusicIterator remote interface from ValueListIterator and implement the methods in the MusicIterator bean class. This has two advantages. One, it separates the general operations of the Value List Iterator Pattern from the application-specific operations we require in the MusicIterator EJB. Second, the ValueListIterator interface is reusable with other EJB applications that require paging.

Listing 5.11 contains the source code for the ValueListIterator interface. This interface defines methods common to all value lists, such as setting page size, fetching the next or previous page, and determining if there are more elements to read. Method resetIndex() resets the index for the data and method setPageSize() returns the old page size.

Listing 5.11 ValueListIterator.java

```java
// ValueListIterator.java
import java.rmi.RemoteException;
import java.util.*;

public interface ValueListIterator {

  public static final int defaultPageSize = 10;

  public int getSize() throws RemoteException;
  public int setPageSize(int numberOfElements)
          throws RemoteException;

  public int getPageSize() throws RemoteException;
  public ArrayList previousPage() throws RemoteException;
  public ArrayList nextPage() throws RemoteException;

  public void resetIndex() throws RemoteException;
  public boolean hasMoreElements() throws RemoteException;
  public boolean hasPreviousElements() throws
          RemoteException;

} // ValueListIterator
```

Design Guideline

When an enterprise bean implements a reusable set of operations, isolate the reusable parts in an interface. Then, extend this "reusable" specification in the enterprise bean's remote interface. Make sure all the methods in this reusable interface have RemoteException *in their* throws *clauses.*

Listing 5.12 is the remote interface for the MusicIterator EJB. Note that this interface *extends* ValueListIterator (in addition to EJBObject). This means we inherit all the method definitions of ValueListIterator implicitly. All we have to do is add getTrackList() to complete the remote interface for our MusicIterator EJB.

Listing 5.12 MusicIterator.java

```
// MusicIterator.java
import javax.ejb.EJBObject;
import java.rmi.RemoteException;
import java.util.*;

public interface MusicIterator extends EJBObject,
        ValueListIterator {

    public ArrayList getTrackList(RecordingVO rec) throws
            NoTrackListException, RemoteException;

} // MusicIterator
```

The only thing left to show you is the MusicIteratorBean implementation class in Listing 5.13. This class contains the code for all methods in the remote interface, including those from ValueListIterator as well as the ejbCreate() method (corresponding to create() in the home interface). Since this is a stateful session bean, the class also includes the declaration and management of client-specific instance variables. These fields keep track of the client's request for reading the recordings from the Music Collection. Recording data can be accessed forwards or backwards with a page size that the client may customize.

As you peruse the code, note that MusicIterator EJB uses instance variable pageBean to forward calls to the MusicPage EJB. This instance variable is initialized in ejbCreate().

Listing 5.13 MusicIteratorBean.java

```java
// MusicIteratorBean.java
import java.rmi.RemoteException;
import javax.rmi.PortableRemoteObject;
import javax.ejb.*;
import javax.naming.*;
import java.util.*;

public class MusicIteratorBean implements SessionBean {

  // Instance variables
  private MusicPage pageBean = null;
  private int currentIndex;
  private int previousStart;
  private int pageSize;
  private int arraySize;

  // Business methods

   public ArrayList getTrackList(RecordingVO rec)
      throws NoTrackListException {

    try {
      return pageBean.getTrackList(rec);
    } catch (Exception ex) {
      throw new EJBException(ex.getMessage());
    }
  }

  public int getSize() { return arraySize; }

  public int setPageSize(int numberOfElements) {
    int oldSize = pageSize;
    if (numberOfElements < 1 )
      { pageSize = 1; }
    else if (numberOfElements > arraySize)
      { pageSize = arraySize; }
    else
      { pageSize = numberOfElements; }
    return oldSize;
  }

  public int getPageSize() { return pageSize; }
```

Listing 5.13 MusicIteratorBean.java *(continued)*

```java
public ArrayList previousPage()
{
  // Return the previous page to the client
  // Perform some basic sanity checks
  // on the parameters

  try {
    currentIndex = previousStart - pageSize;
    if (currentIndex < 0) currentIndex = 0;
    int newIndex = currentIndex;
    previousStart = currentIndex;
    if (previousStart == 0) previousStart = -1;
    currentIndex += pageSize;
    if (currentIndex > arraySize)
        currentIndex = arraySize;
    return pageBean.getPage(newIndex, pageSize);

  } catch (Exception ex) {
    throw new EJBException(ex.getMessage());
  }
}

public ArrayList nextPage()
{
  // Return the next page to the client
  // Perform some basic sanity checks
  // on the parameters

  try {
    int newIndex = currentIndex;
    previousStart = currentIndex;
    currentIndex += pageSize;
    if (currentIndex > arraySize)
        currentIndex = arraySize;
    return pageBean.getPage(newIndex, pageSize);

  } catch (Exception ex) {
    throw new EJBException(ex.getMessage());
  }
}
```

Listing 5.13 MusicIteratorBean.java *(continued)*

```java
public void resetIndex() {
  currentIndex = 0;
  previousStart = 0;
}

public boolean hasMoreElements() {
    return (currentIndex < arraySize);
}

public boolean hasPreviousElements() {
  return (previousStart >=0);
}

// EJB Methods

public MusicIteratorBean() {}

// We must initialize all instance variables here
public void ejbCreate() {
  try {
    Context initial = new InitialContext();
    Object objref =
        initial.lookup("java:comp/env/ejb/MusicPage");
    MusicPageHome pageHome = (MusicPageHome)
        PortableRemoteObject.narrow(objref,
        MusicPageHome.class);
    pageBean = pageHome.create();
    arraySize = pageBean.getSize();

  } catch (Exception ex) {
    throw new EJBException(ex.getMessage());
  }

  // set page size from ValueListIterator default
  pageSize = ValueListIterator.defaultPageSize;
  currentIndex = 0;
  previousStart = 0;
  System.out.println("MusicIteratorBean:ejbCreate()");
}
```

Listing 5.13 MusicIteratorBean.java *(continued)*

```
   public void ejbRemove() {}
   public void ejbActivate() {}
   public void ejbPassivate() {}
   public void setSessionContext(SessionContext sc) {}
} // MusicIteratorBean
```

Deployment Descriptor

Listing 5.14 contains the deployment descriptor for MusicIterator EJB. It indicates that MusicIterator EJB is stateful, and it includes the EJB reference for
MusicPage EJB.

Listing 5.14 MusicIterator EJB Deployment Descriptor

```xml
<ejb-jar>
  <display-name>MIteratorJAR</display-name>
  <enterprise-beans>

   <session>
      <display-name>MusicIteratorBean</display-name>
      <ejb-name>MusicIteratorBean</ejb-name>
      <home>MusicIteratorHome</home>
      <remote>MusicIterator</remote>
      <ejb-class>MusicIteratorBean</ejb-class>
      <session-type>Stateful</session-type>
      <transaction-type>Bean</transaction-type>

      <ejb-ref>
        <ejb-ref-name>ejb/MusicPage</ejb-ref-name>
        <ejb-ref-type>Session</ejb-ref-type>
        <home>MusicPageHome</home>
        <remote>MusicPage</remote>
      </ejb-ref>

      <security-identity>
        <description></description>
        <use-caller-identity></use-caller-identity>
      </security-identity>
    </session>
  </enterprise-beans>
</ejb-jar>
```

Invocation Patterns

Suppose that our application has more than one client active at the same time. How does the EJB container handle multiple client requests? When does the EJB container instantiate the MusicIterator EJB and when does it instantiate the MusicPage EJB?

Figure 5-5 shows three clients, each with their own instance of the stateful MusicIterator EJB. (We show this ownership with a solid arrow from the client to the MusicIterator EJB instance.) The EJB container will instantiate the stateless MusicPage EJB *as needed*. Depending on the timing of the requests, it is possible that a single instance could service all requests. How significant is this?

In the MusicIterator EJB implementation code, the following statement makes a request to instantiate the MusicPage EJB.

```
pageBean = pageHome.create();
```

Recall that when a client invokes the MusicPage EJB's `create()` method, the EJB container maps this call to `ejbCreate()` *unless an instance of the bean already exists*. If an instance exists, the container does not execute the `ejbCreate()` method. This is significant in our example, since the MusicPage EJB uses the MusicDAO to read in the entire database! Fortunately, we can avoid this expensive step because the EJB container is free to assign the same instance of

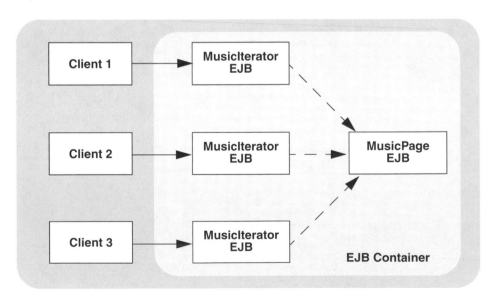

Figure 5-5 Stateful vs. Stateless Session Bean Objects

the MusicPage EJB to another client request. We show this "dynamic-assignable" relationship in Figure 5-5 with a dotted arrow from each MusicIterator EJB to the single instance of the MusicPage EJB.

Because the MusicPage EJB is a stateless bean, we can economize on the expensive resources of reading the database and caching the data. The EJB container must assign one stateful MusicIterator EJB to each client for the duration of the session. However, since the MusicIterator EJB does not consume a lot of resources, we don't pay a high price to make it stateful.

Design Guideline

The MusicPage EJB uses the MusicDAO to read the entire Music Collection database into memory. In the real world, a large database may not make this approach feasible. In this situation, the MusicDAO could implement its own caching scheme to deliver data for paging. Note that this capability does not affect the overall architecture of our application, since the details would be confined to the MusicPage EJB and its helper class, MusicDAO.

5.4 Web Component Client

The MusicCart has a JSP web component client that uses the stateful MusicCart EJB and MusicIterator EJB. This JSP program is more complicated than the examples you've seen previously, so let's take time to explain its structure.

The MusicCart shopping JSP program consists of five JSP files. You've already seen **error.jsp** (see Listing 4.10 on page 119), so we're not going to repeat that program here. Figure 5-6 shows how the other JSP files interact.

The **login.jsp** and **loginPost.jsp** files allow the client to "log in" and establish a customer identity. If successful, the **musicCart.jsp** displays a radio button list of recording titles for one page. The screen also has buttons to add or remove recording titles in the music cart, page through the list of recording titles with Next or Previous, and display tracks from a specific recording.

The **shoppingPost.jsp** file is responsible for handling the shopping requests (adding and removing titles) and for displaying the track list. As the user modifies the contents of the shopping cart, **shoppingPost.jsp** displays its new contents in HTML table format.

The **musicCart.jsp** uses MusicIterator EJB to page through the Music Collection database. File **shoppingPost.jsp** uses the MusicCart EJB to keep track of customer information and the current contents of the shopping cart. It also accesses the MusicIterator EJB to read the selected recording's track list. As you will see, most of the session data is stored in the two stateful session beans

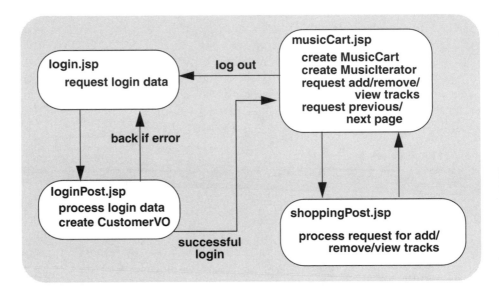

Figure 5-6 Relationship Among JSP Files for the MusicCart JSP Web Component

(MusicCart EJB and MusicIterator EJB), but the JSP session object also stores session data.

Design Guideline

It is always preferable to keep track of session data inside stateful session beans instead of JSP session objects. In the long run, data in stateful session beans is much easier to maintain than data in a web component.

Let's look at several screen shots that illustrate the JSP client. The initial login page (**login.jsp**) prompts for a name and password. After supplying this information (any string will work as long as it's not empty), the user clicks on a "Submit Login" button. The **loginPost.jsp** page acknowledges a successful login and provides access to the Music Collection site. Figure 5-7 shows the initial page after entering the Music Collection site.

Figure 5-7 Screen Shot After the User Successfully Logs In to the Music Collection Site

The **musicCart.jsp** page shows the first three recordings from the Music Collection database on the screen. There are buttons to view the tracks of a recording, add a selected recording to the music cart, or delete a recording from the cart. If a user chooses to view tracks, the screen looks similar to the display in Figure 4–6 on page 111. The Previous and Next buttons allow users to "page" through the recordings in the Music Collection.

With "Imagine" already selected, let's click on "Add Recording to Cart."
Figure 5-8 shows the result.

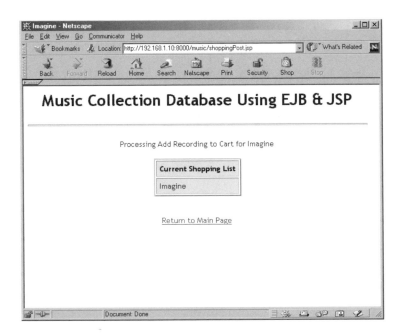

Figure 5-8 Screen Shot After the User Clicks "Add Recording to Cart" for Imagine

We then return to the main page. Here we click on the "Next" button which displays the next set of recordings as shown in Figure 5-9.

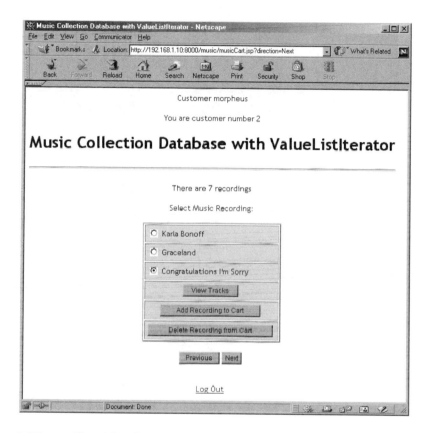

Figure 5-9 Screen Shot After the User Returns to the Main Page and Clicks on the Next Button

If we select "Graceland" and attempt to delete this recording from our shopping cart, we'll see an error page, since this recording is not in our cart. Figure 5-10 shows the result.

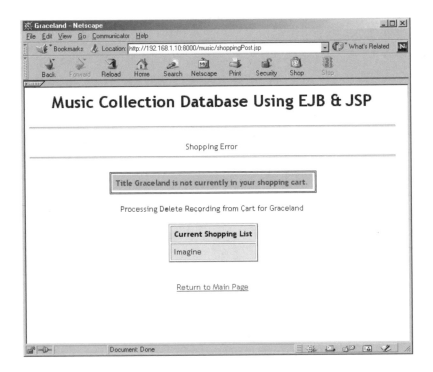

Figure 5-10 Screen Shot After the User Attempts to Remove an Item Not Currently in the Shopping Cart

login.jsp

Listing 5.15 contains **login.jsp**, which presents a login screen to the user. It requests two text fields: a login name and password. A Submit button allows the user to submit the login information to the login processing program, **loginPost.jsp**.

Listing 5.15 login.jsp

```
<%--
  login.jsp
--%>

<%--
  JSP Component to gather user name and password
  information.
--%>

<%@ page errorPage="error.jsp" %>
<%
  String requestURI = request.getRequestURI();
  session.putValue("loginURL", requestURI);
%>

<html>
<head>
<title>Music Collection Database Login Page</title>
</head>

<body bgcolor=white>
<center>
<h1>Login Page</h1>
<hr>

<p>
Please provide the following information
<form method="post" action="loginPost.jsp">
<p>

<table border=2 cellpadding=5 bgcolor=#e0e0e0>
  <tr><td>
  Name:
  </td><td>
  <input TYPE="text" NAME="name" size=20>
  </td></tr>

  <tr><td>
  Password:
  </td><td>
  <input TYPE="password" NAME="password" size=20>
  </td></tr>
```

Listing 5.15 login.jsp *(continued)*

```
  <tr><td align=center colspan=2>
  <input TYPE="submit" NAME="Login" VALUE="Submit Login">
  </td></tr>
</table>
</form>
</body></html>
```

loginPost.jsp

Listing 5.16 contains **loginPost.jsp**, which receives login information submitted by the user. The customer identity is transient; that is, we don't save it to permanent store. As long as neither field is empty, the login is successful. (In the next chapter, we provide a customer name and password verification against a Customer database.) Upon successfully logging in, the program builds a `CustomerVO` value object from the input data and stores it into the session object for the **musicCart.jsp** program. The user also sees a congratulatory message and a link to the Music Collection page.

An unsuccessful login reports an error and displays a link back to the original login page.

Listing 5.16 loginPost.jsp

```
<%--
  loginPost.jsp
--%>

<%--
  JSP Web component to process login information
  making sure user has supplied a value for
  each field.
--%>

<%@ page import="CustomerVO" errorPage="error.jsp" %>
<%
  CustomerVO customer = null;
%>

<html>
<title>Process Login</title>
<body bgcolor=white>
<center>
```

Listing 5.16 loginPost.jsp *(continued)*

```
<%
  String requestURI =
    (String)session.getValue("loginURL");

  // Get name and password values provided by user
  String name = (String)request.getParameter("name");
  String password =
    (String)request.getParameter("password");

  // Check to make sure they're not empty
  if (name.equals("") || password.equals("")) {

  // Empty, report error to user
  // We use html formatting tags to create an error box
  // with red lettering so that it will stand out.
%>

<h1>Login Error</h1>
<hr>
<p>
<p STYLE="background:#bfbfbf;color:red;
font-weight:bold;border:double thin;padding:5">
You have left a field empty. You must provide both a name
and a password.
</font>
<br><br><a href="<%= requestURI %>">
  Return to Login Page</a>

<%
  }
  else {
    customer = new CustomerVO(name, password, "NoEmail");
    session.putValue("customer", customer.getName());
    // a new customer requires a new music cart;
    // put this information in session object for
    // musicCart.jsp
    String newCustomer = "new";
    session.putValue("newCustomer", newCustomer);
%>
```

Listing 5.16 loginPost.jsp *(continued)*

```
<h1>Login Successful</h1>
<p>
<h2>Welcome <%= customer.getName() %> </h2>
<hr>
<p>

<br><br><a href="musicCart.jsp">Enter Music Collection
Site</a>
<%
   }
%>
</body></html>
```

---

musicCart.jsp

Listing 5.17 contains **musicCart.jsp**, which manipulates the MusicCart EJB and
the MusicIterator EJB on behalf of the user. The program presents a radio button list of recording titles for one page of the Music Collection database. We set
the page size to a very small value (3). (We don't have many titles in our database and we want to be able to manipulate them with the Next and Previous
buttons.)

A user may select a title or request a different page of data. Once the user
selects a title, one of three commands can be chosen: add a title to the shopping
cart, remove a title from the shopping cart, or view a track list for that title. The
title and the command are stored in a `request` object for the next JSP file, **shop-
pingPost.jsp**.

Inside `jspInit()`, we initialize the home interfaces for both stateful session
beans and store them in class variables. All clients can share these instances—
we use them to create a stateful session bean for each new customer. Note that
the `customerCounter` integer is also a class wide variable. We initialize it when
the application server first deploys the web component. Each new customer
increments the counter.

This program gets most of its variables from the session object, since the
user returns to this page multiple times. The logic determines when the user is
a new customer. A new customer must have a new instance of both the Music-
Cart EJB and the MusicIterator EJB. A returning customer obtains these objects
from the implicit session object.

Listing 5.17 musicCart.jsp

```jsp
<%--
  musicCart.jsp
--%>

<%--
  JSP Web component to read the Music Collection Database
  using the ValueListIterator Pattern
--%>

<%--
  The following page directive tells the JSP engine
  to import the named classes and packages when compiling
  the generated servlet code and to use
  "error.jsp" for an errorPage.
--%>

<%@ page import="MusicCart,MusicCartHome,CustomerVO,Music-
Iterator,MusicIteratorHome,RecordingVO,java.util.*,
javax.naming.Context, javax.naming.InitialContext,
javax.rmi.PortableRemoteObject" errorPage="error.jsp" %>

<%--
  The following variables appear in a JSP declaration.
  They may be shared.
--%>

<%!
  MusicIteratorHome musicHome;
  MusicCartHome cartHome;
  int customerCounter = 0;

  public void jspInit() {
    try {
      Context initial = new InitialContext();
      Object objref = initial.lookup(
          "java:comp/env/ejb/EJBMusic");

      // a reference to the home interface is shareable
      musicHome = (MusicIteratorHome)
          PortableRemoteObject.narrow(
          objref, MusicIteratorHome.class);
      System.out.println(
          "created MusicIteratorHome object");
```

Listing 5.17 musicCart.jsp *(continued)*

```
        objref = initial.lookup(
            "java:comp/env/ejb/MyMusicCart");
        // a reference to the home interface is shareable
        cartHome = (MusicCartHome)
            PortableRemoteObject.narrow(objref,
            MusicCartHome.class);

    } catch (Exception ex) {
      System.out.println("Unexpected Exception: " +
          ex.getMessage());
    }
  }
%>

<%
  // Initialize variables from session object
  ArrayList albums = null;
  int total = 0;
  String currentTitle =
    (String)session.getValue("curTitle");
  if (currentTitle == null) currentTitle = "";

  String customer =
    (String)session.getValue("customer");
  String newCustomer =
    (String)session.getValue("newCustomer");
  MusicCart cart =
    (MusicCart)session.getValue("musicCart");
  MusicIterator mymusic =
    (MusicIterator)session.getValue("mymusic");

  if (cart == null || newCustomer.equals("new")) {
    // new customer; initialize music cart and
    // music iterator
    customerCounter++;
    System.out.println("New Session or Customer for "
      + customer);
    cart = cartHome.create(customer);
    mymusic = musicHome.create();
```

Listing 5.17 musicCart.jsp *(continued)*

```
    mymusic.setPageSize(3);
    albums = mymusic.nextPage();
    newCustomer = "old";
    session.putValue("newCustomer", newCustomer);
    currentTitle = "";
  }

  else {
    // NOT a new customer; get list from session object
    albums = (ArrayList)session.getValue("albums");
  }

  String requestURI = request.getRequestURI();
  session.putValue("musicURL", requestURI);
  session.putValue("mymusic", mymusic);
  session.putValue("musicCart", cart);
  total = mymusic.getSize();

  // direction indicates user wants Previous or Next page
  String direction =
    (String)request.getParameter("direction");
  if (direction == null) direction = "";

  // use MusicIterator to check status
  // and get next page
  if (direction.equals("Next") &&
        mymusic.hasMoreElements())
    albums = mymusic.nextPage();

  // Check status and get previous page
  else if (direction.equals("Previous") &&
        mymusic.hasPreviousElements())
    albums = mymusic.previousPage();

  // Use the current values in albums if direction does not
  // specify either "Previous" or "Next"
  // Save albums in session object
  session.putValue("albums", albums);
%>
```

Listing 5.17 musicCart.jsp *(continued)*

```
<%--
  The following html code sets up the page to display
  the recording titles in radio buttons and invoke
  page shoppingPost.jsp with the selected user input.
--%>

<html>
<head>
<title>
  Music Collection Database with ValueListIterator</title>
</head>
<body bgcolor=white>
<center>

<p>
Customer <%= customer %>
<p>
You are customer number <%= customerCounter %>
<p>
<h1>Music Collection Database with ValueListIterator</h1>
<hr>

<p>
There are <%= total %> recordings
<form method="post" action="shoppingPost.jsp">
<p>
Select Music Recording:
<p>

<table border=2 cellpadding=5 bgcolor=#e0e0e0>
<%
  // Generate html radio button elements with the recording
  // titles stored in each RecordingVO element.

  String title;
  RecordingVO r;
  Iterator i = albums.iterator();
  boolean checked = false;
  int j = 1;
```

Listing 5.17 musicCart.jsp *(continued)*

```
  while (i.hasNext()) {
    r = (RecordingVO)i.next();
    title = r.getTitle();
    // "check" the radio button if the title
    // matches the previous selection, or if it's the
    // last one and we haven't checked one yet
    if (title.equals(currentTitle) ||
            (j == albums.size() && !checked)) {
      checked = true;
%>

      <tr><td>
      <input type="radio" name="title"
            value="<%=title%>" checked> <%= title %>
      </td></tr>

<%
    }
    else {
%>
      <tr><td>
      <input type="radio" name="title"
            value="<%=title%>" > <%= title %>
      </td></tr>

<%
    } // end else
    j++;
  } // end while
%>

<%--
  Provide buttons to View, Add, Delete titles
  Center them at the bottom of the table
--%>

      <tr><td align=center>
      <input TYPE="submit" NAME="View"
            VALUE="View Tracks">
      </td></tr>
```

Listing 5.17 musicCart.jsp *(continued)*

```
        <tr><td align=center>
        <input TYPE="submit" NAME="Add"
                VALUE="Add Recording to Cart">
        </td></tr>

        <tr><td align=center>
        <input TYPE="submit" NAME="Delete"
                VALUE="Delete Recording from Cart">
        </td></tr>
</table>
</form>

<%--
   Provide buttons to view the previous or next page
   of recording titles
--%>

<form action="musicCart.jsp" method=get>
<input type="submit" name="direction" value="Previous">
<input type="submit" name="direction" value="Next">
</form>
<br><a href="login.jsp">Log Out</a>
</body></html>
```

---

shoppingPost.jsp

Listing 5.18 contains **shoppingPost.jsp**. After obtaining the current values of its variables from the session object, this program performs the appropriate action. If it receives a command to view a recording's track list, the program invokes the MusicIterator EJB's `getTrackList()` method to build a table with the data. To add or remove a title, the program calls the MusicCart EJB's `addRecording()` or `removeRecording()` methods and redisplays the Music-Cart's current list of titles (again in table form).

When deleting a title from the shopping cart, we invoke `removeRecord-ing()` in a try block to specifically check for a `ShoppingException`. Method `removeRecording()` generates this exception when the named recording title is not in the shopping cart. After processing, the user returns to the request page (**musicCart.jsp**).

Listing 5.18 shoppingPost.jsp

```jsp
<%--
  shoppingPost.jsp
--%>

<%--
  Use a page directive to import needed classes and
  packages for compilation. Specify "error.jsp"
  as the page's errorPage.
--%>

<%@ page import="ShoppingException,MusicCart,
MusicCartHome,CustomerVO,MusicIterator,
MusicIteratorHome,RecordingVO,TrackVO,java.util.*,
javax.naming.Context, javax.naming.InitialContext,
javax.rmi.PortableRemoteObject" errorPage="error.jsp" %>

<%--
  Declare and initialize variables.
--%>

<%
  ArrayList tracks;
  ArrayList shoppingList;
  String requestURI =
          (String)session.getValue("musicURL");
  MusicIterator mymusic =
          (MusicIterator)session.getValue("mymusic");
  MusicCart cart =
          (MusicCart)session.getValue("musicCart");
  ArrayList albums =
          (ArrayList)session.getValue("albums");
  String currentTitle = request.getParameter("title");
  session.putValue("curTitle", currentTitle);
%>

<html>
<head>
<title><%= currentTitle %></title>
</head>
```

Listing 5.18 shoppingPost.jsp *(continued)*

```
<body bgcolor=white>
<center>
<h1>Music Collection Database Using EJB & JSP</h1>
<hr>
<p>

<%
  // Access the albums ArrayList to find the RecordingVO
  // object with the selected title.
  RecordingVO r = null;
  Iterator i = albums.iterator();
  boolean found = false;

  while (i.hasNext()) {
    r = (RecordingVO)i.next();
    if (r.getTitle().equals(currentTitle)) {
      found = true;
      break;
    }
  }

  if (found) {                            // found title
    String command = request.getParameter("View");
    if (command != null) {            // command is View
      tracks = mymusic.getTrackList(r);
%>

  <table bgcolor=#e0e0e0 border=2 cellpadding=5>
  <p>
  Processing <%= command %> for <%= currentTitle %>
  <p>
  <tr>
    <th>Track Number</th>
    <th>Track Length</th>
    <th>Track Title</th>
  </tr>
```

Listing 5.18 shoppingPost.jsp *(continued)*

```
<%
     // Use a combination of scriptlet code,
     // html and JSP expressions to build the table
     TrackVO t;
     i = tracks.iterator();
     while (i.hasNext()) {
       t = (TrackVO)i.next();
%>

  <tr>
    <td> <%= t.getTrackNumber() %></td>
    <td> <%= t.getTrackLength() %></td>
    <td> <%= t.getTitle() %></td>
  </tr>

<%
     }
   out.println("</table>");
   }

   else {
     command = request.getParameter("Add");
     if (command != null) {            // command is Add
       cart.addRecording(r);
     }

     else {
       command = request.getParameter("Delete");
       if (command != null) {         // command is Delete
         try {
           cart.removeRecording(r);
         } catch(ShoppingException ex) {
           // begin catch handler
%>
```

Listing 5.18 shoppingPost.jsp *(continued)*

```
<p>
Shopping Error
<hr>
<p>
<p STYLE="background:#bfbfbf;color:red;
font-weight:bold;border:double thin;padding:5">
Title <%= currentTitle %>
is not currently in your shopping cart.
</font>

<%
            } // end catch handler
         }
       }
       // put displaylist code here
%>

    <table bgcolor=#e0e0e0 border=2 cellpadding=5>
    <p>
    Processing <%= command %> for <%= currentTitle %>
    <p>
    <tr>
      <th>Current Shopping List</th>
    </tr>

<%
    // Use a combination of scriptlet code,
    // html and JSP expressions to build the table
    shoppingList = cart.getShoppingList();
    i = shoppingList.iterator();
    while (i.hasNext()) {
      r = (RecordingVO)i.next();
%>
      <tr><td> <%= r.getTitle() %></td></tr>
<%
    } // end while loop
    out.println("</table>");
  }
 }
```

Listing 5.18 shoppingPost.jsp *(continued)*

```
  else {
    out.println("No tracks for " + currentTitle
              + " found.<br>");
  }
%>

<br><br><a href="<%= requestURI %>">Return to Main Page</a>
</body>
</html>
```

Deployment Descriptor

Listing 5.19 contains the deployment descriptor for our web component client. We've specified login in <servlet-name> to match **login.jsp** in <jsp-file>. Note there are two <ejb-ref> definitions in this descriptor file: one for the MusicIterator EJB and one for the MusicCart EJB. The <ejb-ref-name> for each EJB must match the coded name provided to the lookup() method in **musicCart.jsp** (see page 175).

Listing 5.19 Web Component Deployment Descriptor

```
<web-app>
  <display-name>MusicWAR</display-name>
  <servlet>
    <servlet-name>login</servlet-name>
    <display-name>login</display-name>
    <jsp-file>/login.jsp</jsp-file>
  </servlet>

  <servlet-mapping>
    <servlet-name>login</servlet-name>
    <url-pattern>/login</url-pattern>
  </servlet-mapping>

  <session-config>
    <session-timeout>30</session-timeout>
  </session-config>
```

Listing 5.19 Web Component Deployment Descriptor *(continued)*

```
<ejb-ref>
    <ejb-ref-name>ejb/EJBMusic</ejb-ref-name>
    <ejb-ref-type>Session</ejb-ref-type>
    <home>MusicIteratorHome</home>
    <remote>MusicIterator</remote>
</ejb-ref>

<ejb-ref>
    <ejb-ref-name>ejb/MyMusicCart</ejb-ref-name>
    <ejb-ref-type>Session</ejb-ref-type>
    <home>MusicCartHome</home>
    <remote>MusicCart</remote>
</ejb-ref>
</web-app>
```

5.5   Local Interfaces

One of the new features added in the EJB 2.0 specification is local interfaces for session and entity beans. What are local interfaces and when do you use them?

The EJB examples we've presented so far have all had a home interface, remote interface, and bean implementation class. A client accesses an EJB through either its home interface with create() or through its remote interface using a business method. The EJB container intercepts method invocations and, in turn, calls the respective bean implementation method, or, in the case of create() with a stateless session bean, simply grabs a bean instance from the pool (if possible). Each call from the client to the bean is a remote invocation using the Java Remote Method Invocation (RMI) API. This means argument parameters and return values are copied, serialized, and transmitted remotely. While remote calls give an enterprise application its scalability and accessibility, RMI adds overhead to the network. Furthermore, while we do want certain EJBs to have remote clients (such as our MusicIterator EJB, MusicCart EJB, and Loan EJB presented earlier) some EJBs do not *need* remote clients.

To implement the Value List Iterator Pattern, we created a stateful MusicIterator EJB to interface with a stateless MusicPage EJB. Although a remote client could certainly bypass the front-end MusicIterator EJB and invoke methods on the MusicPage EJB directly, we anticipate that clients would rather use the convenient interface provided by the MusicIterator EJB. Thus, we presume that the *only* clients of MusicPage EJB will be instances of MusicIterator EJB. If we're willing to limit our deployment so that all instances of MusicIterator EJB and MusicPage EJB share the same Java Virtual Machine (JVM), then we can say that all clients of MusicPage EJB will be local.

What does it mean to be a local client? A local client runs in the same JVM as the bean it accesses. A local client may be a web component or another EJB, but not an application client. With remote access, the location of the EJB is transparent to the remote client (the remote EJB may execute in the same JVM, or it may be on a machine halfway around the world). Furthermore, argument parameters and return values are passed by *reference* with local calls. This increases performance, since no copies are made. Passing arguments by reference can be risky, however. Methods could use a reference to inadvertently modify an argument passed to it (this is called a ***side effect***). Then, changes to the client's view of an object change the EJB's view as well.

The MusicPage EJB is a good candidate for local access because it is tightly coupled with the MusicIterator EJB. These two enterprise beans were designed to work in tandem, and limiting their execution to the same JVM makes sense in this case. Furthermore, argument passing involves read-only operations, so we don't need to worry about side effects to parameter objects.

Other common uses of local interfaces are with the Session Facade Pattern (see "Session Facade Pattern" on page 250) and entity bean container-managed persistence (see "Introducing Container-Managed Persistence" on page 278).

Implementation Guideline

*It's also possible to implement an enterprise bean with **both** local and remote access, although this is not common in production environments. Since you cannot access an enterprise bean from an application client through its local interface (which is typically how you would test your EJB code), you should consider implementing remote access for testing and debugging.*

Local Interface Implementation

How do you implement an EJB with local access? As you might guess, it's all a matter of the interfaces. Access to the create() methods is through the *local home interface*. Access to the bean's business methods is through the *local interface*. These interfaces are distinct from their "remote cousins" and extend different interfaces. Thus, the local home interface extends EJBLocalHome (instead of EJBHome) and the local interface extends EJBLocalObject (instead of EJBObject). Since access is specifically not remote, do not specify RemoteException in the throws clause for any method in a local interface.

Let's update our filename conventions in Table 5.1 to include local and local home interfaces.

Figure 5-11 shows a class diagram of the classes and interfaces that we write for MusicPage EJB with local interfaces. Interface MusicPageLocalHome is the local home interface extending interface EJBLocalHome. Interface MusicPage-Local is the local interface extending interface EJBLocalObject. And finally,

Table 5.1 Naming Conventions for EJB Class and Interface Names

EJB Class/Interface	Name	Example
Remote Interface	Bean Name	MusicPage
Home Interface	Bean Name + Home	MusicPageHome
Local Interface	Bean Name + Local	MusicPageLocal
Local Home Interface	Bean Name + LocalHome	MusicPageLocalHome
Bean Implementation Class	Bean Name + Bean	MusicPageBean

class MusicPageBean is the bean implementation class that implements class SessionBean (unchanged from the previous implementation). Class ContainerProxy intercepts calls made through the local home and local interfaces and forwards them to the appropriate method in class MusicPageBean.

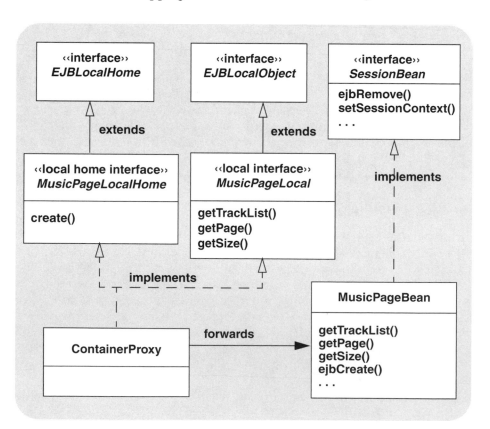

Figure 5-11 Class Diagram Showing the EJB Classes for a Session Bean with Local Interfaces

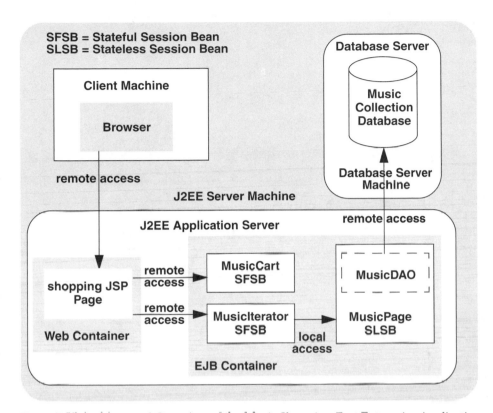

Figure 5-12 Architectural Overview of the Music Shopping Cart Enterprise Application

Before we show you the MusicPage EJB with local interfaces, let's review the component architecture of our MusicCart web application and add in characteristics of the EJBs. In Figure 5-12 we've noted EJB access (remote or local), as well as which EJBs are stateful session beans (SFSB) and which are stateless session beans (SLSB). Note that anytime access is remote, the client and server components may execute in different JVMs (and thus on different machines). For local access, the client and server components must run in the same JVM.

Local Home Interface

We define the local home interface in `MusicPageLocalHome`, shown in Listing 5.20. Note that this interface extends the `EJBLocalHome` interface. Method `create()` does not need a `RemoteException` in its throws clause and it returns a local interface object (`MusicPageLocal`) instead of a remote interface object.

Listing 5.20 MusicPageLocalHome.java

```
// MusicPageLocalHome.java
import javax.ejb.CreateException;
import javax.ejb.EJBLocalHome;

public interface MusicPageLocalHome extends EJBLocalHome {

    MusicPageLocal create() throws CreateException;
}
```

Local Interface

We define local interface MusicPageLocal in Listing 5.21 and extend it from interface EJBLocalObject. Note that none of the methods should have RemoteException in their throws clauses. Although the method names and signatures are all identical to their remote versions, we now pass parameters and return values by reference rather than by value.

Listing 5.21 MusicPageLocal.java

```
// MusicPageLocal.java
import javax.ejb.EJBLocalObject;
import java.util.*;

public interface MusicPageLocal extends EJBLocalObject {

  public ArrayList getTrackList(RecordingVO rec)
      throws NoTrackListException;

  public int getSize();
  public ArrayList getPage(int currentIndex,
      int pageSize);
}
```

Bean Implementation Class

For local interfaces, what changes must be made to our MusicPageBean implementation class? The answer is none. Thus, unless the bean implementation code needs to make some changes because of the way method parameters and return objects are treated, no changes are required.

MusicIterator Client

We must also update the code in **MusicIteratorBean.java** (Listing 5.13 on page 160) to access client MusicPage EJB through the local interfaces. Here are the changes:

- We no longer have to import class
  `javax.rmi.PortableRemoteObject.`
- We change the declaration of state variable `pageBean` from
  `MusicPage` to `MusicPageLocal`:

```
private MusicPageLocal pageBean = null;
```

- Inside method `ejbCreate()`, we change the declaration of variable `pageHome` from `MusicPageHome` to `MusicPageLocalHome`.
- Furthermore, we no longer need
  `PortableRemoteObject.narrow` to create a home object:

```
MusicPageLocalHome pageHome = (MusicPageLocalHome)objref;
```

Deployment Descriptor

The deployment descriptor must reflect changes to both the description of MusicPage EJB (we have local and local home interfaces) and to its client, MusicIterator EJB. The client now specifies the local and local home interfaces for accessing the MusicPage EJB. In assembling our components, we've placed both the MusicPage EJB and the MusicIterator EJB in the same JAR file. Listing 5.22 shows the new deployment descriptor for `<ejb-jar>` (the EJB JAR file). You might want to compare this deployment descriptor to Listing 5.9 on page 156 and Listing 5.14 on page 163.

Listing 5.22 Deployment Descriptor for MusicJAR

```
<ejb-jar>
  <display-name>MusicPageJAR</display-name>
  <enterprise-beans>
    <session>
      <display-name>MusicPageBean</display-name>
      <ejb-name>MusicPageBean</ejb-name>
      <local-home>MusicPageLocalHome</local-home>
```

Listing 5.22 Deployment Descriptor for MusicJAR *(continued)*

```xml
      <local>MusicPageLocal</local>
      <ejb-class>MusicPageBean</ejb-class>
      <session-type>Stateless</session-type>
      <transaction-type>Bean</transaction-type>

<env-entry>
<env-entry-name>MusicDAOClass</env-entry-name>
<env-entry-type>java.lang.String</env-entry-type>
<env-entry-value>MusicDAOCloudscape</env-entry-value>
</env-entry>

  <security-identity>
    <description></description>
    <use-caller-identity></use-caller-identity>
  </security-identity>

  <resource-ref>
    <res-ref-name>jdbc/MusicDB</res-ref-name>
    <res-type>javax.sql.DataSource</res-type>
    <res-auth>Container</res-auth>
    <res-sharing-scope>Shareable</res-sharing-scope>
  </resource-ref>
</session>

<session>
  <display-name>MusicIteratorBean</display-name>
  <ejb-name>MusicIteratorBean</ejb-name>
  <home>MusicIteratorHome</home>
  <remote>MusicIterator</remote>
  <ejb-class>MusicIteratorBean</ejb-class>
  <session-type>Stateful</session-type>
  <transaction-type>Bean</transaction-type>

  <ejb-local-ref>
    <ejb-ref-name>ejb/MusicPage</ejb-ref-name>
    <ejb-ref-type>Session</ejb-ref-type>
    <local-home>MusicPageLocalHome</local-home>
    <local>MusicPageLocal</local>
    <ejb-link>MusicPageBean</ejb-link>
  </ejb-local-ref>
```

Listing 5.22 Deployment Descriptor for MusicJAR *(continued)*

```
      <security-identity>
        <description></description>
        <use-caller-identity></use-caller-identity>
      </security-identity>
    </session>
  </enterprise-beans>
</ejb-jar>
```

You'll note that descriptor tags for MusicPage EJB now include `<local-home>` and `<local>`. Also, the descriptor tags for MusicIterator EJB include `<ejb-local-ref>` (a *local* EJB reference to MusicPage EJB). As before, MusicPage EJB is a *stateless* session bean; MusicIterator EJB is a *stateful* session bean.

5.6   Design Guidelines and Patterns

This chapter contrasts stateless session beans with stateful session beans. We discuss situations where each is the preferable choice for implementing an EJB. To implement the Value List Iterator Pattern, we use a stateful session bean to control a data-intensive stateless session bean.

Value List Iterator Pattern

In situations where an enterprise application requests a large amount of data, the Value List Iterator Pattern eases network load and the resource consumption caused by large data returns. Instead of receiving all the data at once, the client controls the amount by requesting data a page at a time. Furthermore, the client can control how many elements a page contains.

Our implementation of this pattern uses both a stateful bean (MusicIterator EJB) and a stateless bean (MusicPage EJB). The stateful bean keeps track of per-client data: the desired page size and the current location in the data set. It also provides client-friendly routines such as `hasMoreElements()` and `hasPreviousElements()` to help with end-of-data and start-of-data boundary conditions.

Why not eliminate the MusicIterator EJB and place the paging state information in another component? If the MusicPage EJB maintains this information, it would have to be stateful. This affects performance, since the EJB container will possibly have to passivate and activate this data. What if we place the paging state information in the JSP web client? Although we can certainly do this, our attempt here is to separate business logic from the presentation layer. A stateful

MusicIterator EJB allows other clients to page through the database (such as a stand-alone Java application or another web component). And because the MusicIterator EJB is decoupled from the recording data, activating and passivating the stateful MusicIterator EJB does not require much overhead.

The stateless MusicPage EJB (which the EJB container can assign to various clients as needed) performs the data-intensive job of reading the database. To make database access vendor independent, we use the DAO pattern. Depending on the timing of the client requests, it is possible for a single instance of the MusicPage EJB to service many clients.

Design Guideline

When using a ValueListIterator, pick a page size that is appropriate for network load and transmission speed. Use a large page size with a fast network and a smaller page size for slower networks.

Stateful vs. Stateless Session Beans

We've touched on the major issues in this chapter. If a session bean must keep track of client-specific data, then you should make it a stateful session bean. Remember that a stateful session bean is tied to a single client. Because sharing instances is not possible, stateful session beans can become a resource liability within your system. There are several ways to avoid using stateful session beans.

- Encapsulate client data into value objects and pass them to methods of a stateless session bean. The downside to this approach is that it puts the burden on the client to keep track of this data. However, if the data is not complicated and doesn't change much, this is a good approach. (We used this tactic with the Loan EJB in Chapter 3. Each method requires the LoanVO value object which the client creates. See Listing 3.2 on page 41.)
- If you have a session bean that is expensive to create and keep around, you might be able to wrap client-specific functionality into a small, streamlined stateful session bean. This front-end bean can then forward its calls to a stateless session bean that does all the work. This is the approach we use for the stateful MusicIterator EJB as a front end to the stateless MusicPage EJB. With this approach, the EJB container can efficiently manage the stateless, more resource-intensive enterprise bean.

Local Interfaces

Implementing a session or entity bean with local access can potentially improve the performance of an enterprise application. We say potentially, because although local calls are more efficient than corresponding remote calls, EJBs with local access must execute in the same JVM as its clients. In the long run, this restriction might hedge an enterprise application's scalability, since it prohibits the distribution of local clients across machines.

JSP Web Clients

JSP programs seem like quick solutions to provide user input and presentation aspects of an enterprise application. However, you must be careful not to build too much complexity into a JSP client. The example we provide in this chapter is about as complicated as you should get. The goal is to reduce business logic and scriptlet code in JSP files and limit JSP programs to presentation issues.

That said, what other implementation strategies are helpful for creating JSP clients? Pay particular attention to JSP clients that use stateful session beans (such as the example presented in this chapter).

* A JSP client that instantiates a stateful session bean should not use class-wide variables to hold client-specific state. Instead, the client should use variables declared inside the _jspService() routine (that is, in scriptlet code, not in JSP declarations).
* A JSP client that instantiates a stateless session bean can use a class-wide variable. These are declared once during the life of a JSP component and can be easily shared among multiple requests.

5.7 Key Point Summary

This chapter introduces stateful session beans and contrasts them with stateless sessions beans. The MusicCart EJB is a classic example of a stateful session bean since it keeps track of client-specific conversational state. In addition, we implement the Value List Iterator Pattern, leveraging the benefits of both a stateful session bean (MusicIterator EJB) and a stateless session bean (MusicPage EJB). We bring these three EJBs together in one J2EE application with a web component JSP client. We examine how the EJB container manages the life cycles and assignment of EJB objects to clients and how it affects the overall performance of an enterprise application. We use local interfaces to further improve the performance garnered through the Value List Iterator Pattern.

Here are the key points from this chapter.

- A stateful session bean keeps track of client-specific data throughout the session.
- An EJB container assigns an instance of a stateful session bean to a single client. It can assign an instance of a stateless session bean to multiple clients (one at a time).
- The conversational state of a stateful session bean goes away when the session terminates.
- The EJB container can reacquire the resources consumed by a stateful bean by making it passive (this is called passivation). It can make it active when necessary.
- Passivation requires serializing instance variables and writing them to secondary storage. During activation, the EJB container de-serializes the data and reads it back into memory.
- Any instance variable that cannot be serialized must be handled by the bean developer in the `ejbPassivate()` and `ejbActivate()` methods. The EJB container invokes `ejbPassivate()` just before passivation and `ejbActivate()` just after activation.
- The MusicCart EJB is a stateful session bean that allows a client to create a shopping cart and add and remove recordings.
- `CustomerVO` is a value object that encapsulates the data pertaining to a "customer."
- The home interface of a stateful session bean may contain more than one `create()` method. Each `create()` method must have a corresponding `ejbCreate()` method in the bean implementation class with the same signature.
- The purpose of `ejbCreate()` is to properly initialize a stateful session bean's instance variables. If the client provides improper initialization data with `create()`, `ejbCreate()` should throw a `CreateException`.
- A stateful session bean's remote interface contains the EJB's business method definitions.
- A stateful session bean's implementation contains the code for the EJB business methods.
- Class `RecordingVO` implements method `equals()` so that collection utility class `ArrayList` can perform comparison between its `RecordingVO` elements.
- Business method `removeRecording()` throws application exception `ShoppingException` if the `RecordingVO` object is not currently in the shopping cart.
- The Value List Iterator Pattern helps manage large lists by allowing the client to request data a page at a time.

- We implement Value List Iterator by wrapping all client-specific operations in a stateful session bean (MusicIterator EJB). MusicIterator EJB then bundles the appropriate data into calls to a stateless session bean (MusicPage EJB).
- The MusicPage EJB is a modification of the Music EJB presented in Chapter 4 (see "Session Beans and JDBC" on page 85). We replaced `getMusicList()` with `getPage()`, which returns a subset of the entire list.
- The `MusicIterator` remote interface extends the `ValueListIterator` interface. This separates the reusable methods from the domain-specific methods. Methods in `ValueListIterator` must throw `RemoteException` so that interface `MusicIterator` can extend it.
- Because the resource-intensive MusicPage EJB is stateless and the fairly light-weight MusicIterator EJB is stateful, we've leveraged the benefits of both session bean types for optimal performance and client convenience.
- The web component JSP client uses five separate JSP files to allow the user to login and manipulate an online shopping cart. It uses session objects and stateful session beans to maintain client state.
- We've implemented local access for the MusicPage EJB. This requires providing two new interfaces: a local interface (`MusicPageLocal`) for the business methods, and a local home interface (`MusicPageLocalHome`) for the `create()` method.
- Local EJBs and their clients must execute in the same Java Virtual Machine (JVM).
- Local EJBs use pass by reference for method parameters and return values instead of pass by value. This eliminates the overhead of copying arguments as well as the serialization required by RMI.
- Consider using local interfaces for tightly coupled EJBs.

ENTITY BEANS WITH BMP

Chapter 6

Even the most patient reader is likely to wonder when we'll begin using EJB examples that show how to manipulate database records other than to simply read them. We have seen stateless session beans effectively read and cache database records. We've used stateful session beans to track where in the data list the client is currently reading, and we've used stateful session beans to hold objects in a virtual shopping cart for clients. We've even used a stateless session bean to discover the wonders of interest rates, monthly payments, and amortization tables.

The real work and power of enterprise computing, however, lies in being able to create, remove, and update database records with the confidence that the data is always consistent and synchronized with all clients, as well as with the permanent data store. To accomplish this difficult task, you use entity beans. In the J2EE architecture, you define business data with entity beans. These beans that you build work together under the management of the EJB container to provide data integrity.

Entity beans are nothing more than a reflection of data stored in a database (and they also offer helpful "finder" methods). But, by being data in memory and easily accessible, entity beans open up the database so that clients widely distributed can safely access (update, create, remove) this data. Because the entity bean is just a vessel for data, the J2EE architecture must provide the system services that allow the data transactions to occur in a thread-safe, consistent, and efficient manner.

In this chapter we explore the Bean-Managed Persistence (BMP) mechanisms of entity beans, the services provided by the bean, and the services provided by the EJB container. We also explore design techniques for using entity beans efficiently and the importance of using session beans with entity beans in an enterprise application. Best of all, we'll add persistence to our Music Collection application!

6.1   Introducing Entity Beans

Our example entity bean models the customer data for the Music Collection shopping application. We'll delay describing it until after we've characterized entity beans in general.

An entity bean is an in-memory representation of persistent data. The persistence mechanism is either coded by the bean developer (bean-managed persistence) or provided by the container (container-managed persistence). For both bean-managed and container-managed entity beans, the EJB container manages life cycles and keeps the beans synchronized with the underlying database. Because multiple clients may share an entity bean (and possibly alter its state), the container and the bean developer must make sure that any updates occur within an appropriate transaction. In this chapter we present an entity bean example with bean-managed persistence. In the next chapter we discuss Container-Managed Persistence (CMP). We begin by exploring an entity bean's properties.

Properties of Entity Beans

An entity bean is quite different from a session bean. In general, we use a session bean to model a business process. A session bean contains the business logic to accomplish one or more tasks. For example, we've seen a Loan (session) EJB that calculates monthly payments for a long-term, fixed-rate loan. An entity bean, on the other hand, represents business data, and in general, does not provide the capability to model a business process. From that standpoint, we characterize an entity bean as containing minimal logic and being "data heavy."

Persistent and Shareable

Entity beans are persistent. Furthermore, the bean is always synchronized with the database, allowing access by multiple clients. The J2EE architecture provides two ways to persist the data: BMP and CMP. With BMP, the bean provider writes the database access code, either directly in the bean implementation class, or callable through a data access object (DAO). Database access is typically achieved through JDBC calls. However, there is nothing to preclude the bean provider from accessing a nonrelational database system. In fact, one compelling reason for using BMP is that you may have a nonrelational database system and are thus prevented from using container-managed persistence. (We discuss additional points for choosing between BMP and CMP under "Properties of CMP Entity Beans" on page 278.)

Local and Remote Interfaces

Like session beans, entity beans may have either a remote or local interface (or both). For bean-managed persistence, it is a good idea to implement the remote interface for convenient testing (it is more convenient to test from a stand-alone application client, which is necessarily remote) and a local interface for production. We recommend local access to entity beans through a "business smart" session bean. Because entity bean access tends to be many fine-grained calls which read or update persistent variables, performance improves if these calls are local. This avoids RMI overhead and decreases network traffic. The session bean front end is called the Session Facade Pattern, which we present in this chapter.

EJB Methods and Database Access

With entity beans, specific EJB methods cause certain database operations. Table 6.1 summarizes these methods and their associated database behaviors. We discuss these methods in more detail in the upcoming sections.

Table 6.1 EJB Methods and Database Access Operations

Method	Database Access
ejbCreate()	Inserts new record. Returns primary key to container.
ejbFindByPrimaryKey()	Selects record with specified primary key. Returns primary key to container.
ejbFind*XXX*()	Selects one or more records. Returns primary key or collection of primary keys to container.
ejbHome*XXX*()	Custom database access (select or update) not tied to any specific primary key.
ejbLoad()	Selects (refresh in-memory persistent variables).
ejbStore()	Updates (store persistent variables).
ejbRemove()	Deletes record.

Primary Key and Finder Methods

All entity beans have a unique primary key and a method in the home (or local home) interface called `findByPrimaryKey()`. Method `findByPrimaryKey()` maps to `ejbFindByPrimaryKey()` in the entity bean's implementation class. An entity bean's client invokes method `findByPrimaryKey()` to gain access to the bean's business methods (which are generally data access or data update methods). Furthermore, a client can "find" entity beans by other criteria, depending on the finder methods specified in the home interface.

With session beans, the only way to obtain an object that implements the remote or local interface is through the home interface `create()` methods. With entity beans, however, finder methods also obtain an object that implements the remote (or local) interface. We use a finder method when the record already exists in the database. We use `create()` when we want to insert a new record in the database.

Our Customer EJB has several finder methods. Method `findByCustomer-Name()` allows the client to specify a String name as an argument and method `findAll()` returns a collection of Customer entity beans to the client. The finder methods defined will depend on the data that the entity bean represents. The finder methods in the home interface map to `ejbFindXXX()` methods in the bean implementation class. For example, `findByCustomerName()` maps to `ejbFindByCustomerName()` and `findAll()` maps to `ejbFindAll()`. In BMP, the bean provider writes the appropriate SQL Select queries to implement the `ejbFindXXX()` methods. The queries may access more than one database table if the entity bean pulls its persistent fields from related tables.

Create Methods

Entity beans may also have one or more `create()` methods. Like session beans, `create()` methods in the home (or local home) interface map to `ejb-Create()` methods in the bean implementation class. Unlike session beans, however, implementation code for `ejbCreate()` results in database insert commands. Thus, invoking `create()` for an entity bean not only creates an instance of the entity bean, but also creates a corresponding record in the underlying database. If an insert attempts to create a record with a duplicate primary key, the database software throws an SQLException; the bean implementation code will, in turn, throw a `CreateException`.

Home Methods

Entity beans also have home methods. Clients access an entity bean's home methods through the home or local home interface. These methods, therefore, cannot access a specific entity bean. Rather, home methods perform a "bean-wide" query, calculation, or update. This is analogous to a Java *class method* in that a client can invoke the method with the notation `class.method()` without instantiating an object.

In our Customer EJB, for instance, we provide a home method called `get-TotalCustomers()` that counts the number of records in our Customer database. While we must access the database to perform this method, it doesn't require an entity bean instantiation by the container. Home methods map to `ejbHomeXXX()` methods in the bean implementation class. This particular method, then, maps to `ejbHomeGetTotalCustomers()`. (The word "home" is a bit overused here. Although clients also access finder and create methods through the home interface, "home methods" refer specifically to these bean-wide business methods implemented by `ejbHomeXXX()` methods in the bean implementation class.)

EJB Methods

The entity bean's implementation class must implement the `EntityBean` interface. This interface includes the "EJB" methods that the EJB container invokes to manage an entity bean instance. While we've seen some of these methods with our session bean examples (such as `ejbActivate()` and `ejbPassivate()`), entity beans have two additional important methods whose job is to synchronize the entity bean instance with its underlying database. These methods are `ejbLoad()` and `ejbStore()`. In BMP, the bean developer must provide the database access code to read the database with `ejbLoad()` and write new values to the database with `ejbStore()`. Client code never calls these methods directly. They are called by the EJB container to make sure that any business method that affects the entity bean will be correctly applied to the underlying database and that the entity bean and database are properly synchronized.

Let's proceed now to our entity bean example.

6.2   Customer Entity Bean

Entity beans can be more difficult to understand than session beans because the EJB container does more work behind the scenes. Therefore, as we present our example Customer EJB, we'll show you the entity bean code and explain the services that the EJB container provides.

The Big Picture

Our entity bean example consists of a Customer EJB with Bean-Managed Persistence (BMP). It provides persistence for the CustomerVO data we used in the previous chapter (see Listing 5.1 on page 143). With this capability, our J2EE shopping application can now identify customers from a database (and verify a customer's password), or create a new customer. We thus provide a true "login" process. The CustomerVO object includes a customer's name, password, and e-mail address. Our persistent customer will have these fields, as well as a CustomerID primary key and a boolean that indicates whether or not this customer has orders pending in our "virtual" shopping system. Figure 6-1 shows the database table for our Customer EJB and the structure of class `CustomerModel` that holds the persistent data inside the entity bean. At this time, our Customer EJB has no database "relationships" with any other persistent data.

Figure 6-2 shows the architectural overview of these components. Our application's customer identity verification and new customer creation services are provided by both a Customer EJB *entity* bean and a CustomerSession EJB stateless *session* bean. The CustomerSession EJB provides the business logic and the Customer EJB provides the data persistence. The diagram also includes components introduced in previous chapters. These components are unchanged, but we want to show how everything fits together, as well as emphasize their reusability! Note that CustomerSession EJB communicates with Customer EJB through *local* interfaces. The Customer EJB entity bean uses CustomerDAO (DAO pattern) to implement its persistence.

Design Guideline

Because Customer EJB uses bean-managed persistence, it makes sense to implement vendor independent database access. Hence, we use a DAO to implement JDBC calls to the database. Refer to "Data Access Object Pattern" on page 119 in Chapter 4 for more information.

Customers Table

CustomerID (PK)
Name
Password
Email
OrdersPending

```
public class CustomerModel {

    private String customerID;
    private String name;
    private String password;
    private String email;
    private boolean ordersPending;
    . . .

}
```

Figure 6-1 Customers Database Table and CustomerModel Persistent Data

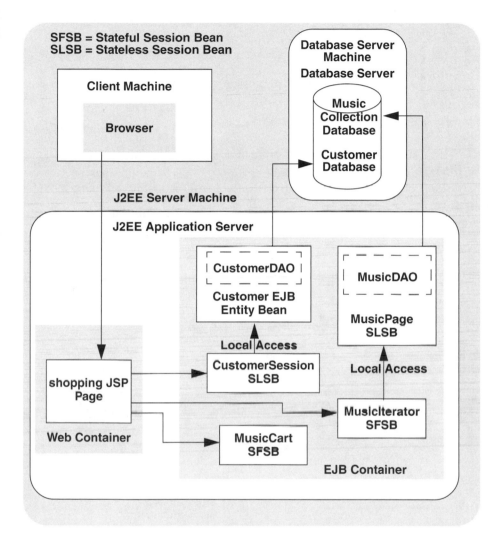

Figure 6-2 Architectural Overview of the Music Shopping Cart Enterprise Application
with Customer Login and Sign Up Capabilities

Structure of Entity Beans

Entity bean structure is similar to session bean structure. The client accesses the
bean initially through the home (or local home) interface, using either one of
the finder methods or a `create()` call. Either of these returns a remote or local
object (or a collection of objects). The remote or local interface object provides
the data access methods (which are business methods from an entity bean's

point of view). As with the session bean, the EJB container intercepts these calls
and forwards them to the bean implementation class.

Figure 6-3 shows the classes and interfaces of our Customer entity bean with
local interfaces. (To avoid cluttering the diagram, we show the local and local
home interfaces only.) The local home interface holds the create() methods,
the finder methods, and any home methods. The local interface contains the

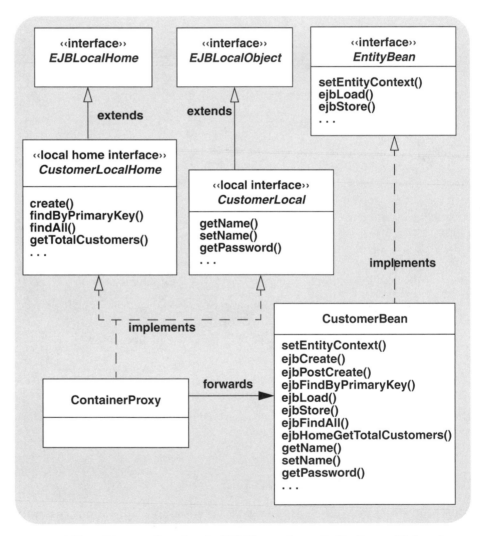

Figure 6-3 Class Diagram Showing the EJB Classes for an Entity Bean with Local
Interfaces

business methods. The bean implementation class implements the `EntityBean` interface and contains the code for the EJB methods and the business methods.

For Customer EJB, we implement *both* local and remote interfaces. As you will see later, the remote interface implementation helps us understand the system with an application test client. We use the local and local home interfaces when accessing the entity bean with CustomerSession EJB.

Design Guideline

Implementing both the remote and local interfaces of BMP entity beans is a good idea. The remote interface lets you rigorously check the code with an application test client. You can then access the entity bean in a production environment with a session bean using the entity bean's local interfaces.

Home and Local Home Interfaces

The home interface contains create methods, finder methods, and home methods. All finder methods begin with "`findBy`," create methods must be called `create()`, and the home methods have no naming restrictions in the home or local home interface.

Listing 6.1 shows the source for the home interface, **CustomerHome.java**. Note that interface `CustomerHome` extends `EJBHome` and provides remote access to its methods. We therefore include `RemoteException` in all of the methods' throw clauses. Furthermore, method `create()` must specify `CreateException`, and all of the finder methods must specify `FinderException`.

Listing 6.1 CustomerHome.java

```
// CustomerHome.java
import java.util.Collection;
import javax.ejb.*;
import java.rmi.RemoteException;

public interface CustomerHome extends EJBHome {

  public Customer create(String name, String password,
    String email) throws RemoteException, CreateException;

  // Finder methods
  public Customer findByPrimaryKey(String customerID)
    throws RemoteException, FinderException;

  public Collection findByCustomerName(String name)
    throws RemoteException, FinderException;
```

Listing 6.1 CustomerHome.java *(continued)*

```
public Collection findAll()
   throws RemoteException, FinderException;

// Home methods
// Return the number of Customers in the database
public int getTotalCustomers()
   throws RemoteException;
}
```

A finder method may return either a single object or a *collection* (an object implementing abstract interface `Collection`), depending on whether the finder method anticipates that more than one database record will satisfy the corresponding database query. For example, `findByPrimaryKey()` always returns a single object. A finder method that returns a single object throws an `ObjectNotFoundException` (a subclass of `FinderException`) when the database query fails to find the requested record. A finder method that returns a collection simply returns an empty collection if it does not find any objects (and no exception is thrown). Note that `findByCustomerName()` and `findAll()` both return collections.

Method `getTotalCustomers()` is a home method, which we access through the home interface, as follows.

```
// Get a home interface object
CustomerHome home =
   (CustomerHome)PortableRemoteObject.narrow(objref,
                 CustomerHome.class);
// Access home method
int count = home.getTotalCustomers();
```

Home methods typically perform database-wide operations. They never invoke business methods that are dependent on a specific entity bean instance.

Why doesn't the `create()` method include either the boolean variable for the `ordersPending` field or the primary key field in its signature? The answer is that when we create a customer, it doesn't yet have an order associated with it. Since the `ordersPending` boolean is always false at creation time, the bean implementation code can initialize this boolean to false. Furthermore, the bean implementation code generates the primary key, so we exclude it from `create()`'s signature as well.

Design Guideline

We have chosen the Customer EJB entity bean to show you BMP because a Customer can exist without an order. This means that this version of Customer EJB is not dependent on other entity beans. In the next chapter, we implement its relationship with Order EJBs (and LineItem EJBs). Until then, the Customer EJB adds a nontrivial but isolated customer "login and sign up" capability to our system using BMP.

Listing 6.2 shows the source for the local home interface, **CustomerLocal-Home.java**. You'll note that its methods are the same as the home interface, but it extends EJBLocalHome and we've removed all RemoteExceptions from the throw clauses. Also, findByPrimaryKey() and create() return objects implementing the CustomerLocal interface instead of the remote interface, Customer. Finders findByCustomerName() and findAll() return collections of CustomerLocal objects.

Listing 6.2 CustomerLocalHome.java

```java
// CustomerLocalHome.java
import java.util.Collection;
import javax.ejb.*;

public interface CustomerLocalHome extends EJBLocalHome {

  public CustomerLocal create(String name,
    String password, String email) throws CreateException;

  // Finder methods
  public CustomerLocal findByPrimaryKey(String customerID)
    throws FinderException;

  public Collection findByCustomerName(String name)
    throws FinderException;

  public Collection findAll() throws FinderException;

  // Home method
  public int getTotalCustomers();
}
```

Remote and Local Interfaces

The remote and local interfaces specify the business methods for the entity bean. With session beans, these business methods carry out a business process. With entity beans, however, business methods typically get or update one or more fields in a database record associated with the entity bean. The business logic ensures that the new data values make sense. More typically, however, the entity bean simply accepts or retrieves data. It leaves any data consistency checking to a separate business component, such as a "business-enabled" session bean. This allows the business logic to reside in the controlling session bean.

Design Guideline

Using a business-enabled session bean is the tactic we take in our virtual shopping application. The CustomerSession EJB provides the consistency checking for new data values (so that, for example, if you change your password, it cannot be the empty string). Then, if the business rules change (say, passwords must be a certain length or they must contain at least one nonalphabetic character), the code in the CustomerSession EJB changes, not the underlying entity bean code. Furthermore, the business-enabled session bean will oftentimes coordinate the behavior of more than one related entity bean. This is yet another reason to place business logic in a controlling session bean.

In the Customer EJB, the remote interface contains methods for setting and getting the entity bean's persistent variables; i.e., those variables that are stored in the database. Note that there is no setter for the primary key (`customerID`), since primary keys never change. All methods specify `RemoteException` in their `throws` clauses. Like session beans, the entity bean's remote interface extends `EJBObject`. Listing 6.3 contains the source for **Customer.java**.

Listing 6.3 Customer.java

```
// Customer.java
import javax.ejb.EJBObject;
import java.rmi.RemoteException;

public interface Customer extends EJBObject {

   public String getCustomerID()
     throws RemoteException;
```

Listing 6.3 Customer.java *(continued)*

```java
public String getName()
  throws RemoteException;
public void setName(String newName)
  throws RemoteException;

public String getPassword()
  throws RemoteException;
public void setPassword(String newPassword)
  throws RemoteException;

public String getEmail()
  throws RemoteException;
public void setEmail(String newEmail)
  throws RemoteException;

public boolean getOrdersPending()
  throws RemoteException;
public void setOrdersPending(boolean pending)
  throws RemoteException;
}
```

We now show you Customer EJB's local interface, CustomerLocal. It contains the same methods as the remote interface without RemoteException in the throw clauses. And, CustomerLocal extends EJBLocalObject. Listing 6.4 contains the source for **CustomerLocal.java**.

Listing 6.4 CustomerLocal.java

```java
// CustomerLocal.java
import javax.ejb.EJBLocalObject;

public interface CustomerLocal extends EJBLocalObject {

  public String getCustomerID();
  public String getName();

  public String getPassword();
  public void setPassword(String newPassword);

  public String getEmail();
  public void setEmail(String newEmail);
```

Listing 6.4 CustomerLocal.java *(continued)*

```
  public boolean getOrdersPending();
  public void setOrdersPending(boolean pending);
}
```

The Role of the EJB Container

Before we delve into the bean implementation code, let's explore what the EJB container does behind the scenes. First we'll show you how to create an object that implements the home interface. Once we have the home interface, we invoke either a `create()` method or a finder method to instantiate objects that implement the remote interface. With the remote interface object, we can call the business methods.

Optimizing Stores

All business methods, even if they only perform a data lookup, must execute within a transaction in order for the EJB container to ensure data integrity between the in-memory entity bean and the database. A key concept in entity beans is that the container wraps each transactional business method invocation with calls to `ejbLoad()` and `ejbStore()`. This guarantees that the in-memory persistent variables are always synchronized with the database.

```
ejbLoad();              // read data from database
business_method();      // possibly modify data
ejbStore();             // update data in database
```

The `ejbLoad()` method reads the database and refreshes the entity bean's persistent variables. This step is crucial. Because the EJB container may instantiate more than one entity bean per database record, we must refresh the persistent variables before each business method in case another client changes their values. After `business_method()` completes, `ejbStore()` writes the persistent variables back to the database. Calls to `ejbStore()` work well with transactional business methods that *modify* the persistent variables. But what if a business method only reads them? In this situation, `ejbStore()` does not need to update the database.

   The use of a ***dirty flag*** in `ejbStore()` helps optimize entity bean behavior. In the entity bean, the bean developer includes a `dirty` flag as an instance variable of the bean. It is initially set to false in either `ejbLoad()` (when the initial values come from the database) or in `ejbCreate()` (when the initial values come from the client). The business methods that *modify* persistent data set the `dirty` flag to `true`. Those business methods that only *read* persistent data do not. When the EJB container calls `ejbStore()`, this method checks the `dirty` flag and updates the database only if the persistent variables have changed.

We'll take a closer look at the `dirty` flag implementation when we present the code for class `CustomerBean` later in the chapter (see Listing 6.10 on page 233 through Listing 6.13 on page 237.)

Method Calls

Figure 6-4 shows a sequence diagram for obtaining an object that implements the home interface and using it to call method `create()`. First, we invoke the `narrow()` method of `PortableRemoteObject` and invoke `CustomerHome`'s `create()` method (passing appropriate values for name, password, and e-mail address). The EJB container intercepts the call, instantiates an instance of `CustomerBean` (the bean implementation class), and invokes the bean's `ejbCreate()` method. Method `ejbCreate()` inserts values for the new Customer into the database. These are the JDBC calls invoked through methods in the `CustomerDAO` implementation class. The EJB container then invokes `ejbPostCreate()` followed by `ejbStore()`. Note that `ejbStore()` invokes the actual DAO

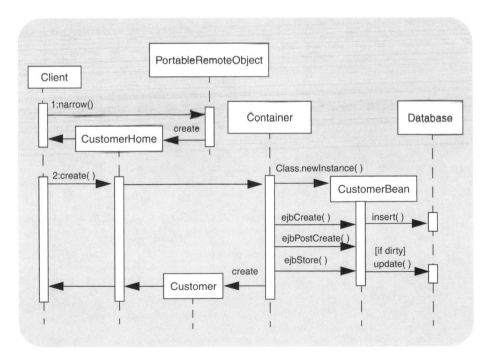

Figure 6-4 Sequence Diagram Showing the Creation of a Customer Entity Bean by Invoking the Home Interface `create()` Method

method to update the database *only* if the `dirty` flag (instance variable boolean `dirty`) is true.

Figure 6-5 shows a sequence diagram for obtaining a `Customer` entity bean with a finder method followed by calls to business methods `setPassword()` and `getName()`. In the client's call to `findByPrimaryKey()`, the container instantiates a `CustomerBean` object. Method `ejbFindByPrimaryKey()` returns a *primary key* to the EJB container. Since the EJB container oversees the life cycle of the entity bean, it may be able to use an already-existing Customer entity bean instance to return to the client. Thus, the EJB container caches entity beans in memory.

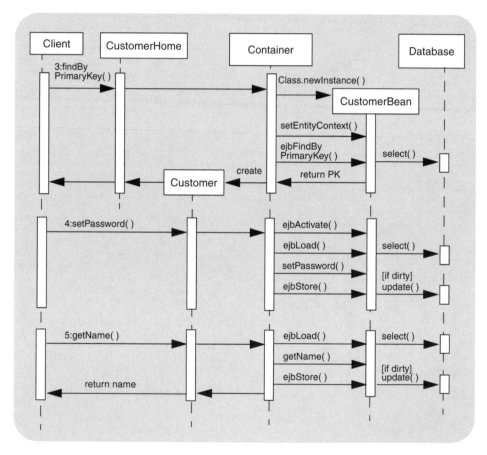

Figure 6-5 Sequence Diagram Showing the Instantiation of a Customer Entity Bean by Invoking `findByPrimaryKey()` Followed by Business Methods `setPassword()` and `getName()`

Once the client has an object that implements the remote interface (`Customer`), it can invoke business methods. Let's begin with the call to `setPassword()`. Note that the EJB container first invokes method `ejbActivate()` followed by `ejbLoad()` and the required database select statement. Method `setPassword()` updates the persistent `password` field and sets the `dirty` flag to `true`. When the EJB container invokes `ejbStore()`, this executes the database update statement which synchronizes the database with the entity bean.

Likewise, when the client invokes business method `getName()`, the EJB container calls `ejbLoad()`. (A call to `ejbActivate()` is not necessary here, since the bean is already activated.) The EJB container then invokes `CustomerBean`'s `getName()` followed by `ejbStore()`. Here, we avoid executing the database update statement because the `dirty` flag is false. (Method `getName()` does not set it.)

Design Guideline

With CMP, the EJB container code can optimize caching behavior for the entity bean. With BMP, however, any optimization is left up to the bean developer. Maintaining a "dirty flag" to track changes to persistent fields can improve performance.

DAO Pattern Implementation

Rather than place JDBC calls in private methods inside the bean implementation class, we'll use a DAO to access the database. This helps isolate database dependent code and provides a flexible way to deploy alternate database implementations. The CustomerDAO pattern is equivalent to the MusicDAO implementation you've already seen in "Data Access Object Pattern" on page 119. We'll use the Cloudscape database (part of the J2EE reference implementation) for the underlying database. Figure 6-6 provides a class diagram illustrating the class relationships.

CustomerModel

The Customer EJB and CustomerDAO must work together to provide access to the database. To do this, we introduce class `CustomerModel`, which contains fields that constitute the persistent data of a Customer entity bean. Class `CustomerModel` is a Value Object, and we use it to transmit the persistent fields between the Customer EJB implementation class and the CustomerDAO implementation class. Note that Customer EJB and the DAO implementation

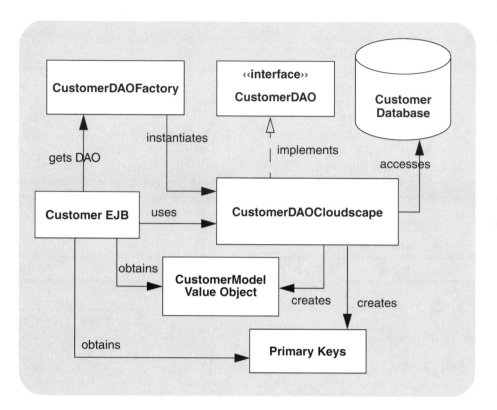

Figure 6-6 Class Relationships in DAO Pattern Implementation for Customer EJB

classes are the only two components that use class CustomerModel. Listing 6.5
contains the source for **CustomerModel.java**.

Listing 6.5 CustomerModel.java

```
// CustomerModel.java
public class CustomerModel {

// Encapsulation of Customer EJB persistent variables
   private String customerID;        // primary key
   private String name;
   private String password;
   private String email;
   private boolean ordersPending;
```

Listing 6.5 CustomerModel.java *(continued)*

```java
public CustomerModel(String customerID, String name,
  String password, String email, boolean ordersPending)
{
  setCustomerID(customerID);
  setName(name);
  setPassword(password);
  setEmail(email);
  setOrdersPending(ordersPending);
}

public void setCustomerID(String id) {
  this.customerID = id;
}

public void setName(String name) {
  this.name = name;
}

public void setPassword(String password) {
  this.password = password;
}

public void setEmail(String email) {
  this.email = email;
}

public void setOrdersPending(boolean ordersPending) {
  this.ordersPending = ordersPending;
}

public String getCustomerID() {
  return customerID;
}

public String getName() {
  return name;
}

public String getPassword() {
  return password;
}
```

Listing 6.5 CustomerModel.java *(continued)*

```java
public String getEmail() {
  return email;
}

public boolean getOrdersPending() {
  return ordersPending;
}
}
```

CustomerDAOSysException

Next we need a system exception class to propagate SQLExceptions from the CustomerDAO to the Customer EJB implementation class. Listing 6.6 contains the source for **CustomerDAOSysException.java**.

Listing 6.6 CustomerDAOSysException.java

```java
// CustomerDAOSysException.java
// System Exception
import java.lang.RuntimeException;

// CustomerDAOSysException extends standard
// RuntimeException.
// Thrown by CustomerDAO subclasses when there is an
// unrecoverable system error (typically SQLException)

public class CustomerDAOSysException extends
        RuntimeException {

  public CustomerDAOSysException(String msg) {
    super(msg);
  }

  public CustomerDAOSysException() {
    super();
  }
}
```

CustomerDAO

The CustomerDAO interface defines the database access methods required by the Customer EJB bean implementation class. Listing 6.7 contains the source for **CustomerDAO.java** interface.

Listing 6.7 CustomerDAO.java

```
// CustomerDAO.java
import java.util.Collection;
import javax.ejb.CreateException;

public interface CustomerDAO {

  // generate primary key
  public String dbGetKey();

  // inserts new CustomerModel record in database
  public void dbInsertCustomer(CustomerModel data)
    throws CreateException;

  // find specified primary key
  public boolean dbSelectByPrimaryKey(String primaryKey)
    throws CustomerDAOSysException;

  // the following 'dbSelect' methods
  // return a collection of primary keys
  public Collection dbSelectByCustomerName(String name)
    throws CustomerDAOSysException;
  public Collection dbSelectAll()
    throws CustomerDAOSysException;

  // load CustomerModel data from database
  public CustomerModel dbLoadCustomer(String primaryKey)
    throws CustomerDAOSysException;

  // store CustomerModel data to database
  public void dbStoreCustomer(CustomerModel data)
    throws CustomerDAOSysException;
```

Listing 6.7 CustomerDAO.java *(continued)*

```
   // delete Customer data from database with primary key
   public void dbRemoveCustomer(String primaryKey)
      throws CustomerDAOSysException;

   // database access method required by home method
   public int dbCountTotalCustomers()
      throws CustomerDAOSysException;
}
```

CustomerDAOCloudscape

The `CustomerDAOCloudscape` class is the implementation of `CustomerDAO` for the Cloudscape database. You'll note that besides containing the JDBC database access code, it also calls the Cloudscape `KeyGen` class to obtain a primary key.

Creating a unique primary key is a nontrivial problem, since multiple clients may attempt to create new Customer entity beans simultaneously. The Cloudscape utility `KeyGen.getUniversalKeyStringValue()` generates primary keys unique to the database. This routine is proprietary, however. If portability is an issue (and it usually is), techniques that dole out *blocks of primary keys* per request provide an efficient way to generate primary keys. The current value can be stored in a database. Furthermore, many database systems support an auto-generated primary key through a stored procedure.

Design Guideline

There are several ways to tackle the problem of generating unique primary keys. If you generate your own primary keys, using blocks of keys is efficient. A scheme which simply gets the next primary key from a database might create a bottleneck with a high-usage system.

The `CustomerDAOCloudscape` load and store routines encapsulate Customer persistent data fields into a `CustomerModel` value object. These methods all exhibit the same structure we used in the MusicDAO implementation class: we call `getConnection()` prior to each database access and use a `finally` block to release JDBC resources (closing statements and result sets and releasing the connection). Let's discuss several of these methods.

The `dbInsertCustomer()` method (see page 223) is called from `ejbCreate()` to insert a new Customer in the database. It builds a database insert command from its arguments. An error during this operation generates an `SQLException` that we catch and rethrow as a `CreateException`. Attempting to insert a record with a duplicate primary key causes the database software to throw an SQLException.

We invoke method dbSelectByPrimaryKey() (see page 224) from ejbFind-ByPrimaryKey(). This method specifies a query to select a record with a specific primary key as follows:

```
select CustomerID from Customers where CustomerID = ?
```

We don't read the data in the result set, but simply invoke ResultSet's next() method. If this method returns true, the current row is valid; false means there are no more rows. Thus, if our query returns false, then a record matching the specified primary key does not exist in the database.

We invoke method dbSelectByCustomerName() (see page 225) from ejbFindByCustomerName(). Here we specify the following query to select all records that match the specified name and fetch only the primary key from the database record.

```
select distinct CustomerID from Customers where Name = ?
```

Note that this method builds an ArrayList of primary keys, which we return to the finder method (and to the container). It is the EJB container's job to return the matching entity beans to the client.

Finally, look at method dbLoadCustomer() (see page 227) which we invoke from ejbLoad(). Here our select statement requests the named fields from the record that matches the specified primary key.

```
Select Name, Password, Email, OrdersPending from Customers
Where CustomerID = ?
```

We then extract each value from the result set and assign it to the matching persistent variable in value object CustomerModel.

Listing 6.8 contains the source for **CustomerDAOCloudscape.java**.

Listing 6.8 CustomerDAOCloudscape.java

```
// CustomerDAOCloudscape.java
import java.util.*;
import javax.ejb.*;
import javax.naming.*;
import javax.sql.DataSource;
import java.sql.*;
import COM.cloudscape.util.KeyGen;
```

Listing 6.8 CustomerDAOCloudscape.java *(continued)*

```java
// Implements CustomerDAO for Cloudscape database.
public class CustomerDAOCloudscape implements CustomerDAO {

  private Connection con = null;
  private DataSource datasource = null;

  public CustomerDAOCloudscape()
        throws CustomerDAOSysException {
    String dbName = "java:comp/env/jdbc/CustomerDB";
    try {
      InitialContext ic = new InitialContext();
      datasource = (DataSource) ic.lookup(dbName);

    } catch (NamingException ex) {
      throw new CustomerDAOSysException(
        "Cannot connect to database: " +
        dbName + ":\n" + ex.getMessage());
    }
  }

  // Cloudscape propriety routine to generate
  // primary key
  // called by ejbCreate()
  public String dbGetKey() {
    return KeyGen.getUniversalKeyStringValue();
  }

  // Obtain a JDBC Database connection
  private void getConnection()
        throws CustomerDAOSysException {
    try {
      con = datasource.getConnection();
    } catch (SQLException ex) {
      throw new CustomerDAOSysException(
        "Exception during DB Connection:\n"
        + ex.getMessage());
    }
  }
```

Listing 6.8 CustomerDAOCloudscape.java *(continued)*

```java
// Release JDBC Database connection
private void disConnect()
      throws CustomerDAOSysException {
  try {
    if (con != null) con.close();
  } catch (SQLException ex) {
    throw new CustomerDAOSysException(
      "SQLException during DB close connection:\n" +
      ex.getMessage());
  }
}

private void closeStatement(PreparedStatement s)
      throws CustomerDAOSysException {
  try {
    if (s != null) s.close();
  } catch (SQLException ex) {
    throw new CustomerDAOSysException(
      "SQL Exception during statement close\n"
      + ex.getMessage());
  }
}

private void closeResultSet(ResultSet rs)
      throws CustomerDAOSysException {
  try {
    if (rs != null) rs.close();
  } catch (SQLException ex) {
    throw new CustomerDAOSysException(
      "SQL Exception during result set close\n"
      + ex.getMessage());
  }
}

// called by ejbCreate()
public void dbInsertCustomer(CustomerModel newData)
    throws CreateException {

  String insertStatement =
    "insert into Customers values " +
    "( ? , ? , ? , ?, ? )";
  PreparedStatement prepStmt = null;
```

Listing 6.8 CustomerDAOCloudscape.java *(continued)*

```java
    try {
      getConnection();
      prepStmt =
        con.prepareStatement(insertStatement);

      prepStmt.setString(1, newData.getCustomerID());
      prepStmt.setString(2, newData.getName());
      prepStmt.setString(3, newData.getPassword());
      prepStmt.setString(4, newData.getEmail());
      prepStmt.setBoolean(5, newData.getOrdersPending());
      prepStmt.executeUpdate();

    } catch (SQLException ex) {
      throw new CreateException(ex.getMessage());
    } finally {
      closeStatement(prepStmt);
      disConnect();
    }
  }

  // called by ejbFindByPrimaryKey()
  public boolean dbSelectByPrimaryKey(String primaryKey)
        throws CustomerDAOSysException {

    String selectStatement =
      "select CustomerID " +
      "from Customers where CustomerID = ? ";

    PreparedStatement prepStmt = null;
    ResultSet rs = null;
    boolean result = false;
    try {
      getConnection();
      prepStmt =
        con.prepareStatement(selectStatement);
      prepStmt.setString(1, primaryKey);
      rs = prepStmt.executeQuery();
      result = rs.next();

    } catch (SQLException ex) {
      throw new CustomerDAOSysException(
        "dbSelectByPrimaryKey: SQL Exception caught\n"
        + ex.getMessage());
```

Listing 6.8 CustomerDAOCloudscape.java *(continued)*

```
    } finally {
      closeResultSet(rs);
      closeStatement(prepStmt);
      disConnect();
    }
    return result;
}

// called by ejbFindByCustomerName()
public Collection dbSelectByCustomerName(String name)
        throws CustomerDAOSysException {

    System.out.println("dbSelectByCustomerName for "
          + name);

    String selectStatement =
      "select distinct CustomerID " +
      "from Customers where Name = ? ";

    PreparedStatement prepStmt = null;
    ResultSet rs = null;
    ArrayList a = null;
    try {
      getConnection();
      prepStmt =
        con.prepareStatement(selectStatement);

      prepStmt.setString(1, name);
      rs = prepStmt.executeQuery();
      a = new ArrayList();

      while (rs.next()) {
        a.add(new String(rs.getString(1)));
      }

    } catch (SQLException ex) {
      throw new CustomerDAOSysException(
        "dbSelectByCustomerName: SQL Exception caught\n"
        + ex.getMessage());
```

Listing 6.8 CustomerDAOCloudscape.java *(continued)*

```java
    } finally {
      closeResultSet(rs);
      closeStatement(prepStmt);
      disConnect();
    }
    return a;
  }

  // called by ejbFindAll()
  public Collection dbSelectAll()
        throws CustomerDAOSysException {

    String selectStatement =
      "select distinct CustomerID " +
      "from Customers ";
    PreparedStatement prepStmt = null;
    ResultSet rs = null;
    ArrayList a = null;

    try {
      getConnection();
      prepStmt =
        con.prepareStatement(selectStatement);

      rs = prepStmt.executeQuery();
      a = new ArrayList();

      while (rs.next()) {
        a.add(new String(rs.getString(1)));
      }

    } catch (SQLException ex) {
      throw new CustomerDAOSysException(
        "dbSelectAll: SQL Exception caught\n"
        + ex.getMessage());

    } finally {
      closeResultSet(rs);
      closeStatement(prepStmt);
      disConnect();
    }
    return a;
  }
```

Listing 6.8 CustomerDAOCloudscape.java *(continued)*

```java
// called by ejbLoad()
public CustomerModel dbLoadCustomer(String primaryKey)
    throws CustomerDAOSysException,
    NoSuchEntityException {
  String selectStatement =
    "Select Name, Password, Email, OrdersPending " +
    "from Customers " +
    "Where CustomerID = ? ";

  PreparedStatement prepStmt = null;
  ResultSet rs = null;
  String name = null;
  String password = null;
  String email = null;
  boolean ordersPending = false;

  try {
    getConnection();
    prepStmt =
      con.prepareStatement(selectStatement);
    prepStmt.setString(1, primaryKey);
    rs = prepStmt.executeQuery();


    if (rs.next()) {
      // Read the data from the resultset
      name = rs.getString(1);            // Name
      password = rs.getString(2);        // Password
      email = rs.getString(3);           // Email
      ordersPending = rs.getBoolean(4); // OrdersPending
    }

    else {
      throw new NoSuchEntityException(
        "Row for customerID " + primaryKey +
        " not found in database.");
    }

    System.out.println("dbLoadCustomer: " + name);
    // Create CustomerModel to return to CustomerEJB
    return new CustomerModel(primaryKey,
            name, password, email, ordersPending);
```

Listing 6.8 CustomerDAOCloudscape.java *(continued)*

```java
      } catch (SQLException ex) {
        throw new CustomerDAOSysException(
          "dbLoadCustomer: SQL Exception caught\n"
          + ex.getMessage());
      } finally {
        closeResultSet(rs);
        closeStatement(prepStmt);
        disConnect();
      }
    }

    // called by ejbStore()
    public void dbStoreCustomer(CustomerModel data)
        throws CustomerDAOSysException {
      System.out.println("dbStoreCustomer: "
            + data.getName());
      String updateStatement =
        "update Customers set " +
        "Name = ? , " +
        "Password = ? , " +
        "Email = ? , " +
        "OrdersPending = ? " +
        "where CustomerID = ?";

      PreparedStatement prepStmt = null;
      try {
        getConnection();
        prepStmt =
          con.prepareStatement(updateStatement);

        // Grab values from persistent fields
        // to store in database
        prepStmt.setString(1, data.getName());
        prepStmt.setString(2, data.getPassword());
        prepStmt.setString(3, data.getEmail());
        prepStmt.setBoolean(4, data.getOrdersPending());
        prepStmt.setString(5, data.getCustomerID());
```

Listing 6.8 CustomerDAOCloudscape.java *(continued)*

```java
        int rowCount = prepStmt.executeUpdate();
        if (rowCount == 0) {
          throw new SQLException(
               "Storing row for CustomerID " +
               data.getCustomerID() + " failed.");
        }

    } catch (SQLException ex) {
      throw new CustomerDAOSysException(
        "dbStoreCustomer: SQL Exception caught\n"
        + ex.getMessage());
    } finally {
      closeStatement(prepStmt);
      disConnect();
    }
  }

  // called by ejbRemove()
  public void dbRemoveCustomer(String primaryKey)
        throws CustomerDAOSysException {
    String removeStatement =
      "delete from Customers where CustomerID = ?";
    PreparedStatement prepStmt = null;
    try {
      getConnection();
      prepStmt =
        con.prepareStatement(removeStatement);

      prepStmt.setString(1, primaryKey);
      int result = prepStmt.executeUpdate();

      if (result == 0) {
        throw new SQLException("Remove for CustomerID " +
          primaryKey + " failed.");
      }
```

Listing 6.8 CustomerDAOCloudscape.java *(continued)*

```
    } catch (SQLException ex) {
      throw new CustomerDAOSysException(
        "dbRemoveCustomer: SQL Exception caught\n"
        + ex.getMessage());
    } finally {
      closeStatement(prepStmt);
      disConnect();
    }
  }

  // Use a Select query to count
  // the number of records in the database
  // called by ejbHomeGetTotalCustomers()
  public int dbCountTotalCustomers()
        throws CustomerDAOSysException {

    String selectStatement =
      "select distinct CustomerID " +
      "from Customers ";
    PreparedStatement prepStmt = null;
    ResultSet rs = null;
    int count = 0;

    try {
      getConnection();
      // Request a resultset that is scrollable
      // so we can easily count rows
      prepStmt =
        con.prepareStatement(selectStatement,
          ResultSet.TYPE_SCROLL_INSENSITIVE,
          ResultSet.CONCUR_UPDATABLE);
      rs = prepStmt.executeQuery();

      // go to the last row
      // and get its row number
      rs.last();
      count = rs.getRow();

    } catch (SQLException ex) {
      throw new CustomerDAOSysException(
        "dbCountTotalCustomers: SQL Exception caught\n"
        + ex.getMessage());
```

Listing 6.8 CustomerDAOCloudscape.java *(continued)*

```
    } finally {
      closeResultSet(rs);
      closeStatement(prepStmt);
      disConnect();
    }
    return count;
  }
} // CustomerDAOCloudscape
```

JDBC 2.0 API

The JDBC 2.0 API includes result sets that are scrollable. Previously, result sets were only accessible in the forward direction. Scrollable result sets allow forward and backward reading, as well as skipping (for example, to the end). In the CustomerDAOCloudscape method dbCountTotalCustomers() *(see page 230), we define a scrollable result set so we can access the last row and easily obtain the row count. Otherwise, we would have to loop through the result set and increment a counter.*

CustomerDAOFactory

The CustomerDAOFactory class performs a JNDI lookup to obtain the name of the class it should instantiate for the CustomerDAO. We specify the name of the class in the deployment descriptor. Listing 6.9 contains the source for **CustomerDAOFactory.java**.

Listing 6.9 CustomerDAOFactory.java

```
// CustomerDAOFactory.java
import javax.naming.NamingException;
import javax.naming.InitialContext;

public class CustomerDAOFactory {

  // Instantiate a subclass that implements the abstract
  // CustomerDAO interface.
  // Obtain subclass name from the deployment descriptor
```

Listing 6.9 CustomerDAOFactory.java *(continued)*

```java
public static CustomerDAO getDAO()
        throws CustomerDAOSysException {

    CustomerDAO customerDAO = null;
    String customerDAOClass =
            "java:comp/env/CustomerDAOClass";
    String className = null;

    try {
        InitialContext ic = new InitialContext();
        // Lookup value of environment entry for
        // DAO classname
        // Value is set in deployment descriptor
        className = (String) ic.lookup(customerDAOClass);

        // Instantiate implementation class
        // for the CustomerDAO interface
        customerDAO = (CustomerDAO)
                Class.forName(className).newInstance();

    } catch (Exception ex) {
        throw new CustomerDAOSysException(
            "CustomerDAOFactory.getDAO: " +
            "NamingException for <" + className +
            "> DAO class : \n" + ex.getMessage());
    }
    return customerDAO;
    }
} // CustomerDAOFactory
```

Bean Implementation

The CustomerBean implementation class contains the implementation of the business methods as well as all the finder methods, home methods, and EJB methods. To organize the presentation of the code, we'll display it in sections as shown in Table 6.2.

Table 6.2 CustomerBean.java Code Location

Listing and Page	Contents
Listing 6.10 on page 233	Persistent Variables and Business Methods
Listing 6.11 on page 235	Finder Methods
Listing 6.12 on page 237	Home Method
Listing 6.13 on page 237	EJB Methods

Since we're using a DAO, the database access code has all been gathered into the CustomerDAO implementation class, CustomerDAOCloudscape, which you've just seen.

Listing 6.10 contains the persistent variables and business methods. Note the simplicity of the business methods; they update the persistent data fields as if the in-memory data fields and the records in the database were the same! We can write the business methods this way, because the EJB container calls ejb-Load() before each business method and ejbStore() afterwards. Note also that the business methods that *modify* persistent variables set the dirty flag.

Listing 6.10 CustomerBean.java—Persistent Variables and Business Methods

```
// CustomerBean.java
import java.sql.*;
import javax.sql.*;
import java.util.*;
import javax.ejb.*;
import javax.naming.*;

public class CustomerBean implements EntityBean {

  // Persistent data
  CustomerModel customerData;

  // Variable for DAO access
  private CustomerDAO customerDAO = null;

  // EJB variables
  private EntityContext context;
  private boolean dirty;
```

```java
// Business methods

public String getCustomerID() {
  return customerData.getCustomerID();
}

public String getName() {
  return customerData.getName();
}

public void setName(String name) {
  customerData.setName(name);
  dirty = true;
}

public String getPassword() {
  return customerData.getPassword();
}

public void setPassword(String newPassword) {
  customerData.setPassword(newPassword);
  dirty = true;
}

public String getEmail() {
  return customerData.getEmail();
}

public void setEmail(String newEmail) {
  customerData.setEmail(newEmail);
  dirty = true;
}

public boolean getOrdersPending() {
  return customerData.getOrdersPending();
}

public void setOrdersPending(boolean pending) {
  customerData.setOrdersPending(pending);
  dirty = true;
}
```

The finder methods call methods in the CustomerDAO interface to carry out the database select queries. Listing 6.11 contains the finder methods from file **CustomerBean.java**. Method `ejbFindByPrimaryKey()` returns the primary key; all the other finder methods return a collection of primary keys (or an empty collection if no database records are returned in the select query).

Again, the EJB container's role is significant here and helps explain the implementation code for finder methods. When a finder method returns a primary key, the EJB container matches the entity bean (possibly already instantiated in the container's cache of active entity beans) with the primary key. The EJB container, then, can simply return the cached bean to the client. Thus, by having the implementation code return a primary key, the EJB container is able to optimize an entity bean's life cycle. If the entity bean is not already activated, the EJB container invokes the `ejbActivate()` method, which causes `ejbLoad()` to read the persistent data from the database into the newly activated entity bean.

Listing 6.11 CustomerBean.java—Finder Methods

```
// Finder methods
// returns a primary key
// or throws ObjectNotFoundException

public String ejbFindByPrimaryKey(String primaryKey)
    throws FinderException {

    boolean result;

    try {
        CustomerDAO dao = getDAO();
        result = dao.dbSelectByPrimaryKey(primaryKey);
    } catch (CustomerDAOSysException ex) {
        ex.printStackTrace();
        throw new EJBException("ejbFindByPrimaryKey: " +
            ex.getMessage());
    }
    if (result) {
        return primaryKey;
    }
    else {
        throw new ObjectNotFoundException
            ("Row for id " + primaryKey + " not found.");
    }
}
```

Listing 6.11 CustomerBean.java—Finder Methods *(continued)*

```java
// returns a Collection of primary keys
// or an empty Collection if no objects are found

public Collection ejbFindByCustomerName(String name)
  throws FinderException {
  System.out.println("ejbFindByCustomerName: name="
        + name);
  Collection result;

  try {
    CustomerDAO dao = getDAO();
    result = dao.dbSelectByCustomerName(name);
  } catch (CustomerDAOSysException ex) {
    ex.printStackTrace();
    throw new EJBException("ejbFindByCustomerName: " +
      ex.getMessage());
  }
  // if we don't find any matching objects,
  // result is an empty collection
  return result;
}

// returns a Collection of primary keys
// or an empty Collection if no objects are found

public Collection ejbFindAll()
  throws FinderException {

  System.out.println("ejbFindAll()");
  Collection result;

  try {
    CustomerDAO dao = getDAO();
    result = dao.dbSelectAll();
  } catch (CustomerDAOSysException ex) {
    ex.printStackTrace();
    throw new EJBException("ejbFindAll: " +
      ex.getMessage());
  }
  // if we don't find any matching objects,
  // result is an empty collection
  return result;
}
```

Listing 6.12 contains the home method in **CustomerBean.java**. The client invokes this home method through the home (or local home) interface. While these methods access the database, they don't cause the EJB container to instantiate entity beans like the finder methods.

Listing 6.12 CustomerBean.java—Home Method

```
// EJB Home Method
public int ejbHomeGetTotalCustomers() {
   System.out.println("ejbHomeGetTotalCustomers()");
   int result;

   try {
     CustomerDAO dao = getDAO();
     result = dao.dbCountTotalCustomers();
   } catch (CustomerDAOSysException ex) {
     ex.printStackTrace();
     throw new EJBException("ejbHomeGetTotalCustomers: "
         + ex.getMessage());
   }
   return result;
 }
```

Listing 6.13 contains the EJB methods. We've placed several System.out.println statements in some of the methods. This not only helps test our EJB implementation code, but also shows when the EJB container invokes these methods (since the client does not invoke them directly).

Note that ejbStore() does not call the DAO method dbStoreCustomer() unless the boolean flag dirty is true. Recall that only the business methods that modify persistent variables (the setters) set the dirty flag to true.

The EJB container calls ejbLoad() before executing a business method. If the entity bean is being activated (after a finder call) then ejbLoad() initializes the persistent variables. Otherwise, it just refreshes them. The call to the bean context's getPrimaryKey() method ensures that we obtain a valid primary key.

Listing 6.13 CustomerBean.java—EJB Methods

```
// EJB Methods

// Call the Factory to get the
// CustomerDAO implementation class only
// when necessary; called by EJB Methods
```

Listing 6.13 CustomerBean.java—EJB Methods *(continued)*

```java
private CustomerDAO getDAO()
            throws CustomerDAOSysException {
  if (customerDAO == null) {
    customerDAO = CustomerDAOFactory.getDAO();
  }
  return customerDAO;
}

public String ejbCreate(String name, String password,
  String email) throws CreateException {

  System.out.println("ejbCreate(), name=" + name);
  CustomerModel newCust = null;

  try {
    CustomerDAO dao = getDAO();
    String newKey = dao.dbGetKey();
    newCust = new CustomerModel(
            newKey, name, password, email, false);
    dao.dbInsertCustomer(newCust);

  } catch (CustomerDAOSysException ex) {
    throw new CreateException("ejbCreate: " +
        ex.getMessage());
  }
  // initialize persistent data
  customerData = newCust;
  dirty = false;
  return customerData.getCustomerID();
}

public void setEntityContext(EntityContext context) {
  this.context = context;
  System.out.println("setEntityContext()");
}

public void unsetEntityContext() {
  System.out.println("unsetEntityContext()");
}
```

Listing 6.13 CustomerBean.java—EJB Methods *(continued)*

```java
// invoked by container just after activation
public void ejbActivate() {
  System.out.println("ejbActivate()");
}

// invoked by container just before passivation
public void ejbPassivate() {
  customerDAO = null;
}

public void ejbLoad() {
  System.out.println("ejbLoad()");
  try {
    CustomerDAO dao = getDAO();
    // Get the primary key from the context
    // and refresh persistent data from database
    customerData = dao.dbLoadCustomer(
            (String)context.getPrimaryKey());
    dirty = false;

  } catch (CustomerDAOSysException ex) {
    ex.printStackTrace();
    throw new EJBException("ejbLoad: " +
        ex.getMessage());
  }
}

public void ejbStore() {
  System.out.println("ejbStore(), name="
      + customerData.getName());
  try {
    if (dirty) {
      CustomerDAO dao = getDAO();
      // Synchronize the database with
      // the in-memory values of the persistent data
      dao.dbStoreCustomer(customerData);
      dirty = false;
    }
```

Listing 6.13 CustomerBean.java—EJB Methods *(continued)*

```
    } catch (CustomerDAOSysException ex) {
      ex.printStackTrace();
      throw new EJBException("ejbStore: " +
        ex.getMessage());
    }
  }

  public void ejbPostCreate(String name, String password,
      String email) {
    System.out.println("ejbPostCreate(), name=" + name);
  }

  public void ejbRemove() {
    System.out.println("ejbRemove()");
    try {
      CustomerDAO dao = getDAO();
      dao.dbRemoveCustomer(
              (String)context.getPrimaryKey());

    } catch (CustomerDAOSysException ex) {
      ex.printStackTrace();
      throw new EJBException("ejbRemove: " +
        ex.getMessage());
    }
  }
} // CustomerBean
```

Deployment Descriptor

Listing 6.14 contains some of the declarative information found in the deployment descriptor for the Customer EJB. Note that the descriptor specifies the interface names for both the local and remote interfaces, as well as the home and local home interfaces. Because Customer EJB is an entity bean, we must also specify its persistence type (we're using bean-managed persistence). Tag <prim-key-class> specifies the primary key type (here, java.lang.String). Under the <resource-ref> tag we specify the database resource name "jdbc/CustomerDB." Under the <env-entry> tag we specify the CustomerDAO implementation class name "CustomerDAOCloudscape."

Listing 6.14 Deployment Descriptor for Customer EJB

```
<ejb-jar>
 <display-name>CustomerJAR</display-name>
 <enterprise-beans>
    <entity>
      <display-name>CustomerBean</display-name>
      <ejb-name>CustomerBean</ejb-name>

      <home>CustomerHome</home>
      <remote>Customer</remote>
      <local-home>CustomerLocalHome</local-home>
      <local>CustomerLocal</local>
      <ejb-class>CustomerBean</ejb-class>
      <persistence-type>Bean</persistence-type>
      <prim-key-class>java.lang.String</prim-key-class>
      <reentrant>False</reentrant>

      <env-entry>
        <env-entry-name>CustomerDAOClass</env-entry-name>
        <env-entry-type>java.lang.String</env-entry-type>
        <env-entry-value>
             CustomerDAOCloudscape</env-entry-value>
      </env-entry>
      <security-identity>
        <description></description>
        <use-caller-identity></use-caller-identity>
      </security-identity>

      <resource-ref>
        <res-ref-name>jdbc/CustomerDB</res-ref-name>
        <res-type>javax.sql.DataSource</res-type>
        <res-auth>Container</res-auth>
        <res-sharing-scope>Shareable</res-sharing-scope>
      </resource-ref>
    </entity>
 </ejb-jar>
```

6.3 Entity Bean Test Client

Before integrating the Customer EJB into our Music Collection application, let's test it with an independent Java test client. The test client also helps show the role that the EJB container plays in managing entity beans. We've loaded several test records into our Customers database table (by accessing the database directly). Table 6.3 shows the initial test data.

Table 6.3 Initial Database Values for Customers Table

Customer ID	Name	Password	Email	Orders Pending
101	Catherine	Password101	cm@asgteach.com	false
102	Maheu	Password102	mh@asgteach.com	true
103	Cecile	Password103	cc@asgteach.com	false
104	Chaval	Password104	cv@asgteach.com	true
105	Levaque	Password105	lv@asgteach.com	true

Listing 6.15 shows the source for our test program contained in file **CustomerTestClient.java**. Because this is a stand-alone Java client, we access our Customer EJB through the remote interface.

We first perform the JNDI lookup associated with the EJB coded name "ejb-MyCustomer" and use the `PortableRemoteObject` class to obtain an object that implements the home interface. We then create a new `Customer` record (using the name "Lydia"). Because Customer EJB generates the primary key, we can run this program more than once without duplicating primary keys, creating a distinct "Lydia" customer each time. Our CustomerSession EJB will disallow customers sharing the same name. However, we by-pass this restriction here since the test client accesses the Customer EJB directly.

Next, we call `findByPrimaryKey()` with `customerID` 101 and obtain an object that implements the remote interface (`Customer`). Now we can invoke business methods. After changing the password, we access the customer name. We then call `findAll()` to display information about each record in the database. The last call to home method `getTotalCustomers()` displays the total number of records. (Note that we can also determine the number of records by accessing the `size()` method of the collection returned by `findAll()`.)

Listing 6.15 CustomerTestClient.java

```java
// CustomerTestClient.java
import java.util.*;
import javax.naming.Context;
import javax.naming.InitialContext;
import javax.rmi.PortableRemoteObject;
import javax.ejb.CreateException;

public class CustomerTestClient {

   public static void main(String[] args) {
     try {
       Context initial = new InitialContext();
       Object objref =
           initial.lookup("java:comp/env/ejb/MyCustomer");

       // Get a home interface object
       System.out.println("get a home interface object");
       CustomerHome home =
         (CustomerHome)PortableRemoteObject.narrow(objref,
               CustomerHome.class);

       // Create Customer entity bean.
       Customer lydia = home.create("Lydia",
           "Lydiapassword", "lydia@asgteach.com");

       // Call findByPrimaryKey for PK 101
       // This instantiates a different Customer EJB.
       Customer findPK = home.findByPrimaryKey("101");

       // Call a business method for Customer object
       // just returned
       // Must update the database
       System.out.println("Call setPassword()");
       findPK.setPassword("New Password");

       // Now call a second business method
       // using the same Customer object
       System.out.println(
               "Call getName()");
       String name = findPK.getName();
       System.out.println("name = " + name);
```

Listing 6.15 CustomerTestClient.java *(continued)*

```
            // Call finder method findAll()
            // and display information about
            // each Customer
            Collection c = home.findAll();
            Iterator i = c.iterator();
            while (i.hasNext()) {
              Customer cust = (Customer)i.next();
              System.out.println(cust.getName() + ": "
                    + cust.getPassword());
            }

            // home method
            System.out.println(home.getTotalCustomers()
                    + " customers in database.");

        } catch (CreateException ex) {
          System.err.println("Error creating object." );
          System.err.println(ex.getMessage());

        } catch (Exception ex) {
          System.err.println(
              "Caught an unexpected exception." );
          System.err.println(ex.getMessage());

        } finally {
          System.exit(0);
        }
      }
    }
} // CustomerTestClient
```

Let's run this client and show you the output from both the server and the client program (mixed together to show sequencing). We show the client output in bold. You'll want to refer to the client source, as well as the bean implementation code, for **CustomerBean.java** in Listing 6.13 on page 237 as you examine this output. Here's the output (with annotations in *italics* following each chunk).

get a home interface object
```
setEntityContext()
ejbCreate(), name=Lydia
ejbPostCreate(), name=Lydia
ejbStore(), name=Lydia
```

The EJB container calls setEntityContext() *before calling*
ejbCreate() *with the client's values. Method* ejbCreate() *inserts a new*
record in the database. Method ejbStore() *does not update the database.*

```
setEntityContext()
```
Call setPassword()
```
ejbActivate()
ejbLoad()
dbLoadCustomer: Catherine
ejbStore(), name=Catherine
dbStoreCustomer: Catherine
```
Call getName()
```
ejbLoad()
dbLoadCustomer: Catherine
ejbStore(), name=Catherine
```
name = Catherine

The EJB container calls setEntityContext() *before invoking*
method ejbFindByPrimaryKey() *with key 101. The container*
must activate this entity bean and call ejbLoad()
to read the database (through dbLoadCustomer()*).*
After we change the password, ejbStore() *must write the*
new values to the database (through dbStoreCustomer()*).*
The container invokes ejbLoad() *again before invoking business method*
getName(). *Method* getName() *does not modify the persistent variables, so*
ejbStore() *does not update the database this time.*

```
setEntityContext()
ejbFindAll()
ejbLoad()
dbLoadCustomer: Catherine
ejbStore(), name=Catherine
ejbLoad()
dbLoadCustomer: Catherine
ejbStore(), name=Catherine
```
Catherine: New Password

We now get all Customer records using findAll(). *The container invokes*
setEntityContext() *just once for the finder method.*
For primary key 101 (name Catherine), the bean is already activated (no call to
ejbActivate() *appears). (Note that for each record*
the container invokes ejbLoad() *and* ejbStore() *twice: once for*
getName() *and again for* getPassword().*) For these business methods,*
ejbStore() *does not update the database.*

```
ejbActivate()
ejbLoad()
dbLoadCustomer: Maheu
ejbStore(), name=Maheu
ejbLoad()
dbLoadCustomer: Maheu
ejbStore(), name=Maheu
```
Maheu: Password102

. . .

*For the next Customer record (Maheu), the container
calls* ejbActivate() *to activate this bean and* ejbLoad() *to initialize
the persistent variables. Calls to* ejbStore() *do not update the database.*

```
ejbLoad()
dbLoadCustomer: Lydia
ejbStore(), name=Lydia
ejbLoad()
dbLoadCustomer: Lydia
ejbStore(), name=Lydia
```
Lydia: Lydiapassword
```
setEntityContext()
ejbHomeGetTotalCustomers()
```
6 customers in database.

*Our newly created Customer record (Lydia)
is the final record returned by* findAll()*. Again,*
ejbActivate() *is not necessary since this entity
bean is already activated. Following the output for customer Lydia,
the next two lines show the server output for accessing the home method*
getTotalCustomers() *(with the client output appearing in the last line).*

6.4 Transaction Overview

Business transactions are frequently carried out in a series of separate steps.
Consider the following example where a customer purchases an airline ticket
online. Here we use pseudocode that shows the required steps in a transactional environment.

```
try {
  startTransaction();
    reserveFlight();
    payForFlight();
  commitTransaction();
} catch (Exception ex) {
    rollbackTransaction();
}
```

For this transaction to complete, all steps must be successful. Otherwise, data may be inconsistent. These separate steps make up a *transaction context*, which is viewed as a single operation.

A transaction that *commits* means that all steps in the transaction were successful and data is saved. A transaction that *rolls back* means that one or more steps failed and all work performed in the previous steps must be "undone." Rollbacks are important because they guarantee that any modified data returns to its original state before the transaction began. The start transaction and commit transaction steps form the boundary of a transaction. This is often called a *transaction demarcation*.

A big part of how entity beans work within the J2EE architecture is the role the EJB container plays in managing transactions and synchronizing requests from multiple clients. Transactions delineate critical code in multithreaded enterprise applications. While one client searches for certain database records in a database, another client may be updating those same records. How do we guarantee that the database is consistent and correct?

First of all, the application server provides transaction resource management services. By interfacing with the database server, the transaction manager can lock records involved in a transaction so that other queries or updates are temporarily blocked. Furthermore, if any step within a transaction fails, the transaction manager must make sure that the database returns to its stable state and any intermediate steps are "undone."

Properties of Transactions

All transactions must exhibit the properties of Atomicity, Consistency, Isolation, and Durability. The importance and immutability of these properties is emphasized in the industry through the acronym ACID. What do these properties mean and why are they important?

Atomicity means that all operations of a transaction, even those involving multiple steps, must be treated as a single unit of work. If any step fails, all of the steps must be "undone" so that the database is in its original state. This property helps ensure *Consistency*. Any database operation must leave the data in a consistent state. Any half-completed steps must be either finished to completion or returned to the original state.

Isolation has to do with the resource manager locking the database. This makes a set of operations complete before another transaction's operation modifies the same data. Without isolation, it is possible that one transaction could modify data that is in an intermediate (and inconsistent) state.

Durability means that the operations completed by a transaction must be permanent, regardless of system failures.

Another example that illustrates the need for transactions is the simple procedure of a bank customer transferring money from one account to another. At some point, the first account must be debited the correct amount and the second account credited that same amount. If the first account doesn't have sufficient funds, both accounts must remain unchanged (atomicity and consistency). And, if coincidentally, another owner of the account tries to make a withdrawal, this transaction must be blocked until the first one is complete (isolation). Finally, after the transaction, the account should forever reflect the customer's actions (durability).

Transactions Within the J2EE Platform

The fact that the J2EE platform supports transactions lifts a tremendous burden from the EJB developer. It spares developers from having to worry about process management, threading, and multiuser scenarios. Developers can focus more on the business logic of their systems.

The J2EE platform provides two kinds of transactions: programmatic and declarative. Programmatic transactions use the Java Transaction API (JTA). Declarative transactions use deployment descriptors to specify which methods require container-managed transactions and the attributes of those transactions. The application server supplies the transaction management services for declarative transactions. Entity beans must use (declarative) container-managed transactions; session beans may use either declarative or programmatic.

When you specify that a method executes within a transaction, the EJB container starts and completes the transaction for you. The architecture does not support nested transactions. However, the EJB container can suspend the current transaction context and start a new one.

If a method within a transaction throws a system exception, the EJB container automatically performs a transaction "rollback." This means any database modifications are undone, ensuring that the database remains in a consistent state (even if a database update fails). Any intermediate, partially completed operations are rolled back so that the database is in its original state.

A transaction's attribute defines how the container manages the transaction context for a method. The J2EE architecture defines six different transaction attributes as listed in Table 6.4. J2EE guidelines specified by Sun Microsystems recommend using the **Required** attribute for most EJB methods. This guarantees that the method executes within a transaction. By using the current transaction if it exists, **Required** allows nested method invocations to execute within a single transaction. Thus, all operations are treated as a single work unit, assuring atomicity. This also means that if any operation fails, all database modifications will be "rolled back."

Table 6.4 J2EE Transaction Attributes

Required	If a thread is executing within a transaction, the EJB container uses the current transaction's context. If the thread is not executing within a transaction, the EJB container initiates a new transaction context and attempts to complete the transaction when the method returns.
RequiresNew	The EJB container initiates a new transaction context before invoking the method, suspending the current one if it exists. It attempts to complete the transaction when the method returns.
NotSupported	The method will not execute within a transaction. If the current thread is in a transaction context, the EJB container will suspend the current transaction context and resume it after the method returns.
Supports	If the thread is executing within a transaction, the EJB container uses the current transaction's context. If the thread is not executing within a transaction, the method will not execute within a transaction (it will not initiate a new transaction).
Mandatory	If the thread is executing within a transaction, the EJB container uses the current transaction's context. If the thread is not executing within a transaction, the container throws a `TransactionRequiredException`.
Never	If the thread is executing within a transaction, the EJB container throws a `RemoteException`. If the thread is not executing within a transaction, the container invokes the method without initiating a transaction.

Sometimes, you need to execute a method outside of the current transaction. That is, you don't want it grouped with the current, possibly multiple-step operation. You also may not want this method to block out other clients if it is tied to a lengthy, database locking procedure. However, it still must execute within its own transaction. In this case, you should use attribute **RequiresNew**. For example, let's say you need to access a database to obtain a generated primary key and you're in the middle of a lengthy database update. However, the primary key generation step is a high-use, prone-to-bottleneck operation. It's also not dependent on the current database update. Therefore, you can specify attribute **RequiresNew**. The EJB container will suspend the current transaction and initiate a new transaction just for obtaining the primary key. When the primary key generation method returns, the transaction completes and other clients can now obtain their needed primary keys. You resume executing within the previously suspended transaction.

Transactions Within the Music Collection Application

In general, all business methods, finder methods, and create methods of an entity bean should execute within a transaction. Executing a business method within a transaction guarantees that the corresponding data in the entity matches the underlying persistent data. Finder methods (even though they only perform read operations) must synchronize the in-memory entity bean with the underlying database in case another client has changed the data. In our Customer EJB, we declare (through the deployment tool) all methods to have transaction attribute **Required**. For example, let's say a client invokes method setPassword(). The EJB container will initiate a new transaction if the client thread is not currently executing within a transaction. Otherwise, it will use the current transaction. Because we're executing within a transaction, the EJB container will synchronize the entity bean with the underlying database by invoking ejbLoad(). During this time, if another client requests access to the same entity bean, this second client will be blocked until the transaction completes. When the setPassword() method executes, the entity bean's persistent variable is changed. The EJB container will then resynchronize the entity bean and the database with ejbStore(). If we're in a new transaction, it completes before returning to the client.

In the next section we present the CustomerSession EJB. You will see that encapsulating a multiple-step business process into a session bean business method allows the whole operation to execute within a single transaction. This will be even more advantageous when we integrate other entity beans under the CustomerSession EJB controlling session bean, and it is one of the motivations for using the Session Facade Pattern.

6.5   Session Facade Pattern

Consider what we need to do to integrate our Customer EJB into the Music Collection virtual shopping application (return to Figure 6-2 on page 205). When a user accesses the "login" web page, the JSP client asks for a login name and password. The client must determine if the user name is valid and if the password matches the given user name. We accomplish this multiple-step process by invoking method `findByCustomerName()`, which returns a collection. The client must then verify that only one `Customer` instance is in the collection. It then must call `getPassword()` and check to see if the entity bean's password matches the one provided by the user.

For a JSP client or stand-alone Java client to accomplish this task, we must issue more than one remote call. Multiple remote calls from many clients can quickly cause a network bottleneck. A better approach is to encapsulate the steps of a business process into a single method. Using the *Session Facade Pattern*, we can create a session bean that delegates multiple-step business methods to our Customer EJB entity bean. Figure 6-7 shows the approach. The diagram illustrates the difference between having the remote client access the Customer EJB directly (top half) compared to accessing the entity bean through the Session Facade (bottom half). Within the Session Facade implementation, the `identifyCustomer()` method is a remote call, whereas `findByCustomer-Name()` and `getPassword()` are local calls. Not only does a Session Facade improve performance here, but it also provides a simpler interface to the client.

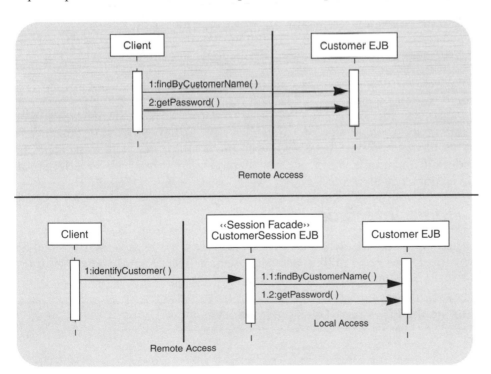

Figure 6-7 Sequence Diagram Showing the Advantages of Using a Session Facade

The Session Facade can (and typically will) implement more than one business process.

A session facade can use a stateless or stateful session bean and offers the following advantages:

- The session bean encapsulates the business process in one place and is callable from any client. Only one remote call is necessary, which replaces the multiple-remote call sequence. Using a session bean facade thus simplifies the client.
- The session bean can access the entity bean with local interfaces, minimizing the number of remote calls. Thus, the multiple, fine-grained calls become local calls, improving performance.
- Using a session facade isolates the entity bean from general clients. If we need to change our underlying database structure, changes to the client are unlikely. And (depending on how radically we alter the interface to our entity bean), changes will be limited to the session facade.
- Since session bean methods execute within transactions, we can perform multiple-step entity bean accesses (which may include database updates) easily within a single transaction. Thus, a session facade simplifies multiple-step operations with entity beans by creating a single, transactional session bean method.

Because we store customer data information in the database only, our session bean can be *stateless*. This session bean provides a simplified interface to the Customer EJB and isolates the entity bean from general clients such as web components or stand-alone Java clients. The CustomerSession EJB will only access methods in the Customer EJB. In the next chapter we'll implement the Order EJB and LineItem EJB, and add methods for a coordinated interface to all three entity beans.

Home Interface

CustomerSession EJB's home interface contains a single `create()` method since CustomerSession EJB is a stateless session bean. Listing 6.16 contains the source for **CustomerSessionHome.java**.

Listing 6.16 CustomerSessionHome.java

```
// CustomerSessionHome.java
import java.io.Serializable;
import java.rmi.RemoteException;
import javax.ejb.CreateException;
import javax.ejb.EJBHome;
```

Listing 6.16 CustomerSessionHome.java *(continued)*

```java
public interface CustomerSessionHome extends EJBHome {

    CustomerSession create()
        throws RemoteException, CreateException;
}
```

Remote Interface

CustomerSession EJB's remote interface contains the business methods. These methods manipulate the Customer EJB and perform such tasks as creating a new customer (method createCustomer()) or verifying a particular customer's password (identifyCustomer()). Listing 6.17 contains the source for **CustomerSession.java**.

Listing 6.17 CustomerSession.java

```java
// CustomerSession.java
import javax.ejb.*;
import java.rmi.RemoteException;
import java.util.*;

public interface CustomerSession extends EJBObject {

  public int getTotalCustomers()
    throws RemoteException;

  public void createCustomer(CustomerVO customer)
      throws CreateException, RemoteException;

  public void changePassword(String name, String password)
      throws CustomerIdentityException, CustomerException,
      RemoteException;

  public void changeEmail(String name, String email)
      throws CustomerIdentityException, CustomerException,
      RemoteException;

  public void identifyCustomer(String name,
      String password)
      throws CustomerIdentityException, RemoteException;

  public boolean getOrdersPending(String name)
      throws CustomerIdentityException, RemoteException;
```

Listing 6.17 CustomerSession.java *(continued)*

```
   public Collection getCustomers() throws RemoteException;
}
```

Method `identifyCustomer()` throws a `CustomerIdentityException` if the specified password does not match the Customer's record as identified by argument `name`. Method `getOrdersPending()` returns the `OrdersPending` field of the customer specified in `name`; it throws a `CustomerIdentityException` if customer `name` cannot be found. Method `getCustomers()` returns a collection of `CustomerVO` objects built from the Customer database.

Application Exceptions

The CustomerSession EJB uses two application exceptions to detect and send errors back to the client. The `CustomerIdentityException` indicates that the client is attempting to perform some task involving a customer identified by name, but the name cannot be located in the database. We also use the `CustomerIdentityException` to indicate that the given name and password combination do not match.

The `CustomerException` indicates any other problems associated with the Customer EJB or the underlying database.

These two exceptions are used exclusively by the CustomerSession EJB to manage error detection between client requests and the Customer EJB. Listing 6.18 shows the source for **CustomerIdentityException.java**.

Listing 6.18 CustomerIdentityException.java

```java
// CustomerIdentityException.java
// Application Exception
public class CustomerIdentityException extends Exception {

    public CustomerIdentityException() { }

    public CustomerIdentityException(String msg) {
        super(msg);
    }
}
```

Listing 6.19 contains the source for **CustomerException.java**.

Listing 6.19 CustomerException.java

```java
// CustomerException.java
// Application Exception
public class CustomerException extends Exception {

    public CustomerException() { }

    public CustomerException(String msg) {
        super(msg);
    }
}
```

Bean Implementation

Listing 6.20 is the implementation code for the CustomerSession EJB. Its primary job is to translate client requests into the proper sequence of business method invocations on the Customer EJB. The business method identifyCustomer(), for example, must use the Customer EJB finder method to find the correct Customer entity bean and compare the password in its argument with the password stored in the bean. The client can assume that the Customer is correctly identified as long as the CustomerSession EJB does not throw a CustomerIdentityException.

Note that the createCustomer() method performs parameter checking on the values in the CustomerVO object before creating a Customer entity bean. It also makes sure that the name does not already exist in the database.

The business methods in the CustomerSession EJB all execute within a transaction. During deployment, we specify container-managed transactions and assign transaction attribute **Required** to each business method. For business methods that perform multiple-step operations, this provides all the ACID properties we need for transactional processing. In createCustomer(), for instance, we call findByCustomerName() to verify that a customer name is not already in use. If the name does not exist, we proceed to create the new customer record using that name. If this method doesn't execute within a single transaction, another client could conceivably create a customer record using the same name in between the return of findByCustomerName() and the completion of the create() call. By using a transaction in createCustomer(), we ensure that this multiple-step procedure is treated as a single unit of work (satisfying the requirements for atomicity and consistency).

Listing 6.20 CustomerSessionBean.java

```java
// CustomerSessionBean.java
import java.rmi.RemoteException;
import javax.ejb.*;
import javax.naming.*;
import java.util.*;

public class CustomerSessionBean implements SessionBean {

  // initialize in ejbCreate()
  private CustomerLocalHome customerHome;

  // Business methods
  // Return the number of Customers in the database
   public int getTotalCustomers() {
     return customerHome.getTotalCustomers();
   }

  // Create a new Customer in the CustomerDB
  // verify that the name is unique and the password
  // is non-empty.

  public void createCustomer(CustomerVO customer)
      throws CreateException, FinderException {
    if (customer.getName() == null
        || customer.getPassword() == null
        || customer.getEmail() == null) {
      throw new CreateException("Customer data is null");
    }

    if (customer.getName().equals("")
        || customer.getPassword().equals("")
        || customer.getEmail().equals("")) {
      throw new CreateException(
              "Customer fields cannot be empty.");
    }
```

Listing 6.20 CustomerSessionBean.java *(continued)*

```
  Collection c =
    customerHome.findByCustomerName(customer.getName());
  if (c.size() == 0) {
    customerHome.create(
      customer.getName(),
      customer.getPassword(),
      customer.getEmail());
  }
  else {
    throw new CreateException(
          "Customer name already in use.");
  }
}

// Change the password identified by customer 'name'.
// Make sure customer is in the database
// Throws CustomerIdentityException if no match.
// Throws CustomerException for other problems.

public void changePassword(String name, String password)
    throws CustomerIdentityException, CustomerException,
    FinderException {
  if (password.equals("")) {
    throw new CustomerException(
          "Password cannot be empty");
  }

  Collection c = customerHome.findByCustomerName(name);
  if (c.size() == 1) {
    Iterator i = c.iterator();
    CustomerLocal cust = (CustomerLocal)i.next();
    cust.setPassword(password);
  }
  else {
    throw new CustomerIdentityException(
      "Cannot find customer " + name);
  }
}
```

Listing 6.20 CustomerSessionBean.java *(continued)*

```java
// Change the email for the customer 'name'.
// Make sure customer is in the database
// Throws CustomerIdentityException if no match.
// Throws CustomerException for other problems.

public void changeEmail(String name, String email)
    throws CustomerIdentityException, CustomerException,
    FinderException {
  if (email.equals("")) {
    throw new CustomerException(
            "Email cannot be empty");
  }

  Collection c = customerHome.findByCustomerName(name);
  if (c.size() == 1) {
    Iterator i = c.iterator();
    CustomerLocal cust = (CustomerLocal)i.next();
    cust.setEmail(email);
  }
  else {
    throw new CustomerIdentityException(
            "Cannot find customer " + name);
  }
}

// Given a customer name, make sure the password
// matches the customer's name in the database
// Throws CustomerIdentityException if no match.

public void identifyCustomer(String name,
    String password) throws CustomerIdentityException,
    FinderException {

  Collection c = customerHome.findByCustomerName(name);
```

Listing 6.20 CustomerSessionBean.java *(continued)*

```java
    if (c.size() == 1) {
      Iterator i = c.iterator();
      CustomerLocal cust = (CustomerLocal)i.next();
      if (!cust.getPassword().equals(password)) {
        throw new CustomerIdentityException(
            "Incorrect Password for customer " + name);
      }
    }
    else {
      throw new CustomerIdentityException(
          "Cannot find customer " + name);
    }
  }

  // For customer 'name', return the ordersPending field.
  // Throw CustomerIdentityException if customer
  // cannot be found.

  public boolean getOrdersPending(String name)
      throws CustomerIdentityException,
      FinderException {

    Collection c = customerHome.findByCustomerName(name);

    if (c.size() == 1) {
      Iterator i = c.iterator();
      CustomerLocal cust = (CustomerLocal)i.next();
      return cust.getOrdersPending();
    }
    else {
      throw new CustomerIdentityException(
          "Cannot find customer " + name);
    }
  }
```

Listing 6.20 CustomerSessionBean.java *(continued)*

```java
// Get all the customers in the customer database:
// Return an ArrayList of CustomerVOs

public Collection getCustomers()
            throws FinderException {

  // return an ArrayList of CustomerVOs
  ArrayList customerList = new ArrayList();

  Collection a = customerHome.findAll();
  Iterator i = a.iterator();

  while (i.hasNext()) {
    CustomerLocal customerEJB = (CustomerLocal)i.next();

    CustomerVO customer =
      new CustomerVO(customerEJB.getName(),
        customerEJB.getPassword(),
        customerEJB.getEmail());
    customerList.add(customer);
  }
  return customerList;
}

 // EJB Methods
public CustomerSessionBean() {}

public void ejbCreate() {
  try {
    Context initial = new InitialContext();

    // Find Local Home Interface to CustomerEJB
    Object objref =
          initial.lookup("java:comp/env/ejb/Customer");
    customerHome = (CustomerLocalHome)objref;

  } catch (Exception ex) {
    ex.printStackTrace();
    throw new EJBException(ex.getMessage());
  }
}
```

Listing 6.20 CustomerSessionBean.java *(continued)*

```
    public void ejbRemove() {}
    public void ejbActivate() {}
    public void ejbPassivate() {}
    public void setSessionContext(SessionContext sc) {}

} // CustomerSessionBean
```

Deployment Descriptor

Listing 6.21 shows portions of the deployment descriptor for the EJB JAR file that holds the CustomerSession EJB. The CustomerSession EJB is a stateless session bean with container-managed transactions. It references the Customer entity bean through its local and local home interfaces. Under the <assembly-descriptor> tag, the deployment descriptor lists all its transactional methods, along with the transaction attribute we assign (in all cases, attribute **Required**). The <method> tag identifies methods with transactions. We show the <method> tags for getTotalCustomers() and createCustomer() only.

Listing 6.21 Deployment Descriptor for Customer JAR File

```
<ejb-jar>
  <display-name>CustomerJAR</display-name>
  <enterprise-beans>
    <session>

      <display-name>CustomerSessionBean</display-name>
        <ejb-name>CustomerSessionBean</ejb-name>
        <home>CustomerSessionHome</home>
        <remote>CustomerSession</remote>
        <ejb-class>CustomerSessionBean</ejb-class>
        <session-type>Stateless</session-type>
        <transaction-type>Container</transaction-type>

       <ejb-local-ref>
         <ejb-ref-name>ejb/Customer</ejb-ref-name>
         <ejb-ref-type>Entity</ejb-ref-type>
         <local-home>CustomerLocalHome</local-home>
         <local>CustomerLocal</local>
         <ejb-link>CustomerBean</ejb-link>
       </ejb-local-ref>
```

Listing 6.21 Deployment Descriptor for Customer JAR File *(continued)*

```
<security-identity>
      <description></description>
      <use-caller-identity></use-caller-identity>
   </security-identity>
  </session>
</enterprise-beans>

<assembly-descriptor>
  <container-transaction>
    <method>
      <ejb-name>CustomerSessionBean</ejb-name>
      <method-intf>Remote</method-intf>
      <method-name>getTotalCustomers</method-name>
      <method-params />
    </method>
    <trans-attribute>Required</trans-attribute>
  </container-transaction>

  <container-transaction>
    <method>
      <ejb-name>CustomerSessionBean</ejb-name>
      <method-intf>Remote</method-intf>
      <method-name>createCustomer</method-name>
      <method-params>
         <method-param>CustomerVO</method-param>
      </method-params>
    </method>
    <trans-attribute>Required</trans-attribute>
  </container-transaction>
    . . .
  </assembly-descriptor>
</ejb-jar>
```

6.6   Web Component Client

Armed with the Customer (entity) EJB and CustomerSession (session) EJB, we now add login and sign up functionality to our Music Collection shopping application. Figure 6-8 depicts the web component's structure and the JSP files that supply the functionality. The new or updated components are white. (You may want to compare its structure to the previous version shown in Figure 5-6 on page 166.)

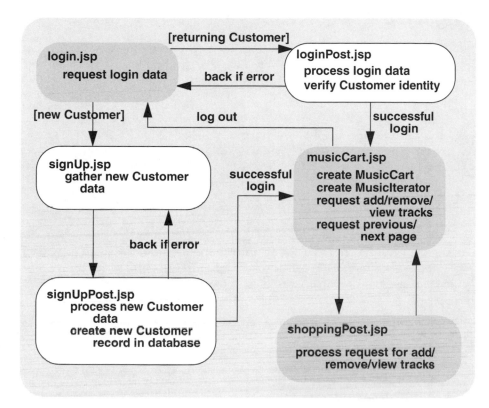

Figure 6-8 Relationship Among JSP Files After Adding Customer Database Verification and Creation

The sign up process requires files **signUp.jsp** to collect the new customer data and **signUpPost.jsp** to process it. The login page (file **login.jsp**) has an added link for new customers (its only change). The biggest modification from the version we presented in Chapter 5 is in **loginPost.jsp**, which now provides customer verification. These programs access the CustomerSession EJB to either create a new customer or verify an existing customer by name and password.

This section presents the sources for **signUp.jsp**, **signUpPost.jsp**, and **login-Post.jsp**. As you look through the code, note that accessing the Customer database is simple because we go through the session facade CustomerSession EJB. Let's start with **login.jsp**.

login.jsp

File **login.jsp** now has a link that accesses the new customer page (**signUp.jsp**). Since there are no other modifications, we display this link (shown in bold) between the last two lines of the code, as follows:

```
</form>
<br><br>If you are a new Customer
<a href="signUp.jsp">Sign Up Here</a>
</body></html>
```

signUp.jsp

This JSP program creates an HTML table to help format the input form that asks for the required new customer information: name, password (typed in twice), and e-mail address. We use an HTML input form and specify page **sign-UpPost.jsp** as the action parameter. Listing 6.22 shows the source for **signUp.jsp**.

Listing 6.22 signUp.jsp

```
<%--
  signUp.jsp
--%>

<%--
  JSP Component to gather new Customer
  information.
--%>

<%@ page errorPage="error.jsp" %>

<%
  String requestURI = request.getRequestURI();
  session.putValue("signUpURL", requestURI);
%>
<html>
<head>
<title>New Customer Sign Up Page</title>
</head>
```

Listing 6.22 signUp.jsp *(continued)*

```
<body bgcolor=white>
<center>
<h1>Sign Up Page</h1>
<hr>
<p>
Please provide the following information
<form method="post" action="signUpPost.jsp">

<p>
<table border=2 cellpadding=5 bgcolor=#e0e0e0>
  <tr><td>
  Name:
  </td><td>
  <input TYPE="text" NAME="name" size=30>
  </td></tr>

  <tr><td>
  Password:
  </td><td>
  <input TYPE="password" NAME="password" size=30>
  </td></tr>

  <tr><td>
  Retype Password:
  </td><td>
  <input TYPE="password" NAME="password_2" size=30>
  </td></tr>

  <tr><td>
  Email:
  </td><td>
  <input TYPE="text" NAME="email" size=30>
  </td></tr>

  <tr><td align=center colspan=2>
  <input TYPE="submit" NAME="SignUp" VALUE=" Sign Me Up ">
  <input TYPE="reset" VALUE=" Clear Form ">
  </td></tr>
</table>
</form>
</body></html>
```

signUpPost.jsp

Listing 6.23 shows the source for **signUpPost.jsp**. This JSP program processes the new customer data provided by the user. It makes sure that none of the fields are empty and checks that both password fields are the same. If there are no problems, the program uses the CustomerSession EJB to create a new customer with the user-supplied information. If this succeeds (no exceptions are thrown), we display a successful login message and a link to enter the Music Collection site. Otherwise, we check the errorString variable. If there was a problem, errorString will be non-null. A text box appears with an error message and provides a link to the previous page, allowing the user to correct the problem.

Listing 6.23 signUpPost.jsp

```
<%--
   signUpPost.jsp
--%>

<%--
   JSP Web component to process new Customer
   information.
   Make sure user has supplied a value for
   each field.
--%>

<%@ page import="CustomerSession,CustomerSessionHome,
CustomerVO,CustomerException,
CustomerIdentityException,java.util.*,
javax.ejb.CreateException, javax.naming.Context,
javax.naming.InitialContext,
javax.rmi.PortableRemoteObject"
errorPage="error.jsp" %>

<%!
   CustomerSession mysession = null;
   public void jspInit() {
     try {
       Context initial = new InitialContext();
       Object objref = initial.lookup(
           "java:comp/env/ejb/CustomerSession");
```

Listing 6.23 signUpPost.jsp *(continued)*

```
        // get a home interface to CustomerSession EJB
        CustomerSessionHome home = (CustomerSessionHome)
            PortableRemoteObject.narrow(
            objref, CustomerSessionHome.class);
        // get a remote interface to CustomerSession EJB
        mysession = home.create();

    } catch (Exception ex) {
        System.out.println("Unexpected Exception: " +
            ex.getMessage());
    }
  }
%>

<%
  CustomerVO customer = null;
%>
<html>
<title>Process New Customer Information</title>
<body bgcolor=white>
<center>

<%
  String requestURI =
    (String)session.getValue("signUpURL");

  // Get name, password & email values provided by user
  String name = (String)request.getParameter("name");
  String password =
    (String)request.getParameter("password");
  String password2 =
    (String)request.getParameter("password_2");
  String email = (String)request.getParameter("email");

  // Check to make sure no fields are empty
  String errorString = null;
  if (name.equals("")
    || password.equals("") || email.equals("")) {
    errorString = "You have left a field empty. " +
      "You must provide a Name, " +
      "a Password, and an Email address.";
  }
```

Listing 6.23 signUpPost.jsp *(continued)*

```
    // make sure both password fields are the same
    else if (!password.equals(password2)) {
      errorString =
        "The passwords you provided were not the same. " +
        "Please try again.";
    }

    else { // everything is ok; create new customer
      try {
        customer = new CustomerVO(name, password, email);
        mysession.createCustomer(customer);
        session.putValue("customer", name);
        String newCustomer = "new";
        session.putValue("newCustomer", newCustomer);
%>

<h1>Login Successful</h1>
<p><h2>Welcome <%= customer.getName() %> </h2>
<hr><p>
<br><br><a href="musicCart.jsp">
Enter Music Collection Site</a>

<%
      } catch (CreateException ex) {
        errorString = ex.getMessage();
      }
    } // end else
    if (errorString != null) { // we have a problem

      // We use html formatting tags to create an error box
      // with red lettering so that it will stand out.

%>

<h1>Customer Information Error</h1>
<hr>
<p>
<p STYLE="background:#bfbfbf;color:red;
font-weight:bold;border:double thin;padding:5">
<%= errorString %>
</font>
<br><br><a href="<%= requestURI %>">
  Return to Sign Up Page</a>
```

Listing 6.23 signUpPost.jsp *(continued)*

```
<%
  } // end if
%>
</body></html>
```

Design Guideline

*Recall that stateless session beans are shareable because they do not contain client-specific state information. In **signUpPost.jsp**, we can initialize* CustomerSession *variable* mysession *in a JSP declaration and share its instance with as many clients as necessary. We'll perform this same initialization in **loginPost.jsp**.*

---

loginPost.jsp

The previous version of this web component requested customer login information, but only checked if the user-supplied fields were non-null. Any customer name and password were accepted. No actual customer was created and no information was saved. Since we've implemented CustomerSession EJB and Customer EJB, we can now create new customers and provide a login process that checks a user-supplied name and password with values stored in our customer database.

Listing 6.24 contains the source for file **loginPost.jsp**. This JSP program processes login information and verifies name and password fields with the underlying database by calling CustomerSession EJB's identifyCustomer(). You'll notice that its structure is very similar to **signUpPost.jsp**. Here, instead of creating a new customer record, we look up a preexisting record and verify that its name and password are correct.

Listing 6.24 loginPost.jsp

```
<%--
  loginPost.jsp
--%>

<%--
  JSP Web component to process login information.
  Make sure user has supplied a value for
  each field.
--%>
```

Listing 6.24 loginPost.jsp *(continued)*

```
<%@ page import="CustomerSession,CustomerSessionHome,
CustomerException,CustomerIdentityException,java.util.*,
javax.naming.Context, javax.naming.InitialContext,
javax.rmi.PortableRemoteObject"
errorPage="error.jsp" %>

<%!
  CustomerSession mysession = null;
  public void jspInit() {
    try {
      Context initial = new InitialContext();
      Object objref = initial.lookup(
          "java:comp/env/ejb/CustomerSession");
      // get a home interface to CustomerSession EJB
      CustomerSessionHome home = (CustomerSessionHome)
          PortableRemoteObject.narrow(
          objref, CustomerSessionHome.class);
      // get a remote interface to CustomerSession EJB
      mysession = home.create();

    } catch (Exception ex) {
      System.out.println("Unexpected Exception: " +
          ex.getMessage());
      ex.printStackTrace();
    }
  }
%>

<html>
<title>Process Login</title>
<body bgcolor=white>
<center>
<%
  String requestURI =
    (String)session.getValue("loginURL");

  // Get name and password values provided by user
  String name = (String)request.getParameter("name");
  String password =
    (String)request.getParameter("password");
```

Listing 6.24 loginPost.jsp *(continued)*

```
  // Perform error checking on Customer input fields
  String errorString = null;
  // Check to make sure they're not empty
  if (name.equals("") || password.equals("")) {
    errorString = "You have left a field empty. " +
      "You must provide both a name " +
      "and a password.";
  }

  else {
    try {
      // see if name and password match
      mysession.identifyCustomer(name, password);
      session.putValue("customer", name);
      String newCustomer = "new";
      session.putValue("newCustomer", newCustomer);
%>

<h1>Login Successful</h1>
<p>
<h2>Welcome <%= name %> </h2>
<hr>
<p>
<br><br><a href="musicCart.jsp">
Enter Music Collection Site</a>

<%
    } catch (CustomerIdentityException ex) {
      errorString = ex.getMessage();
    }
  } // end else
  if (errorString != null) {            // we have a problem

    // We use html formatting tags to create an error box
    // with red lettering so that it will stand out.

%>

<h1>Login Error</h1>
<hr>
<p>
```

Listing 6.24 loginPost.jsp *(continued)*

```
<p STYLE="background:#bfbfbf;color:red;
font-weight:bold;border:double thin;padding:5">
<%= errorString %>
</font>
<br><br><a href="<%= requestURI %>">
  Return to Login Page</a>

<%
  } // end if
%>
</body></html>
```

6.7   Design Guidelines and Patterns

With the introduction of entity beans, our enterprise application can safely and efficiently model business data that updates a database. Let's review some of the design decisions we've made in implementing our Customer entity bean and associated session facade, CustomerSession EJB.

Using BMP

General wisdom dictates using Container-Managed Persistence (CMP) whenever possible. However, not all entity beans can be implemented with CMP. Bean-managed persistence requires that the bean developer write the database access code for an entity bean. This means writing `ejbLoad()` and `ejbStore()` routines to synchronize the database, as well as implementing the `ejbFind-XXX()`, `ejbCreate()`, and `ejbRemove()` methods. To minimize actual database updates with `ejbStore()`, we maintain a `dirty` flag. We set the `dirty` flag in any business method that modifies persistent variables and only update the database when persistent variables have changed.

DAO Pattern

An entity bean with BMP is a good candidate to use the DAO pattern. This promotes database independence and allows the bean developer to use alternate DAO implementation classes by changing only the deployment descriptor. We define a `CustomerDAO` interface that contains the database access routines required by the Customer EJB bean implementation code. In addition, we define the `CustomerModel` class to hold the persistent data. Like the DAO pattern we presented with the Music Database, we also define a factory class,

`CustomerDAOFactory`, a DAO implementation class for the Cloudscape database, `CustomerDAOCloudscape`, and a system exception class, `CustomerDAO-SysException`.

Local Interfaces

Performance will improve if you implement entity beans with local interfaces. Because entity beans typically contain find-grained setter and getter methods, remote access in a high-usage system can quickly cause network bottlenecks. Use a session bean to access entity beans through local interfaces. The session bean may be stateless or stateful; however, a stateless bean is more efficient.

Transactions

Since entity beans are persistent and shareable, they are managed by an EJB container that supports transactions. Entity beans must use container-managed transactions. This means that during the deployment process, the bean developer specifies which methods require transactions and the attribute of those transactions. In general, the entity bean finder, `create()`, `remove()`, and business methods all execute within transactions. The **Required** attribute is typical and covers most scenarios. Thus, if the client thread is already in a transaction, the EJB container continues to use this transaction context. If the client thread is not currently executing within a transaction, the EJB container initiates a new transaction.

Session Facade Pattern

The session facade pattern delegates a session bean as an interface to one or more entity beans. The session bean accesses the entity beans using local interfaces and provides a simplified interface for clients to the entity beans. It implements one or more business processes in its business methods. The session facade pattern not only improves performance of entity bean access by using local interfaces, it offers many other advantages.

- A session bean models a business process and it can therefore encapsulate the business rules that affect entity beans.
- A session bean is callable from any client.
- A session bean isolates the entity bean from general clients.
- A session bean's multiple-step business method can execute within a single transaction, providing support for the ACID transaction properties.
- A session bean simplifies the interface between clients and entity beans.

Entity Bean Testing

Since BMP is more complicated than CMP, you may want to implement remote interfaces to the entity bean for testing purposes. You can then write a stand-alone Java client to test your entity bean. Once testing is complete, you may create the local and local home interfaces for access through a session bean.

6.8   Key Point Summary

This chapter introduces entity beans and Bean-Managed Persistence (BMP). The EJB container provides services to keep the entity bean synchronized with the underlying database, as well as providing support for transactions. The EJB container manages the life cycle of entity beans, keeping them activated for efficient access by clients.

Although entity beans and session beans have similar structure (they both have home/local home and remote/local interfaces and bean implementations), entity beans and session beans are quite different in the roles they occupy.

- An entity bean models persistent business data. A session bean models a business process and is not persistent.
- An entity bean's `create()` method inserts data into an underlying database. A session bean's `create()` method only instantiates a bean instance.
- An entity bean has finder methods that locate records from an underlying database to instantiate a bean instance. A session bean has no equivalent process.
- An entity bean has home methods that provide services not tied to a particular record, but can be applied to the database as a whole. You could use a session bean business method to provide this same kind of service.
- An entity bean's business methods provide setter and getter routines to update or obtain persistent variables. These methods are purely data driven. A session bean's business method provides a business service (a process).
- Entity beans have unique primary keys that map to primary keys in the underlying database.

Additionally, we've encountered the following important topics with entity beans.

- A bean developer may not be able to take advantage of CMP and will therefore have to use BMP.
- A finder method returns an entity bean instance (or a collection) to the client , but the corresponding `ejbFindXXX()` method returns a primary key (or a collection of primary keys) to the container.
- A finder method that returns a single object throws an `ObjectNotFoundException` if that primary key is not in the underlying database. A finder method that returns a collection returns an empty collection if no matching records exist.
- An entity bean's `ejbCreate()` method performs database inserts. The `ejbFindXXX()` methods perform database selects. The `ejbRemove()` method performs database deletes.
- The finder methods must specify `FinderException` in their `throws` clauses.
- A `dirty` flag minimizes database updates in `ejbStore()` and will help optimize entity beans.
- Use the Session Facade Pattern to access entity beans with local interfaces. This reduces the number of remote calls to the entity bean and improves performance.
- Encapsulate business processes in the session facade and use a single transaction for multiple-step entity bean updates.

ENTITY BEANS WITH CMP

Chapter 7

ow that we've slugged through the swamp of BMP, tackling dirty flags, DAOs, and the underlying workings of finder methods, we're ready to take on the challenge of Container-Managed Persistence. With CMP, the bean developer does not write the database access code that entity beans use to insert, select, update, and delete records. If business methods modify persistent variables, the CMP mechanism automatically records these changes in the underlying datastore. And, database independent persistent mechanisms are no longer necessary. Instead, the container provides these services. As an added bonus, the source of your bean implementation class shrinks dramatically with CMP. All you have to do is figure out how to tell the container what you want. Simple enough? Not quite. A big part of CMP is communicating to the container how you want your entity bean to behave under the watchful eye of the application server and its EJB container.

In this chapter we'll explore writing entity beans using CMP, including how to specify an entity bean's persistent fields, its relationship fields, customized finder methods, and select methods. We'll also expand the CustomerSession EJB Session Facade bean from the previous chapter. Not only will this approach provide an appealing client interface to our Customer EJB, but we'll also describe the related Order EJB and LineItem EJB. All three entity beans will use CMP in their implementations and have the CustomerSession Facade as the remote client access mechanism.

7.1   Introducing Container-Managed Persistence

Previous to the EJB 2.0 specification, a bean developer could only use container-managed persistence with *isolated* entity beans—that is, beans with no relationship fields (foreign keys) to other entity beans. This restriction made CMP possible for simple entity beans only and prevented CMP use with real-world, enterprise applications.

That all changed with the EJB 2.0 specification. With the addition of local interfaces, bean developers can now specify entity bean relationships and build enterprise systems with data that models real-world requirements more effectively. As we explore the properties of entity beans with container-managed persistence, keep in mind that CMP and BMP entity beans still share a common structure. In fact, a BMP and CMP entity bean can have identical local home and local interface classes. The differences are in the details of the bean implementation class and the deployment descriptor that holds the necessary relationship and query descriptions.

Design Guideline

*Although a bean developer may implement the remote interface and remote home interface for CMP entity beans, local and local home interfaces are **required** for container-managed entity bean relationships. In this chapter, we will use only local interfaces with our CMP entity bean examples.*

Properties of CMP Entity Beans

Like BMP entity beans, CMP entity beans represent business data. They consist of a local interface with business methods and a local home interface with create, finder, and home methods. As with BMP, CMP bean developers must specify the underlying representation of the bean's persistent data. This persistent data constitutes the bean's **Container-Managed Persistence (CMP) fields**. CMP bean developers must also specify the bean's **Container-Managed Relationship (CMR) fields**. The CMR fields hold the local interface (or a collection thereof) of related entity beans. The bean implementation class of CMP entity beans defines **abstract access methods** to all its CMP and CMR fields. An entity bean's local interface may expose one or more of these access methods to clients. The governing business rules will typically dictate the required visibility of the CMP field and CMR field access methods.

Recall that our Customer EJB (BMP) example in Chapter 6 contains no relationships with other entity beans; consequently, that version of the Customer EJB does not have any access methods to relationship fields or database access code to implement entity bean relationships. In this chapter, however, we will show you relationships with our entity bean examples.

Like BMP entity beans, clients instantiate CMP entity beans through the `create()` method (which inserts data into the underlying data store) or one of the finder methods (which performs a select on the database). The `remove()` method performs a database delete operation.

The advantages of CMP include increased portability with the database access mechanism and a large reduction in the amount of code that the bean developer must write. Since database access is managed by the container, CMP entity beans do not contain any database access (SQL) code. Furthermore, as CMP implementations improve, performance improvements will undoubtedly follow.

However, CMP has some limitations. The current EJB Query Language (which bean developers must use to create custom finder methods) lacks the Order By directive. With CMP you cannot persist SQL Date types (but you can convert Java Date or Calendar objects to longs—we'll show you how). CMP entity beans require detailed deployment descriptor tags. You must describe the persistent data fields, relationships with other entity beans, and custom queries (using EJB QL). This task's level of difficulty and tedium depends on the elegance of the application server's tools. Finally, since the container generates the persistence code, it's more difficult to track down problems.

That all said, we think CMP offers a promising approach. CMP removes the burden of trying to optimize database updates for tricky concurrency scenarios. In the long run, this promise (and eventual realization) of optimization by the container is a true gain for enterprise businesses.

Abstract Persistence Schema

An entity bean's *abstract persistence schema* is the description of its persistent (CMP) fields and relationship (CMR) fields. The bean developer provides this description through a deployment tool or an administrative program provided by the application server. Through both code inspection and declarative statements provided by the bean developer, the deployment tool builds the appropriate schema in the entity bean's deployment descriptor. How is this done? To answer this question, let's examine three entity beans that model the business data of a virtual shopping application.

Figure 7–1 shows three entity beans (Customer EJB, Order EJB, and LineItem EJB), the business data that each bean models, and their relationship to each other. Note that a customer may have zero or more associated orders (`0..*`), but an order must have one customer. A line item has exactly one order. An order has one or more line items (`1..*`). A line item cannot exist without an order and an order cannot exist without a customer. A customer, however, may exist without an order. Also, an order must have at least one line item. Each entity bean has CMP fields and its own primary key (denoted PK).

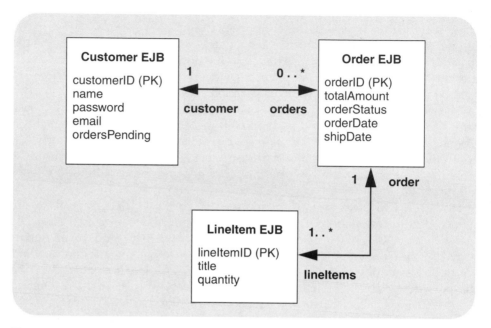

Figure 7–1 Abstract Schema for the Music Collection Virtual Shopping Application

We've labeled the CMR relationship fields next to the navigational arrows. For example, **orders** designates the zero or more Order EJBs associated with a Customer EJB, and **customer** is the one Customer EJB associated with an Order EJB. Likewise, **lineItems** denotes the one or more LineItem EJBs associated with an Order EJB. Finally, **order** is the one Order EJB associated with a LineItem EJB.

Listing 7.1 shows a portion of the XML deployment descriptor for Customer EJB. As we explore CMP, we'll cover the details of this entity bean and the related Order EJB and LineItem EJB. For now, simply note the correspondence between the persistent data fields for Customer EJB shown in Figure 7–1 and their identification in the deployment descriptor (tag `<cmp-field>`). The `<primkey-field>` tag identifies persistent field `customerID` as the primary key. Also, compare the Customer EJB - Order EJB relationship shown in Figure 7–1 to its description in Listing 7.1 (tag `<ejb-relation>`). Finally, note that the abstract persistence schema name for Customer EJB is defined in the deployment descriptor (tag `<abstract-schema-name>`).

Listing 7.1 Deployment Descriptor for Customer EJB

```xml
<entity>
    <display-name>CustomerBean</display-name>
    <ejb-name>CustomerBean</ejb-name>
    <local-home>CustomerLocalHome</local-home>
    <local>CustomerLocal</local>
    <ejb-class>CustomerBean</ejb-class>

    <persistence-type>Container</persistence-type>
    <prim-key-class>java.lang.String</prim-key-class>
    <reentrant>False</reentrant>
    <cmp-version>2.x</cmp-version>
    <abstract-schema-name>customerEJB
    </abstract-schema-name>
    <cmp-field>
      <description>no description</description>
      <field-name>name</field-name>
    </cmp-field>

    <cmp-field>
      <description>no description</description>
      <field-name>password</field-name>
    </cmp-field>
    <cmp-field>
      <description>no description</description>
      <field-name>email</field-name>
    </cmp-field>

    <cmp-field>
      <description>no description</description>
      <field-name>customerID</field-name>
    </cmp-field>
    <cmp-field>
      <description>no description</description>
      <field-name>ordersPending</field-name>
    </cmp-field>

    <primkey-field>customerID</primkey-field>
    <security-identity>
      <description></description>
      <use-caller-identity></use-caller-identity>
    </security-identity>
  </entity>
```

Listing 7.1 Deployment Descriptor for Customer EJB *(continued)*

```
<ejb-relation>
    <ejb-relation-name></ejb-relation-name>
    <ejb-relationship-role>
      <ejb-relationship-role-name>CustomerBean
       </ejb-relationship-role-name>
      <multiplicity>One</multiplicity>

      <relationship-role-source>
        <ejb-name>CustomerBean</ejb-name>
      </relationship-role-source>
      <cmr-field>
        <cmr-field-name>orders</cmr-field-name>
        <cmr-field-type>java.util.Collection
         </cmr-field-type>
      </cmr-field>
    </ejb-relationship-role>

    <ejb-relationship-role>
      <ejb-relationship-role-name>OrderBean
       </ejb-relationship-role-name>
      <multiplicity>Many</multiplicity>
      <cascade-delete />
      <relationship-role-source>
        <ejb-name>OrderBean</ejb-name>
      </relationship-role-source>
      <cmr-field>
        <cmr-field-name>customer</cmr-field-name>
      </cmr-field>
    </ejb-relationship-role>
  </ejb-relation>
```

Relationship Multiplicity

As you can see from Figure 7–1, entity bean relationships are not always one to one. The relationship between customer and order, for instance, is *one to many,* where "many" is zero or more. Conversely, the relationship between order and customer is *many to one*. We express relationship multiplicity as a specific one-way designation. That's because each relationship depends on your viewpoint.

Furthermore, multiplicity *many* can be either 0..* (meaning zero or more) or 1..* (meaning one or more). When multiplicity many allows zero, this implies that the collection of "many" objects may be empty. On the other hand, when multiplicity many specifies one or more, this implies that the collection of "many" objects must contain at least one element.

Multiplicity *one* implies *always* one, and multiplicity *optional* (0..1) means zero *or* one. Either of these can be used with the other (one to one, one to optional) or with many (one to many, optional to many). An example of a one-to-one relationship is a capital city for each state. Each state has exactly one capital city, and each capital city belongs to exactly one state. An example of an optional-to-optional relationship is a seat on an airline flight. Each seat may have at most one passenger, but it is also possible for the seat to be vacant (unassigned). The passenger may exist without a seat assignment (although we hope an assignment is eventually made).

Table 7.1 describes various entity bean relationships *from* entity bean A *to* entity bean B. We provide an example for each listed relationship. Note that for one or optional multiplicity (a *singular* multiplicity), the representing type is the *local interface* of the entity bean. For multiplicity many, the representing type is a *collection* of local interface entity bean objects. For each collection, you may choose either java.util.Collection (when duplicates are allowed) or java.util.Set (which disallows duplicate elements). We won't list all possibilities in the following table, but you can deduce other relationship multiplicities (i.e., optional to many where many is 1..*) from what we describe here. Also, we use a Collection for multiplicity *many* in our examples.

Table 7.1 Entity Bean Relationship Multiplicities

A to B	Description	Type of A	Type of B
One to One *capital city to state*	Each A is associated with one B, and each B is associated with one A.	Local interface of A (CityLocal). Initialize at creation time.	Local interface of B (StateLocal). Initialize at creation time.
One to Many (1..*) *order to line item*	Each A is associated with one or more Bs. Each B must be associated with one A.	Local interface of A (OrderLocal). Initialize at creation time.	Collection of local interface to B (Collection of LineItemLocal). Collection must not be empty. Initialize at creation time.
One to Many (0..*) *customer to order*	Each A is associated with zero or more Bs. Each B must be associated with one A.	Local interface of A (CustomerLocal). Initialize at creation time.	Collection of local interface to B (Collection of OrderLocal). Collection may be empty. Initialize when required by business rules.

Table 7.1 Entity Bean Relationship Multiplicities *(continued)*

A to B	Description	Type of A	Type of B
Optional to Optional *passenger to seat*	Each A may be associated with a B. Each B may be associated with an A.	Local interface of A (PassengerLocal). Initialize when required by business rules.	Local interface of B (SeatLocal). Initialize when required by business rules.
Optional to Many (0..*) *library member to library book*	Each A is associated with zero or more Bs. B may or may not be associated with an A.	Local interface of A (MemberLocal). Initialize when required by business rules.	Collection of local interface to B (Collection of BookLocal). Collection may be empty. Initialize when required by business rules.
Many (0..*) to Many (0..*) *students to courses*	Each A is associated with zero or more B. Each B is associated with zero or more A.	Collection of local interface to A (Collection of StudentLocal). Collection may be empty. Initialize when required by business rules.	Collection of local interface to B (Collection of CourseLocal). Collection may be empty. Initialize when required by business rules.

Choosing between the zero or more version of "many" and the one or more version of "many" depends on whether you want to allow an empty collection. For example, in Table 7.1 we've described the relationship between student and course to be many to many, where both "many" multiplicities are zero or more. Thus, a student may exist who has not signed up for any courses, and a course may exist with no enrolled students. This seems reasonable. Perhaps a student with no courses will eventually lose student status, and a course with no enrollment will eventually be cancelled. But, the business rules of the system will determine these scenarios. It's important for the bean developer to recognize that these associations are not necessarily established when the entity bean is created.

Relationship Navigability

Returning to Figure 7–1 on page 280, you'll note that double-headed arrows mark the relationship between entity beans. We can therefore navigate from Customer EJB to Order EJB and back. The Customer EJB and Order EJB CMR fields provide *two-way navigation*, or a *bidirectional relationship*. That is, if you have a Customer EJB, you can find the collection of Order EJBs associated with that customer. Similarly, given an Order EJB, you can determine the associated Customer EJB. The same two-way navigation exists between Order EJB and LineItem EJB. From the Order EJB you can determine the line items and from the LineItem EJB you can fetch the order.

Bean developers implement two-way navigation when it's important to find related records from a given entity bean. However, maintaining relationship fields requires extra work by the container. (Depending on implementation details, the container may create cross reference database tables using foreign keys that relate one entity's primary key to another entity's primary key. One to many relationships produce multiple entries in the cross reference table for the "one" end.)

As an alternative, bean developers may choose to implement *one-way navigation*, or a *unidirectional relationship*, for some of its relationship fields. One-way navigation means that you may determine a related entity bean in one direction only. For example, we may decide that to navigate from a LineItem EJB to its Order EJB is not necessary. Thus, while we can determine the line items that belong to an order, we can no longer navigate to the order from the line item.

Design Guideline

When you initialize or update a CMR field on one end of a bidirectional relationship, the container updates the other end within the same transaction. For example, when you create an Order EJB and initialize its customer *CMR field, the container adds that Order EJB to the* orders *collection CMR field of the corresponding Customer EJB. Initializing or updating CMR fields results in corresponding database insert or update operations (within the current transaction).*

Note that the relationship multiplicity is *the same* regardless of whether you implement one-way or two-way navigation. In other words, a one to many multiplicity still exists between Order EJBs and LineItem EJBs irrespective of providing a bidirectional or unidirectional relationship.

For our example, we implement a bidirectional relationship between both the Customer EJB and Order EJB, and the Order EJB and LineItem EJB.

Life Cycle Relationships

When does a relationship between two entity beans begin? When does it end? The answers depend on whether a singular multiplicity specifies optional (and thus allows zero) or one (requiring exactly one at all times). For multiplicity many, does the relationship allow zero elements in the collection, or must there be at least one? If there must always be at least one related entity bean in a relationship, then that relationship is initialized during the *create* process. If, on the other hand, multiplicity many allows zero elements in a collection or a singular relationship is optional, then the *business rules* determine when the relationship is initialized. For example, in our virtual shopping application, a user must sign in as a new or returning customer before placing orders. Thus, the application creates a customer entity bean before it can create an order for that customer. Therefore, we cannot initialize the relationship between customer and order at the time we create the Customer EJB.

However, when the application creates an Order EJB, the customer who placed the order is known. Since an order must have one customer associated with it, the application initializes the relationship to the "correct" Customer EJB when it creates the order.

The bean developer must therefore decide if a relationship exists throughout the life cycle of the entity bean. In the case where the relationship is required, singular multiplicity becomes *one* instead of optional and multiplicity many is *one or more* rather than zero or more. When business rules dictate that relationships begin and end with events other than creation and destruction, multiplicity reflects this with *optional* for singular multiplicity and *zero or more* for multiplicity many.

Cascading Deletes

What happens when we remove a customer from our system? That is, what happens when the application calls `remove()` for a Customer EJB? For all entity beans that have relationship fields with other entity beans, we must specify the actions in this scenario. Since our premise is that an order cannot exist without a customer, we must remove any related orders (there may be more than one) when the application removes a customer. Furthermore, since a line item cannot exist without an order, we must also remove all the related line items (there will be at least one) when removing an order. This sequence of *cascading deletes* occurs when the destruction of one bean dictates the destruction of related beans. For each relationship, bean developers specify if cascading deletes should apply.

Business logic may prevent the removal of a customer from the database if that customer has pending orders (and in turn prevent the destruction of possibly unfilled orders). If, for example, a controlling session facade has a business method `removeCustomer()`, the method should throw an application exception if that customer has orders pending, disallowing its removal.

On the other hand, it is perfectly acceptable to remove an order from the database (for example, if a customer cancels an order) and possibly leave a customer with no orders. We have already said the relationship between customer and order is one to many where many is zero or more. We, therefore, *allow* the removal of an order without removing the related customer. In fact, we *cannot* remove the related customer. The removal of the customer would cause *all* the customer's orders to be destroyed (through the cascading delete feature). For this reason, cascading deletes never apply to the opposite end of a "many" relationship.

Access Methods for Persistent Fields

Once we define an abstract persistent schema, we can design an entity bean so that the deployment tool can generate the correct deployment descriptor. Here's the approach.

For each CMP field, the bean developer provides abstract access methods inside the bean implementation class.

Return to Figure 7–1 on page 280. Each entity bean specifies its CMP fields. In the Customer EJB, for example, we have (among other persistent fields) a customerID and name, both Strings. Here are the corresponding abstract access methods for these CMP fields in the Customer EJB bean implementation class, CustomerBean.

```
public abstract class CustomerBean implements EntityBean {

  // Access methods for persistent fields
  public abstract String getCustomerID();
  public abstract void setCustomerID(String id);
  public abstract String getName();
  public abstract void setName(String name);
  . . .
}
```

Note that the bean developer provides getter and setter access methods for each CMP field. In fact, the bean developer must adhere to the following naming conventions and rules.

- All access methods must be abstract.
- Getter methods return the CMP's type (here, String).
- Setter methods return void and take the CMP's type as its argument (here, String).
- For getters, the method name get is followed by the CMP field name with its first letter in upper case.
- For setters, the method name set is followed by the CMP field name with its first letter in upper case.

The container generates code to produce the Java persistent fields from these methods. For Customer EJB, for example, the container would *generate* these persistent fields.

```
String customerID;
String name;
   . . .
```

Design Guideline

---

*Note that CMP fields are **virtual** fields only and are accessed through the abstract getter and setter access methods. For example, the only way that a bean developer can read the Customer EJB CMP field* name *is through its getter method* getName().

The deployment tool determines the field names and their data types from the abstract access methods for each persistent field.

Access Methods for Relationship Fields

Not all access methods are for persistent fields, however. Bean developers must provide abstract access methods for relationship (CMR) fields, too.

For each CMR field that requires navigability, the bean developer provides abstract access methods inside the bean implementation class. Relationships that specify many must provide arguments and returns types that are collections (either Collection *or* Set*). Relationships that are singular must specify the local interface of the related entity bean for arguments and return types.*

The naming conventions for CMR access methods are the same as CMP access methods. The argument and return types, however, must be the local interface of the related entity bean. For multiplicity many, argument and return types are either java.util.Collection or java.util.Set.

For example, the Customer EJB is an entity bean that represents a customer. By logging into the Music Collection virtual shopping web site, customers can choose recordings and submit orders. We represent each order with an Order EJB. In our system, customers may have zero or more orders. Thus, we write the following access methods to define this relationship.

```
public abstract class CustomerBean implements EntityBean {
   . . .
   // Access methods for relationship fields
   public abstract Collection getOrders();
   public abstract void setOrders(Collection orders);
   . . .
}
```

Since customers may have more than one order, we use type `Collection`. The container generates a `Collection` relationship field for the Customer EJB as follows.

```
Collection orders;
```

The `orders` collection contains zero or more `OrderLocal` (the Order EJB local interface) objects.

Now let's examine how the corresponding access method would appear in the Order EJB bean implementation class. Here, an order is associated with just one customer.

```
public abstract class OrderBean implements EntityBean {
   . . .
   // Access methods for relationship fields
   public abstract CustomerLocal getCustomer();
   public abstract void setCustomer(
            CustomerLocal customer);
   . . .
}
```

The container generates the following CMR field in the Order EJB.

```
CustomerLocal customer;
```

Design Guideline

*Note that we define relationship fields for the classes on **both ends** of a bidirectional relationship (one to many for customer to orders). In the* `CustomerBean` *implementation class, we define access methods for CMR field* `orders`. *In the* `OrderBean` *implementation class, we define access methods for CMR field* `customer`. *To implement a **unidirectional** (one-way navigation) relationship, simply omit the access methods in the class that does not require navigation.*

We can similarly specify the bidirectional one to many relationship between order and line items. In the `OrderBean` implementation class, we provide abstract access methods to CMR field `lineItems`, as follows.

```
public abstract class OrderBean implements EntityBean {
  . . .
  // Access methods for relationship fields
  public abstract Collection getLineItems();
  public abstract void setLineItems(Collection lineItems);
  . . .
}
```

Since this is the many end of the relationship, the argument and return type is a collection. In the LineItemBean implementation class, we provide the corresponding access methods to CMR field order. Since the multiplicity is singular, the argument and return type is the local interface (OrderLocal) of the related entity bean, Order EJB.

```
public abstract class LineItemBean implements EntityBean {
  . . .
  // Access methods for relationship fields
  public abstract OrderLocal getOrder();
  public abstract void setOrder(OrderLocal order);
  . . .
}
```

Custom Finder and Select Methods

Part of the EJB 2.0 specification defines an EJB Query Language. Similar to SQL, the EJB Query Language allows bean developers to implement bean finder methods and build customized select statements that are portable. Before we show you the EJB Query Language, let's discuss CMP entity bean finder and select methods.

Finder Methods

With CMP, the container implements all finder methods. The bean developer provides finder method definitions in the local home interface, but *does not write* the corresponding ejbFind*XXX*() methods in the bean implementation class. Finder methods specified in the local home interface return either a *single* object that implements the local interface or a *collection* of local interface objects.

All entity beans must provide finder method findByPrimaryKey() in the local home (or remote home) interface. In CMP, we provide access methods to the persistent field that represents the primary key. During the deployment process, the bean developer specifies which persistent field represents the primary key. This allows the container to generate the proper SQL select code to implement `ejbFindByPrimaryKey()`. What about the other finder methods?

Entity bean finder methods can be arbitrarily complex. A finder method, for instance, might find all customers with orders earlier than a specific date. Since CMP must implement all database access code (including SQL select statements for finder methods), a mechanism to specify arbitrarily complex finders becomes necessary. Let's look at an example.

Like the BMP version of Customer EJB, we need to include `findByCustomerName()` in the CMP version as well. Here's the definition of this custom finder method in the `CustomerLocalHome` interface.

```
public interface CustomerLocalHome extends EJBLocalHome {
  . . .
  // Custom finder methods
  public Collection findByCustomerName(String name)
    throws FinderException;
  . . .
}
```

This finder method returns a collection, since we cannot guarantee that only a single object will be found. With CMP, we specify an EJB QL statement so that the deployment tool can generate the correct SQL for the finder method. Whereas SQL may vary from database to database, all EJB 2.0-compliant application servers are required to interpret EJB QL. The container/deployment tool can then generate the SQL that is correct for its underlying database server.

You specify the EJB QL during the deployment process, usually with a tool provided by the application server. Then, the deployment tool builds XML `<query>` tags for each custom finder. Here is the XML `<query>` tag for `findByCustomerName()`.

```
<query>
  <description></description>
  <query-method>
    <method-name>findByCustomerName</method-name>
    <method-params>
      <method-param>java.lang.String</method-param>
    </method-params>
  </query-method>
  <ejb-ql>select distinct object (c)
from customerEJB c where c.name = ?1</ejb-ql>
</query>
```

Don't worry about the EJB QL query yet. We'll discuss it in detail in the next section. Note that with CMP, we must provide the EJB QL queries for custom finders, but this is still much less work than providing a complete BMP implementation.

To implement this finder, the deployment tool generates the appropriate SQL and builds additional XML tags at deployment time. The SQL code depends on specific application and database servers, and is not necessarily portable. Here is the corresponding SQL for findByCustomerName() on our machine using the Cloudscape database server and the Sun reference implementation application server. (We shade the display to indicate generated SQL.)

```xml
<sql-statement>
  <method>
    <ejb-name>CustomerBean</ejb-name>
    <method-intf>LocalHome</method-intf>
    <method-name>findByCustomerName</method-name>
    <method-params>
      <method-param>java.lang.String</method-param>
    </method-params>
  </method>
  <sql>SELECT DISTINCT "c"."customerID" FROM
"CustomerBeanTable" "c" WHERE ("c"."name" = ? )</sql>
</sql-statement>
```

Select Methods

Although finder methods can be arbitrarily complex, they return only an object or a collection of objects implementing the local interface. It may also be necessary to perform database select queries that return other result sets (such as CMP fields or local interface objects of *related* entity beans). Bean developers can use **select methods** when return objects must be more general than the local interface return objects produced by finders. To provide select methods, the bean developer specifies a public *abstract* method with the prefix ejbSelect inside the bean implementation class. Exception FinderException must be included in the select method's throws clause. Like finders, select methods (as the name implies) may perform complex select queries on the database. Bean developers use EJB QL to specify the semantics of the query.

Think of select methods as private helper methods. This means clients do not call select methods directly. Consequently, the bean developer does not expose select methods in either the local or local home interface. You may use either a business method (specified in the local interface) or a home method (specified in the local home interface) to call `ejbSelectXXX()` methods.

Let's look at an example. Suppose that in `CustomerLocalHome`, we specify home method `getTotalCustomers()`, which returns the number of customers in a customer database.

```
public interface CustomerLocalHome extends EJBLocalHome {
    . . .
    // Home method
    public int getTotalCustomers() throws FinderException;
    . . .
}
```

To provide the underlying database select query that the implementation of this home method can call, we use an abstract select method called `ejbSelect-TotalCustomers()` in the CustomerBean implementation class. Then, in the implementation of `ejbHomeGetTotalCustomers()`, we invoke method `size()` as shown to return the number of customers in the database.

```
public abstract class CustomerBean implements EntityBean {
    . . .
    // Select method
    public abstract Collection ejbSelectTotalCustomers()
        throws FinderException;

    // EJB Home Methods
    public int ejbHomeGetTotalCustomers()
            throws FinderException {
      // invoke method size() to get count
      return ejbSelectTotalCustomers().size();
    }
    . . .
}
```

Like finders, the deployment tool builds <query> tags for each select method. Here is the <query> tag for `ejbSelectTotalCustomers()`.

```
<query>
   <description></description>
   <query-method>
      <method-name>ejbSelectTotalCustomers</method-name>
      <method-params />
```

```
    </query-method>
    <ejb-ql>select object (c)
from customerEJB c</ejb-ql>
</query>
```

We'll discuss the EJB QL select statement shortly. And, like finders, the deployment tool generates the appropriate SQL and builds additional XML tags at deployment time. Here is the `<sql-statement>` tag for this select method (again, the generated SQL is not necessarily portable).

```
<sql-statement>
  <method>
  <ejb-name>CustomerBean</ejb-name>
  <method-intf>Bean</method-intf>
  <method-name>ejbSelectTotalCustomers</method-name>
  <method-params />
  </method>
  <sql>SELECT "c"."customerID" FROM
"CustomerBeanTable" "c"</sql>
</sql-statement>
```

This particular select statement returns all customer records from the database in a collection.

Introducing the EJB Query Language

An entity bean is represented by its abstract persistence schema. The bean developer names an entity bean's abstract schema at deployment time. The schema name must be unique within the deployment descriptor. All related entity beans share the same deployment descriptor (and, therefore, the same JAR file).

Bean developers use the EJB Query Language (EJB QL) to define queries for custom finder and select methods with CMP entity beans. To access an entity bean, an EJB QL query references the entity bean's abstract schema. Some queries may need to access relationship fields to complete the query. Queries can navigate to abstract schemata of related entity beans through the bean's relationship fields.

Although much of EJB QL is a subset of SQL, EJB QL has syntax differences. EJB QL allows you to navigate related beans, whereas SQL joins only database tables. An EJB QL query consists of a Select clause, a From clause, and an optional Where clause. EJB QL keywords match equivalent SQL keywords and are not case sensitive. EJB QL identifiers are also case insensitive.

To see how EJB QL works, let's use the abstract schemata describing the Customer EJB, Order EJB, and LineItem EJB entity beans. Most of the examples we'll show you are hypothetical queries, but a few correspond to real methods in our code. You can refer to Figure 7–1 on page 280 as you work through the examples.

Select Clause

The Select clause defines object types returned by the query. The return type is an entity bean's local interface, remote interface, or persistent field. The return type can even be the local interface of a related entity bean.

The Select clause typically names an *identification variable* representing an object in the abstract schema. The syntax object (c), for example, names c as an identification variable. A Select clause can also name a *path expression*. In the Customer EJB schema, the path expression c.name is a persistent field (String). The path expression c.orders is a *relationship field* representing a collection of local interface objects (OrderLocal) of the related entity bean Order EJB.

Design Guideline

If a path expression represents a collection (because the multiplicity of a relationship is many), you cannot use it with a Select clause or subsequent expression. However, you can specify items from a collection using operator IN within a From clause.

From Clause

The From clause defines the source of the data. It also defines identification variables and path expressions used in the Select clause. All identification variables must be defined in the From clause using operators IN or AS, where AS is optional.

Our first example is the EJB QL statement we showed you earlier (see the deployment descriptor on page 294). This query implements the Customer EJB select method ejbSelectTotalCustomers().

```
select object (c) from customerEJB AS c
```

The following is equivalent since operator AS is optional.

```
select object (c) from customerEJB c
```

These queries use c as an identification variable. Both queries access the Customer EJB and return the entire collection of CustomerLocal objects.

Where Clause

The Where clause consists of conditional expressions that narrow the number of objects selected. Here is the EJB QL for custom finder findByCustomer-Name(String name) defined in the CustomerLocalHome interface (see the deployment descriptor on page 291).

```
select distinct object (c) from customerEJB c
where c.name = ?1
```

The distinct keyword eliminates duplicates. Identification variable c refers to the Customer EJB in our schema and c.name is a persistent field in this entity bean. The Where clause restricts the customers retrieved by checking their names. The ?1 corresponds to the string name passed to the findByCustomer-Name() method. This query returns a collection of CustomerLocal objects.

Navigating to Related Beans

In EJB QL, a path expression may navigate to related beans. This is typically used in a From clause with operator IN to specify a new identification variable. To see how this works, let's build a query from the Customer EJB schema that navigates to the Order EJB.

Here's a query that implements findByHigherAmount(double amt) in the CustomerLocalHome interface. Such a query could be used to find "big spenders."

```
select distinct object (c) from customerEJB c, IN
(c.orders) AS o where o.totalAmount > ?1
```

This query returns all customers (a collection of CustomerLocal objects) with an order whose total amount is more than the amount passed to the finder method (?1). Identification variable c represents the Customer EJB abstract schema, and c.orders is a path expression that follows the IN operator. The relationship field (orders) is what names o as our related bean (Order EJB). In the Where clause, o.totalAmount is a persistent field of the Order EJB. The AS is optional in this query but adds clarity when used with the IN operator.

Here's a similar query that implements findByNameAndDate(String name, long date).

```
select distinct object (c) from customerEJB c, IN
(c.orders) AS o where c.name = ?1 and o.orderDate >= ?2
```

The Where clause uses keyword and to form a compound expression. This specifies the condition that name in the Customer EJB is equal to the first argument of findByNameAndDate(), and orderDate in the Order EJB is equal to or more recent than the second argument. As before, the query returns a collection of CustomerLocal objects.

Query Language Examples

Let's show you several more examples of EJB QL. Again, these queries implement finder and select methods that are hypothetical (don't look for them in our source code) and we describe them only to illustrate EJB QL.

Our first query example returns a collection of names (Strings) rather than a collection of CustomerLocal objects.

```
select distinct c.name from customerEJB c
```

Instead of a Select object, we use path expression c.name, which refers to persistent field name in our Customer EJB. This query returns a unique collection of customer names from the database. Such a query can implement select method ejbSelectNames(), for instance.

Design Guideline

*A finder method **must** return its local interface object (or a collection thereof). That is, a finder in the CustomerLocalHome interface must return a CustomerLocal object (or a collection of CustomerLocal objects). If an EJB QL query returns something else (a related local interface object or a persistent data field), then you **must** use an ejbSelectXXX() method for its implementation.*

Our next query implements findByHigherAmount(double   amt) in the Order EJB home interface, OrderLocalHome.

```
select distinct object (o) from orderEJB o
where o.totalamount > ?1
```

In this query, o is an identification variable referring to Order EJB. The Where clause narrows the result set to objects whose persistent field totalAmount is greater than the argument of the finder method (?1). Note that the data retrieved from the query is a collection of OrderLocal objects.

In the next query, we start from the Order EJB and navigate to the Customer EJB. Here's a query that implements select method `ejbSelectNameByHigherAmount(double amt)`.

```
select distinct c.name from orderEJB o, IN
(o.customer) AS c where o.totalamount > ?1
```

The path expression `c.name` refers to persistent field `name` in the Customer EJB. This is found by accessing the customer relationship field of the Order EJB (`o.customer`). The Where clause narrows the selection of `orderEJB` objects to those whose persistent field `totalAmount` is greater than the argument of `ejbSelectNameByHigherAmount()`. The data retrieved from this query is a collection of unique names (Strings). Note that this query cannot be used with a finder method.

The next query implements `findByOrderDate(long date)` in the `CustomerLocalHome` interface.

```
select distinct object (c) from customerEJB c,
IN (c.orders) AS o where o.orderDate > ?1
```

The path expression `c.orders` specifies relationship field `orders` in the Customer EJB, whereas `o.orderDate` specifies persistent field `orderDate` in the Order EJB. This query returns a collection of `CustomerLocal` objects.

Our last query example navigates to the LineItem EJB from the Customer EJB. This query implements `findByTitleImagine()` in the `CustomerLocalHome` interface.

```
select distinct object (c) from customerEJB c,
IN (c.orders) AS o, IN (o.lineitems) AS i
where i.title = 'Imagine'
```

The query selects customers who have orders that include a line item with the recording title 'Imagine.' The path expression `c.orders` accesses customer relationship field `orders`. The path expression `o.lineitems` accesses order relationship field `lineitems`. Since both expressions represent collections, operator `IN` is required, producing new identification variables o (for Order EJB) and i (for LineItem EJB). The path expression `i.title` accesses the persistent field `title` in the LineItem EJB. This query returns a collection of `CustomerLocal` objects.

7.2 The Three Entity Beans

We're now ready to examine the entity beans for LineItem EJB, Order EJB, and Customer EJB. Because we're using container-managed persistence, the implementation code is much shorter than comparable code with bean-managed persistence. The trade-off is that we'll spend more effort on the deployment descriptor since more information is now declarative.

As we present code for each entity bean, we'll also present the relevant declarative information. This information appears in the XML deployment descriptor stored in the JAR file with the entity beans. We package the three entity beans in the same JAR file along with the session facade bean, Customer-Session EJB, which we will show you later in this chapter.

The Big Picture

Let's begin with our familiar architectural component picture. Figure 7–2 shows the components of our enterprise application using CMP entity beans to provide customer and order persistence. The Session Facade stateless session bean, CustomerSession EJB, provides the interface to the entity beans for general clients. The CustomerSession EJB accesses the entity beans using local and local home interfaces. Because the entity beans have relationship fields, we show their interactions with arrows as well. CMP requires that relationships be implemented using local interfaces. Thus, we label the relationship arrows with local access.

While access to the Music Collection Database is through the MusicDAO (as before), access to the Customer Orders Database is through container-managed persistence (CMP), designated by the thick arrow labeled CMP. Since the EJB container provides this service, we show the CMP access from the container to the database.

Note that we package the three entity beans in one JAR file since they must share the same deployment descriptor. CMR fields in one bean require a shared scope for abstract schema names, CMP field names, and CMR field names in other beans. We also place the CustomerSession EJB in the same JAR file, although this is not required.

Structure of CMP Entity Beans

CMP entity bean structure is not too different from BMP entity bean structure. Both allow client access through remote home and local home interfaces to create, finder, and home methods. Both allow access through remote and local interfaces to invoke business methods or CMP field access methods. However,

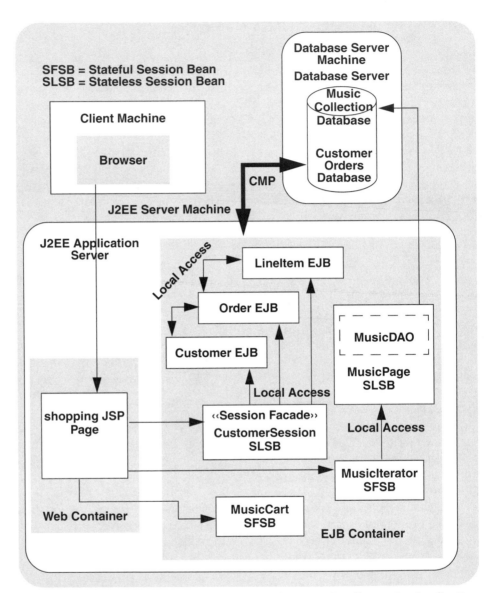

Figure 7–2 Architectural Overview of the Music Shopping Cart Enterprise Application with Customer, Order, and LineItem Persistence

the bean developer cannot expose CMR field access methods in the remote interface; these are restricted to local clients. Also, the bean developer does not expose the setter access method to the primary key field in the component (remote or local) interface of an entity bean. Once a primary key field is set, it should not change.

When you use CMP, the bean implementation class is always *abstract*. Thus, the container generates the concrete implementation class for you. This generated class will contain the code for the abstract CMP field methods, the abstract CMR methods, and the required database access methods the container builds from the declarative information in the deployment descriptor. This includes methods to maintain (and persist) the CMR and CMP fields as well as the implementation of finder and select methods. In short, the bean implementation class provided by the bean developer is short, because so much of its code is generated!

Line Item Entity Bean

Let's start with the simplest bean, LineItem EJB. In addition to the primary key field, a LineItem EJB holds a recording title and the number of recording titles (which is at least one). LineItem EJBs are always associated with an Order EJB. This association is maintained as a relationship field. If fact, you'll see that when we create a LineItem EJB, we associate it with an Order EJB during the create process. Figure 7–3 (a repetition of Figure 7–1 for your convenience) shows the three entity beans, their CMP fields, and their CMR fields (labeled on the arrows). The LineItem EJB database record consists of a `lineItemID` (the primary key), a recording `title`, and a `quantity`.

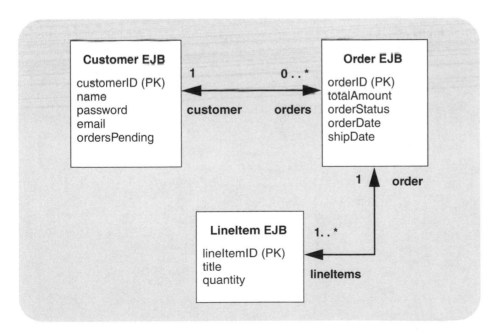

Figure 7–3 Abstract Schema for the Music Collection Virtual Shopping Application

Figure 7–4 shows the classes and interfaces of the LineItem EJB with local interfaces. The local home interface holds the `create()` methods, finder methods, and home methods. The local interface contains the business methods, including any CMP or CMR field access methods the bean developer wants to expose to clients. The abstract bean implementation class (`LineItem-Bean`) implements the `EntityBean` interface and contains the code for the EJB methods, business methods, and the abstract access methods for CMP and CMR fields. Note that the `ejbFindXXX()` methods do not appear in `LineItem-Bean` because the container and deployment tool generate their implementa-

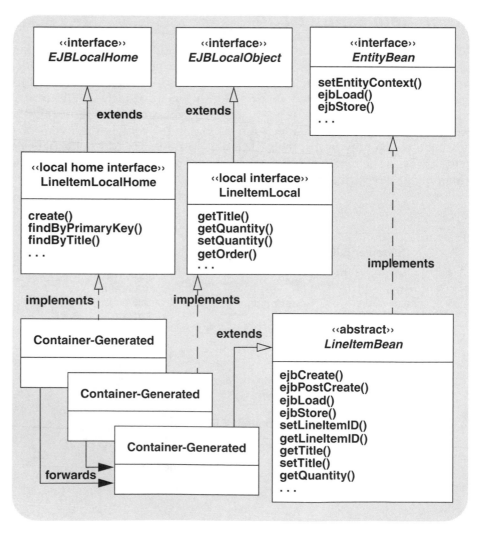

Figure 7–4 Class Diagram Showing the EJB Classes for a CMP Entity Bean

tions using the EJB QL statements. Unlike BMP, a container-generated class extends the bean implementation class (`LineItemBean`). Let's examine LineItem EJB's local home interface first.

Local Home Interface

Listing 7.2 contains the source for **LineItemLocalHome.java**, the local home interface. Here we have the required `findByPrimaryKey()` method, which returns a `LineItemLocal` object. We also have a `create()` method, which requires a title and quantity as arguments. Note that `create()` also specifies an `OrderLocal` object in its argument list. When we show you the bean implementation code, you'll see that this argument allows the LineItem EJB to initialize its relationship field with the Order EJB during the create process.

Finally, we specify custom finder method `findByTitle()`, which returns a collection. Since the LineItem database table will have LineItem EJB records from all the orders, the title field may not be unique. The LineItem EJB does not have any home methods.

Note that with CMP, the bean developer does not implement any of the finder methods. Instead, we use the EJB Query Language during deployment to specify how to generate the appropriate SQL code. We'll show you both the EJB Query Language and the resultant SQL for the finder methods when we examine the deployment descriptor.

Listing 7.2 LineItemLocalHome.java

```
// LineItemLocalHome.java
import javax.ejb.*;
import java.util.*;

public interface LineItemLocalHome extends EJBLocalHome {

    // Method create() includes OrderLocal to
    // initialize relationship field order
    public LineItemLocal create(String title,
        int quantity, OrderLocal order)
        throws CreateException;

    public LineItemLocal findByPrimaryKey(String id)
        throws FinderException;

    // custom finder method
    public Collection findByTitle(String title)
        throws FinderException;
}
```

Local Interface

Listing 7.3 contains the source for file **LineItemLocal.java**, the local interface for the LineItem EJB. Here we have the business methods. These typically include data access methods to one or more of the CMP fields and any CMR fields. In the LineItem EJB, we include getters for persistent fields `lineItemID`, `title`, and `quantity`. The only setter method is for persistent field `quantity`.

Design Guideline

*The local interface defines setters and getters for persistent data fields and relationship fields that are exposed to **external clients only**. Thus, we don't provide "setters" for* `lineItemID` *and* `title`, *since these fields do not change once they are set in home interface method* `create()`. *We **do** provide setters for persistent field* `quantity`, *since we need to update this data field from the CustomerSession EJB client. Finally, we don't provide* `setOrder()`. *We take care of initializing this relationship field during the create process (see* `ejbPostCreate()` *on page 306.)*

We also provide method `getOrder()` for the singular relationship field `order`, which returns `OrderLocal` (Order EJB's local interface object). These setter and getter methods are defined as *abstract* in the bean implementation code since the container is responsible for generating their code.

Listing 7.3 LineItemLocal.java

```
// LineItemLocal.java
import javax.ejb.*;

public interface LineItemLocal extends EJBLocalObject {

    // access methods for persistent fields
    public String getLineItemID();
    public String getTitle();
    public int getQuantity();
    public void setQuantity(int quantity);

    // access methods for relationship fields
    public OrderLocal getOrder();
}
```

Primary Key Generation

Every entity bean has a unique primary key, at least within the database table in which the field is constrained to be a primary key. Therefore, we must either pass the primary key as an argument to ejbCreate(), or generate one within ejbCreate(). In this CMP entity bean example (like our BMP entity bean in the previous chapter), we choose to generate the primary key inside ejbCreate().

Recall that in the BMP example, we include a primary key generation method dbGetKey() in the DAO class (see page 222). Since the Data Access Object pattern is not necessary with CMP, we create a small Java class DBUtil to invoke the Cloudscape KeyGen.getUniversalKeyStringValue() method. Each of our three entity beans invokes this method to obtain a unique primary key. Listing 7.4 contains the source for **DBUtil.java**. Note that we make method dbGetKey() static so we can invoke it with a class name rather than an object.

Listing 7.4 DBUtil.java

```
// DBUtil.java
import COM.cloudscape.util.KeyGen;
public class DBUtil {

  // Cloudscape propriety routine to generate primary key
  public static String dbGetKey() {
    return KeyGen.getUniversalKeyStringValue();
  }
}
```

Design Guideline

Since all three entity beans require primary key generation, we move the call to getUniversalKeyStringValue() out of the bean implementation class and encapsulate it within a utility class. This isolates the proprietary routine. Installing an alternate scheme for primary key generation would require re-implementing method dbGetKey(). See page 220 in the previous chapter for additional issues regarding primary key generation.

Bean Implementation

Listing 7.5 contains the source for the LineItem EJB bean implementation code in file **LineItemBean.java**. You'll notice quite a number of differences between this (relatively compact) CMP code and the code for a BMP entity bean.

Listing 7.5 LineItemBean.java

```java
// LineItemBean.java
import java.util.*;
import javax.ejb.*;
import javax.naming.*;

public abstract class LineItemBean implements EntityBean {

  // EntityBean variables
  private EntityContext context;

  // Access methods for persistent fields

  public abstract String getLineItemID();
  public abstract void setLineItemID(String id);

  public abstract String getTitle();
  public abstract void setTitle(String title);

  public abstract int getQuantity();
  public abstract void setQuantity(int quantity);

  // access methods for relationship fields

  public abstract OrderLocal getOrder();
  public abstract void setOrder(OrderLocal order);

  // EntityBean methods

  public String ejbCreate(String title, int quantity,
      OrderLocal order) throws CreateException {
    String newKey =
        DBUtil.dbGetKey();
    setLineItemID(newKey);
    setTitle(title);
    setQuantity(quantity);
    return newKey;
  }

  public void setEntityContext(EntityContext context) {
    this.context = context;
  }
```

Listing 7.5 LineItemBean.java *(continued)*

```
public void ejbPostCreate(String title, int quantity,
      OrderLocal order) {
  // associate this LineItem EJB with Order EJB
  setOrder(order);
}

public void unsetEntityContext() {
  context = null;
}
public void ejbActivate() { }
public void ejbPassivate() { }

public void ejbLoad() { }
public void ejbStore() { }

public void ejbRemove() { }
} // LineItemBean
```

Note that class `LineItemBean` is *abstract* and contains abstract methods for the CMP and CMR fields. The container provides an implementation for these abstract methods when it extends `LineItemBean` to create a new class.

An entity bean must implement an `ejbCreate()` method for each `create()` method in the local home interface. Since we have just one `create()` method in the local home interface, there is only one `ejbCreate()` in `LineItemBean`. Method `ejbCreate()` initializes the persistent data fields. Because these fields are *virtual*, `ejbCreate()` calls the setter accessor methods to initialize them. This is where we invoke class `DBUtil`'s static method `getKey()` to obtain a primary key. As with BMP entity beans, CMP versions of `ejbCreate()` return the primary key to the container.

One of the parameters for `ejbCreate()` is `OrderLocal order`. Although it is not possible to set a CMR field in `ejbCreate()`, you can set it in `ejbPostCreate()`. Recall that these two methods have identical parameters and the container calls `ejbPostCreate()` after `ejbCreate()`. Inside `ejbPostCreate()`, we initialize the CMR field from the LineItem EJB to Order EJB by invoking `setOrder()` with the `order` argument. The container initializes the other end of the relationship within the same transaction. Thus, after we invoke `setOrder()` in `ejbPostCreate()`, the container adds this newly created LineItem to Order EJB's CMR field `lineItems`, invoking the collection's `add()` method.

Design Guideline

You cannot set a relationship field within ejbCreate() *because the entity instance is not yet fully initialized. However, to set a relationship field during the create process, you may invoke CMR accessor methods in* ejbPostCreate(). *Remember that with two-way navigation, the container sets the other end of the relationship for you.*

The ejbLoad(), ejbStore(), and ejbRemove() methods are all empty. No code is required unless the entity bean requires specific processing right after the load, before the store, or right before the delete. The container loads the bean's CMP fields from the database and then invokes ejbLoad(). Conversely, the container invokes ejbStore() before storing the CMP fields to the database. The container calls ejbRemove() before it deletes the associated database row.

Generated SQL for Container Methods

Now it's time to look at how the deployment process and the container maintain the relationship fields and persistence of our LineItem EJB. The SQL code we show here is specific to the application server, EJB container, and database server that we use (the Sun Microsystems reference implementation). Therefore, other application servers may generate different SQL. However, it helps to understand how the application server is doing its job.

CMP Implementation

Note that the generated SQL code uses database table name "LineItemBeanTable" *to store LineItem EJB's persistent data. This name is generated by the Sun Microsystems Reference Implementation deployment tool. Currently, the only way to change the table name is to edit the generated XML deployment descriptor tags. Unfortunately, you must make this modification each time the deployment tool regenerates SQL.*

Let's examine the SQL generated for the container methods. The deployment tool generates SQL when the bean developer specifies the persistent data fields and indicates which field represents the primary key. Here is a selection of the generated code for the LineItem EJB. We show all generated SQL with a shaded background. (The -- before a text line is an SQL comment.)

```
-- create row SQL Query
INSERT INTO "LineItemBeanTable" ("lineItemID", "quantity",
"title") VALUES ( ?, ?, ? )
```

```
-- delete row SQL Query
DELETE FROM "LineItemBeanTable" WHERE "lineItemID" = ?

-- findByPrimaryKey
SELECT "lineItemID" FROM "LineItemBeanTable" WHERE
"lineItemID" = ?

-- load row
SELECT "quantity", "title" FROM "LineItemBeanTable" WHERE
"lineItemID" = ?

-- store row
UPDATE "LineItemBeanTable" SET "quantity" = ?, "title" = ?
WHERE "lineItemID" = ?
```

EJB Query for Custom Finders

The LineItem EJB has one custom finder method, findByTitle(). In order for the container to generate code for this finder method, we must specify the proper select method for the custom finder. Note that this specification is intended to be portable for all EJB-compliant application servers. The EJB Query Language text appears in the deployment descriptor. We also show the generated SQL code (which is dependent on the application server and is not intended to be portable). Here is the EJB QL query for findByTitle(String title) followed by the generated (shaded) SQL code.

```
select distinct object (i) from lineitemEJB i
where i.title = ?1
```

```
-- Generated SQL Query for findByTitle()
SELECT DISTINCT "i"."lineItemID" FROM "LineItemBeanTable"
"i" WHERE ("i"."title" = ?)
```

The EJB QL query specifies object i (entity bean object LineItem EJB) for the select data return type. The corresponding SQL query specifies the primary key (lineItemID) as its data return type. Why? Recall that although finder methods return *entity bean objects* (such as LineItemLocal), the corresponding ejbFindXXX() method returns *primary keys*. It's the responsibility of the container to return the entity bean instance to the client.

Container-Managed Persistence

The deployment descriptor contains information about the persistent data fields the container must maintain. Listing 7.6 contains portions of the deployment descriptor for LineItem EJB that describes its persistent fields, as well as its local and local home interfaces, its bean implementation class, the persistent mechanism (Container, 2.x), and its abstract schema. The abstract schema name (**lineitemEJB**) is the identifier we use with the EJB Query Language to specify the LineItem database table.

The LineItem EJB persistent fields include lineItemID, quantity, and title. Field lineItemID is identified as the primary key.

Listing 7.6 Generated XML Tags for LineItem CMP

```
<entity>
    <display-name>LineItemBean</display-name>
    <ejb-name>LineItemBean</ejb-name>
    <local-home>LineItemLocalHome</local-home>
    <local>LineItemLocal</local>
    <ejb-class>LineItemBean</ejb-class>
    <persistence-type>Container</persistence-type>
    <prim-key-class>java.lang.String</prim-key-class>
    <reentrant>False</reentrant>
    <cmp-version>2.x</cmp-version>
    <abstract-schema-name>lineitemEJB
     </abstract-schema-name>

    <cmp-field>
      <description>no description</description>
      <field-name>lineItemID</field-name>
    </cmp-field>

    <cmp-field>
      <description>no description</description>
      <field-name>quantity</field-name>
    </cmp-field>

    <cmp-field>
      <description>no description</description>
      <field-name>title</field-name>
    </cmp-field>

    <primkey-field>lineItemID</primkey-field>
    <security-identity>
      <description></description>
      <use-caller-identity></use-caller-identity>
    </security-identity>
  </entity>
```

Container-Managed Relationships

The deployment descriptor also contains information about the relationships that the bean developer provides during the deployment process. Here we show you the CMR fields that apply to our LineItem EJB.

Listing 7.7 contains portions of the deployment descriptor that describe the CMR fields and multiplicity for LineItem EJB and its relationship with Order EJB. The deployment descriptor defines a relationship between OrderBean (one) and LineItemBean (many). OrderBean contains CMR field lineItems (a collection) and LineItemBean contains CMR field order (an OrderLocal type). The <cascade-delete/> tag means that LineItem EJBs are deleted when the related OrderBean EJB is removed. Note that this is a bidirectional relationship because the deployment descriptor describes both ends. Also, from the container's point of view, there is no difference between zero or more and one or more in a many multiplicity. The difference shows up in the business rules implemented by the bean developer.

Listing 7.7 Generated XML Tags for LineItem-Order CMR

```xml
<ejb-relation>
    <ejb-relation-name></ejb-relation-name>
    <ejb-relationship-role>
      <ejb-relationship-role-name>OrderBean
      </ejb-relationship-role-name>
      <multiplicity>One</multiplicity>

      <relationship-role-source>
        <ejb-name>OrderBean</ejb-name>
      </relationship-role-source>
      <cmr-field>
        <cmr-field-name>lineItems</cmr-field-name>
        <cmr-field-type>java.util.Collection
        </cmr-field-type>
      </cmr-field>
    </ejb-relationship-role>

    <ejb-relationship-role>
      <ejb-relationship-role-name>LineItemBean
      </ejb-relationship-role-name>
      <multiplicity>Many</multiplicity>
      <cascade-delete />
      <relationship-role-source>
        <ejb-name>LineItemBean</ejb-name>
      </relationship-role-source>
```

Listing 7.7 Generated XML Tags for LineItem-Order CMR *(continued)*

```
        <cmr-field>
          <cmr-field-name>order</cmr-field-name>
        </cmr-field>
      </ejb-relationship-role>
  </ejb-relation>
```

CMP Implementation

The Sun Microsystems Reference Implementation deployment tool generates SQL to create a cross-reference database table to persist the relationship data. Here is the generated SQL to create the table that persists the relationship between the Order EJB and LineItem EJB (`"CustomerBean_orders_ OrderBean_customerTable"`*). Remember, this is application server dependent!*

```
        <sql-statement>
          <operation>createTable</operation>
          <sql>CREATE TABLE
"CustomerBean_orders_OrderBean_customerTable"
("_CustomerBean_customerID" VARCHAR(255) ,
"_OrderBean_orderID" VARCHAR(255), CONSTRAINT
"pk_CustomerBean_orders_OrderBean_customerTabl" PRIMARY KEY
("_OrderBean_orderID") )</sql>
        </sql-statement>
```

Order Entity Bean

The Order EJB contains bookkeeping information about a customer's order. It holds status information, the order date, ship date, dollar amount, and of course a primary key. The Order EJB also has CMR fields with both the Customer EJB and the LineItem EJB. Recall that the multiplicity between Customer EJB and Order EJB is one to many (where many is zero or more) and the multiplicity between Order EJB and LineItem EJB is one to many (where many is one or more). Therefore, given an Order EJB, we can determine the related Customer EJB. We can also access its collection of related LineItem EJBs. Let's look at the local home interface first.

Local Home Interface

Listing 7.8 contains the source for **OrderLocalHome.java**, the local home interface for Order EJB. The three static final integers represent status codes for the integer `orderStatus` persistent data field. By placing these definitions inside the local home interface, we make them more readily accessible. We only need an object that implements the local home interface to access them.

Note that the parameters for `create()` include the Order EJB CMP fields, as well as the CMR field for Customer EJB. Similar to the LineItem EJB, we set Order EJB's relationship field to Customer EJB during the create process (in `ejbPostCreate()`).

Design Guideline

We set Order EJB's CMR field to Customer EJB during the Order EJB create process because the related Customer EJB already exists. The container will update the associated Customer EJB CMR field for us.

The local home interface also includes the required `findByPrimaryKey()` and custom finder `findByOrderDatePrevious()`. This finder method returns a collection of `OrderLocal` objects whose order date is the same or earlier than the provided argument *and* whose order status matches the status provided. Because this is a custom finder, we must specify EJB QL statements in the deployment descriptor. This allows the container to generate the correct SQL code for its implementation. There are no home methods for Order EJB.

Listing 7.8 OrderLocalHome.java

```java
// OrderLocalHome.java
import java.util.*;
import javax.ejb.*;

public interface OrderLocalHome extends EJBLocalHome {

    public static final int InProcess = 1;
    public static final int Shipped = 2;
    public static final int Closed = 3;

    public OrderLocal create(double totalAmount,
        int orderStatus, long orderDate, long shipDate,
        CustomerLocal customer) throws CreateException;

    public OrderLocal findByPrimaryKey(String id)
            throws FinderException;

    public Collection findByOrderDatePrevious(
        long orderDate, int orderStatus)
        throws FinderException;
}
```

Local Interface

Listing 7.9 contains the source for the local interface in **OrderLocal.java**. The local interface includes getter methods for all the Order EJB CMP fields. There is also one setter method (setOrderStatus()) for CMP field orderStatus, since we need to update this persistent field from the CustomerSession EJB client. We also expose CMR getter methods getCustomer() and getLine-Items(). Finally, the local interface includes business method shipOrder().

Listing 7.9 OrderLocal.java

```java
// OrderLocal.java
import java.util.*;
import javax.ejb.*;

public interface OrderLocal extends EJBLocalObject {
   // Access methods for persistent data fields
   public String getOrderID();
   public double getTotalAmount();
   public int getOrderStatus();
   public long getOrderDate();
   public long getShipDate();
   public void setOrderStatus(int status);

   // Access method for relationship fields
   public CustomerLocal getCustomer();
   public Collection getLineItems();
   // Business methods
   public void shipOrder(long shipDate);
}
```

Bean Implementation

Now that you've seen the bean implementation class for LineItem EJB, the Order EJB should look similar. Listing 7.10 shows the source for **Order-Bean.java**. Class OrderBean is abstract, as are the access methods for the CMP and CMR fields. Note that Order EJB has virtual relationship fields for both Customer EJB (customer) and the collection of LineItem EJBs (lineItems).

Business method shipOrder() sets the shipDate and orderStatus persistent fields. Again, we cannot access these persistent fields directly; we must use their access methods. Also, method shipOrder(), like all business methods, executes within a transaction. This means all CMP and CMR fields will be updated (in the entity bean instance *and* in the database) within a single transaction, maintaining the required properties of atomicity, consistency, isolation, and durability (ACID).

Design Guideline

Although Order EJB's shipOrder() *is a business method, its only client is the Session Facade CustomerSession EJB. Thus our design funnels all entity bean clients through the Session Facade as depicted in Figure 7–2 on page 300. See "Session Facade Pattern" on page 329.*

Method ejbCreate() initializes the persistent data fields using the class setter methods. We get a primary key from DBUtil static method dbGetKey(). After calling ejbCreate(), the container invokes ejbPostCreate(), where we set the customer CMR field (and the container takes care of the "other" end of the bidirectional relationship). Also, the container will initialize the lineItems CMR field during the LineItem EJB create process.

The remaining EJB methods are empty (but required), except setEntity-Context() and unsetEntityContext(), which access the entity bean's context. Remember, the container is responsible for generating code for the finder methods, so you won't find any implementation code here.

Listing 7.10 OrderBean.java

```java
// OrderBean.java
import java.util.*;
import javax.ejb.*;

public abstract class OrderBean implements EntityBean {

    // EntityBean variables
    private EntityContext context;

    // Access methods for persistent fields

    public abstract String getOrderID();
    public abstract void setOrderID(String id);

    public abstract double getTotalAmount();
    public abstract void setTotalAmount(double amount);

    public abstract int getOrderStatus();
    public abstract void setOrderStatus(int status);

    public abstract long getOrderDate();
    public abstract void setOrderDate(long date);
```

Listing 7.10 OrderBean.java *(continued)*

```java
public abstract long getShipDate();
public abstract void setShipDate(long date);

// Access methods for relationship fields

public abstract CustomerLocal getCustomer();
public abstract void setCustomer(
            CustomerLocal customer);

public abstract Collection getLineItems();
public abstract void setLineItems(Collection lineItems);

// Business methods
public void shipOrder(long shipDate) {
  setShipDate(shipDate);
  setOrderStatus(OrderLocalHome.Shipped);
}

// EntityBean methods

public String ejbCreate(double totalAmount,
  int orderStatus, long orderDate, long shipDate,
  CustomerLocal customer)
  throws CreateException {

  String newKey = DBUtil.dbGetKey();
  setOrderID(newKey);
  setTotalAmount(totalAmount);
  setOrderStatus(orderStatus);
  setOrderDate(orderDate);
  setShipDate(shipDate);
  return newKey;
}

public void ejbPostCreate(double totalAmount,
      int orderStatus, long orderDate, long shipDate,
      CustomerLocal customer) {
  setCustomer(customer);
}
```

Listing 7.10 OrderBean.java *(continued)*

```java
public void setEntityContext(EntityContext context) {
  this.context = context;
}

public void unsetEntityContext() {
  context = null;
}

public void ejbActivate() { }
public void ejbPassivate() { }
public void ejbLoad() { }
public void ejbStore() { }
public void ejbRemove() { }

} // OrderBean
```

Generated SQL for Container Methods

Let's now examine the generated code for the Order EJB container methods. Again, remember that this SQL code is dependent on your application server and its underlying database server. So, while this code may not necessarily be portable, it helps you understand what the container is doing behind the scenes. Thus, when you invoke a business method, the container performs a load row and store row. When you create an entity bean, the container inserts a database row. And, when you delete an entity bean, it deletes the corresponding database row.

```sql
-- create row
INSERT INTO "OrderBeanTable" ("orderDate",
"orderID", "orderStatus", "shipDate", "totalAmount")
VALUES ( ?, ?, ?, ?, ? )

-- delete row
DELETE FROM "OrderBeanTable"
WHERE "orderID" = ?

-- findByPrimaryKey()
SELECT "orderID" FROM "OrderBeanTable"
WHERE "orderID" = ?
```

```
-- load row
SELECT "orderDate", "orderStatus", "shipDate",
"totalAmount" FROM "OrderBeanTable"
WHERE "orderID" = ?

-- store row
UPDATE "OrderBeanTable" SET "orderDate" = ?,
"orderStatus" = ?, "shipDate" = ?, "totalAmount" = ?
WHERE "orderID" = ?
```

EJB Query for Custom Finders

The Order EJB has one custom finder method, findByOrderDatePrevious().
In order for the container to generate code for this finder method, we specify
the proper select statement for the custom finder.

Here is the EJB QL text for findByOrderDatePrevious(long orderDate,
int orderStatus) followed by the generated SQL code.

```
select distinct object (o) from orderEJB o where
o.orderDate <= ?1 and o.orderStatus = ?2
```

```
-- Generated SQL Query for findByOrderDatePrevious()
SELECT DISTINCT "o"."orderID" FROM "OrderBeanTable" "o"
WHERE (("o"."orderDate" <= ?) AND ("o"."orderStatus"= ?))
```

In simpler words, this says "select distinct Order objects from abstract schema
orderEJB where the order date is less than or equal to the first parameter, and
the orderStatus equals the second parameter."

Container-Managed Persistence

Listing 7.11 contains deployment descriptor information for Order EJB and its
CMP fields. It identifies the local and local home interfaces, as well as its bean
implementation class (OrderBean). It also identifies the persistent mechanism
as container managed, its abstract schema as **orderEJB**, and its primary field as
orderID.

Listing 7.11 Generated XML Tags for Order CMP

```
<entity>
     <display-name>OrderBean</display-name>
     <ejb-name>OrderBean</ejb-name>
     <local-home>OrderLocalHome</local-home>
     <local>OrderLocal</local>
     <ejb-class>OrderBean</ejb-class>

     <persistence-type>Container</persistence-type>
     <prim-key-class>java.lang.String</prim-key-class>
     <reentrant>False</reentrant>
     <cmp-version>2.x</cmp-version>
     <abstract-schema-name>orderEJB</abstract-schema-name>

     <cmp-field>
       <description>no description</description>
       <field-name>orderDate</field-name>
     </cmp-field>
     <cmp-field>
       <description>no description</description>
       <field-name>shipDate</field-name>
     </cmp-field>

     <cmp-field>
       <description>no description</description>
       <field-name>orderStatus</field-name>
     </cmp-field>
     <cmp-field>
       <description>no description</description>
       <field-name>totalAmount</field-name>
     </cmp-field>

     <cmp-field>
       <description>no description</description>
       <field-name>orderID</field-name>
     </cmp-field>
     <primkey-field>orderID</primkey-field>
     <security-identity>
       <description></description>
       <use-caller-identity></use-caller-identity>
     </security-identity>
  </entity>
```

Container-Managed Relationships

Order EJB has CMR fields with both LineItem EJB and Customer EJB. Listing 7.7 on page 311 shows the deployment information for the relationship between Order EJB and LineItem EJB, so we won't repeat it here. Listing 7.12 contains deployment descriptor information that describes the CMR fields for the Order EJB (customer) and Customer EJB (collection orders) relationship.

Listing 7.12 Generated XML Tags for Order-Customer CMR

```
<ejb-relation>
    <ejb-relation-name></ejb-relation-name>
    <ejb-relationship-role>
      <ejb-relationship-role-name>CustomerBean
       </ejb-relationship-role-name>
      <multiplicity>One</multiplicity>

      <relationship-role-source>
        <ejb-name>CustomerBean</ejb-name>
      </relationship-role-source>
      <cmr-field>
        <cmr-field-name>orders</cmr-field-name>
        <cmr-field-type>java.util.Collection
         </cmr-field-type>
      </cmr-field>
    </ejb-relationship-role>

    <ejb-relationship-role>
      <ejb-relationship-role-name>OrderBean
       </ejb-relationship-role-name>
      <multiplicity>Many</multiplicity>
      <cascade-delete />
      <relationship-role-source>
        <ejb-name>OrderBean</ejb-name>
      </relationship-role-source>
      <cmr-field>
        <cmr-field-name>customer</cmr-field-name>
      </cmr-field>
    </ejb-relationship-role>
  </ejb-relation>
 </relationships>
</ejb-jar>
```

Customer Entity Bean

Our third and final entity bean is Customer EJB. We hope you'll find this entity bean's implementation interesting, since we already presented it using bean-managed persistence in the previous chapter. With the CMP implementation, we now can compare code. This means the bean implementation code will differ dramatically. The differences in the local and local home interfaces, however, are slight. These differences are not due to the persistent mechanism that we use; rather we've added a CMR field (with Order EJB). The local interface has methods to access and update this relationship field.

The local home interface has one small difference. In the BMP version, home method `getTotalCustomers()` does not have `FinderException` in its `throws` clause. In the CMP version we have to add `FinderException` in the `throws` clause because the implementation invokes a CMP select method. Select methods must always specify `FinderException` in their `throws` clauses. In general, however, choosing either CMP or BMP does not affect the local or local home interfaces.

Local Home Interface

Listing 7.13 contains the local home interface for Customer EJB. It is essentially unchanged from **CustomerLocalHome.java** in the previous chapter (see Listing 6.2 on page 209).

Because there are two custom finder methods (`findByCustomerName()` and `findAll()`) we'll need to provide declarative EJB QL statements so that the container can generate the correct SQL code for their implementations. These statements appear in the deployment descriptor, which we'll show you shortly.

Listing 7.13 CustomerLocalHome.java

```
// CustomerLocalHome.java
import java.util.Collection;
import javax.ejb.*;

public interface CustomerLocalHome extends EJBLocalHome {

  // Create method
  public CustomerLocal create(String name,
    String password, String email)
    throws CreateException;
```

Listing 7.13 CustomerLocalHome.java *(continued)*

```
  // Finder methods
  public CustomerLocal findByPrimaryKey(String customerID)
    throws FinderException;

  // Custom finder methods
  public Collection findByCustomerName(String name)
    throws FinderException;

  // Return all Customer EJBs in the database
  public Collection findAll()
    throws FinderException;

  // Home methods
  // Return the number of Customers in the database
  public int getTotalCustomers()
    throws FinderException;
}
```

Local Interface

Listing 7.14 contains the local interface for Customer EJB. It is identical to Listing 6.4 on page 211, except we've included the access method for the relationship field, getOrders(). We've also added business methods addOrder() and dropOrder() to maintain the relationship field with Order EJB.

Design Guideline

Although our CustomerSession EJB client doesn't invoke addOrder() *or* dropOrder() *at this time, we include them as business methods anyway. This makes managing orders of Customer EJBs easy to implement later on.*

Listing 7.14 CustomerLocal.java

```
// CustomerLocal.java
import javax.ejb.EJBLocalObject;
import java.util.*;
public interface CustomerLocal extends EJBLocalObject {
```

Listing 7.14 CustomerLocal.java *(continued)*

```java
    // access methods for persistent fields
    public String getCustomerID();
    public String getName();
    public String getPassword();
    public void setPassword(String newPassword);

    public String getEmail();
    public void setEmail(String newEmail);
    public boolean getOrdersPending();
    public void setOrdersPending(boolean pending);

    // access methods for relationship fields
    public Collection getOrders();

    // business methods
    public void addOrder(OrderLocal order);
    public void dropOrder(OrderLocal order);
}
```

Bean Implementation

Listing 7.15 contains the bean implementation code for Customer EJB. Since you've already seen CMP implementations for Order EJB and LineItem EJB, most of it should be self-explanatory. Remember there is no implementation code for the finder methods, as these will be generated by the container. The custom finder methods will be generated from the query code we provide in the deployment descriptor. Likewise, select method `ejbSelectTotalCus-tomers()` is abstract, since its code will also be generated from our query statements in the deployment descriptor.

Business methods `addOrder()` and `dropOrder()` update the `orders` CMR field that holds the collection of Order EJBs. We use the `getOrders()` access method since we cannot manipulate the (virtual) CMR field directly.

Note that the implementation for `ejbPostCreate()` is empty. That's because at the time we create a Customer EJB, there are no orders in existence for this customer. Therefore, we don't set the relationship field here in the bean implementation code. (It's set by the container when we initialize the "other" end of the relationship in Order EJB's `ejbPostCreate()` method.)

Listing 7.15 CustomerBean.java

```java
// CustomerBean.java
import java.util.*;
import javax.ejb.*;

public abstract class CustomerBean implements EntityBean {

  // EntityBean variables
  private EntityContext context;

  // Access methods for persistent fields

  public abstract String getCustomerID();
  public abstract void setCustomerID(String id);

  public abstract String getName();
  public abstract void setName(String name);

  public abstract String getPassword();
  public abstract void setPassword(String password);

  public abstract String getEmail();
  public abstract void setEmail(String email);

  public abstract boolean getOrdersPending();
  public abstract void setOrdersPending(boolean pending);

  // Access methods for relationship fields
  public abstract Collection getOrders();
  public abstract void setOrders(Collection orders);

  // Select methods
  public abstract Collection ejbSelectTotalCustomers()
    throws FinderException;

  // Business methods
  public void addOrder(OrderLocal order) {
    try {
      Collection orders = getOrders();
      orders.add(order);
    } catch (Exception ex) {
      throw new EJBException(ex.getMessage());
    }
  }
```

Listing 7.15 CustomerBean.java *(continued)*

```java
public void dropOrder(OrderLocal order) {
  try {
    Collection orders = getOrders();
    orders.remove(order);
  } catch (Exception ex) {
    throw new EJBException(ex.getMessage());
  }
}

// EJB Home Methods
public int ejbHomeGetTotalCustomers()
        throws FinderException {
  return ejbSelectTotalCustomers().size();
}

// EntityBean methods

public String ejbCreate(String customerName,
  String password, String email)
        throws CreateException {

  String newKey = DBUtil.dbGetKey();
  setCustomerID(newKey);
  setName(customerName);
  setPassword(password);
  setEmail(email);
  setOrdersPending(false);
  return newKey;
}

public void setEntityContext(EntityContext context) {
  this.context = context;
}

public void unsetEntityContext() {
  context = null;
}

public void ejbActivate() { }
public void ejbPassivate() { }
public void ejbLoad() { }
public void ejbStore() { }
```

Listing 7.15 CustomerBean.java *(continued)*

```
public void ejbPostCreate(String customerName,
   String password, String email) { }

public void ejbRemove() { }

} // CustomerBean
```

Note that the `ejbHomeGetTotalCustomers()` method implements the home method `getTotalCustomers()` from the `CustomerLocalHome` interface. To return the *number* of customers in the database, we invoke `ejbSelectTotal-Customers()` with the `size()` method, since this select method returns a collection.

```
public int ejbHomeGetTotalCustomers()
         throws FinderException {
   return ejbSelectTotalCustomers().size();
}
```

CMP Limitation

The implementation of `ejbHomeGetTotalCustomers()` *is admittedly an inefficient way to count the number of records in the database. However, we are limited by the EJB Query Language in composing our queries. We are also limited in how we can access the result set. Recall that in our BMP example, we implement* `ejbHomeGetTotalCustomers()` *with a scrollable result set. This is more efficient, since we can position the result set cursor at the last row before getting the row number. With CMP, we cannot access the result set directly.*

Generated SQL for Container Methods

After we specify the Customer EJB persistent data fields and the primary key, the deployment tool generates the SQL code to maintain database persistence. Here is the SQL used to perform CMP for our Customer EJB. This code is not meant to be portable; another application server might generate slightly different SQL, depending on the bundled database server.

```
-- create row
INSERT INTO "CustomerBeanTable" ("customerID",
"email", "name", "ordersPending", "password")
VALUES ( ?, ?, ?, ?, ? )

-- delete row
DELETE FROM "CustomerBeanTable" WHERE
"customerID" = ?

-- findByPrimaryKey
SELECT "customerID" FROM "CustomerBeanTable"
WHERE "customerID" = ?

-- load row
SELECT "email", "name", "ordersPending",
"password" FROM "CustomerBeanTable" WHERE
"customerID" = ?

-- store row
UPDATE "CustomerBeanTable" SET "email" = ?,
"name" = ?, "ordersPending" = ?, "password" = ?
WHERE "customerID" = ?
```

EJB Query for Finder and Select Methods

All custom finder methods and select methods require that we specify database lookup code through the EJB Query Language. For Customer EJB, query statements for `ejbSelectTotalCustomers()`, `findAll()`, and `findByCustomerName()` are necessary. We also show SQL code generated by the deployment tool. The deployment tool puts the query statements in the deployment descriptor. Thus, the EJB QL query statements are portable with any EJB-compliant application server. Here is the EJB QL for `ejbSelectTotalCustomers()`, followed by its corresponding generated SQL (shaded).

```
select object (c) from customerEJB c
```

```
-- Generated SQL Query for ejbSelectTotalCustomers()
SELECT "c"."customerID" FROM
"CustomerBeanTable" "c"
```

Next is the EJB QL for `findAll()` and its corresponding generated SQL.

```
select object (c) from customerEJB c
```

```
-- Generated SQL Query for findAll()
SELECT "c"."customerID" FROM
"CustomerBeanTable" "c"
```

Finally, we show you the EJB QL for `findByCustomerName(String name)` and its generated SQL.

```
select distinct object (c) from customerEJB c
where c.name = ?1
```

```
-- SQL Query for findByCustomerName()
SELECT DISTINCT "c"."customerID" FROM
"CustomerBeanTable" "c" WHERE ("c"."name" = ?)
```

Container-Managed Persistence

Listing 7.16 contains deployment descriptor information for Customer EJB, including its interface names, abstract schema, persistence type, CMP field names, and primary key.

Listing 7.16 Generated XML Tags for Customer CMP

```
<entity>
     <display-name>CustomerBean</display-name>
     <ejb-name>CustomerBean</ejb-name>
     <local-home>CustomerLocalHome</local-home>
     <local>CustomerLocal</local>
     <ejb-class>CustomerBean</ejb-class>

     <persistence-type>Container</persistence-type>
     <prim-key-class>java.lang.String</prim-key-class>
     <reentrant>False</reentrant>
     <cmp-version>2.x</cmp-version>
     <abstract-schema-name>customerEJB
     </abstract-schema-name>
     <cmp-field>
       <description>no description</description>
       <field-name>name</field-name>
     </cmp-field>
```

Listing 7.16 Generated XML Tags for Customer CMP*(continued)*

```xml
<cmp-field>
  <description>no description</description>
  <field-name>password</field-name>
</cmp-field>
<cmp-field>
  <description>no description</description>
  <field-name>email</field-name>
</cmp-field>

<cmp-field>
  <description>no description</description>
  <field-name>customerID</field-name>
</cmp-field>
<cmp-field>
  <description>no description</description>
  <field-name>ordersPending</field-name>
</cmp-field>

<primkey-field>customerID</primkey-field>
<security-identity>
  <description></description>
  <use-caller-identity></use-caller-identity>
</security-identity>
</entity>
```

Container-Managed Relationships

Customer EJB's CMR field is a collection of Order EJBs (`Collection orders`). You've already seen the deployment descriptor information for this relationship (Listing 7.12 on page 320), so we won't repeat it here.

7.3 Session Facade Pattern

Now that you've seen the three entity beans in our enterprise application, it's time to present the Session Facade session bean, CustomerSession EJB. The CustomerSession EJB is an enhanced version of the session bean we presented in Chapter 6 (see Listing 6.20 on page 256). For a detailed explanation of the Session Facade Pattern (and why you'd want to use it), see "Session Facade Pattern" on page 250. As you examine the code for the session facade, you'll see how it provides the business logic for a consistent interface to the three entity beans.

Figure 7–5 contains a more detailed diagram of the Session Facade implementation, including the three entity beans. The remote client access to the entity beans is through the Session Facade only. We show the methods in the Session Facade that the remote client uses to fulfill the requirements of the web site. The CustomerSession EJB accesses the entity beans through local interfaces. We also show the multiplicity relationships among the entity beans.

There are additional motivations for using the Session Facade Pattern here. Although we presented this pattern in the previous chapter, its role becomes much more pronounced in designs with multiple related entity beans.

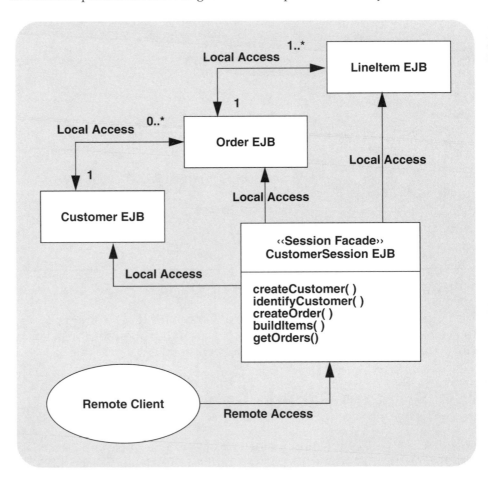

Figure 7–5 Architectural Overview of the Session Facade CustomerSession EJB, Its Client, and the Underlying Entity Beans Customer EJB, Order EJB, and LineItem EJB

Design Guideline

*The Session Facade bean provides the interface to **each of the entity beans**, Customer EJB, Order EJB, and LineItem EJB. It also provides the **business logic** that controls the three entity beans. It fulfills the life cycle creation and subsequent destruction control to maintain the correct business relationship among the entity beans. Without the Session Facade, this business logic would become the responsibility of the remote client. Not only would the business logic be duplicated in all general clients and require multiple remote methods, but it would unnecessarily complicate the interface between the remote client and entity beans. This approach would also adversely affect performance.*

Value Object Pattern Revisited

Suppose a remote client (either a web component, a stand-alone Java client, or even another Enterprise JavaBeans component) wants to create an order, create a customer, or get all of the orders in a system. How does the remote client communicate with the CustomerSession EJB? Recall that we used the Value Object Pattern to encapsulate customer data with `CustomerVO`. "Value Objects" on page 42 discusses both the convenience factor and the performance reasons for encapsulating data to communicate between remote clients and session beans. Listing 5.1 on page 143 lists the code for the customer value object, which we continue to use unchanged in this chapter. We'll also need `LineItemVO` and `OrderVO` value objects, too. Let's look at `LineItemVO` first.

LineItemVO

Listing 7.17 contains the source for the `LineItemVO` class **LineItemVO.java**. A line item represents the recording selected by the customer. We store the recording title and the number of copies of this recording selected by this customer. Class `LineItemVO` must implement interface `Serializable`, since we transmit it remotely.

Note that we implement method `equals()` for `LineItemVO` objects to compare recording titles. Recall that the Java collection classes rely on `equals()` to perform comparisons.

Listing 7.17 LineItemVO.java

```
// LineItemVO.java
import java.util.*;

public class LineItemVO implements java.io.Serializable {
```

Listing 7.17 LineItemVO.java *(continued)*

```java
private String title;
private int quantity;

public LineItemVO(String title, int quantity)
{
  setTitle(title);
  setQuantity(quantity);
}

// getters
public String getTitle() { return title; }
public int getQuantity() { return quantity; }

// setters
public void setTitle(String title) {
  this.title = title;
}

public void setQuantity(int quantity) {
  this.quantity = quantity;
}

public boolean equals(Object lineItem) {
  return (title.equals(
    ((LineItemVO)lineItem).getTitle()));
}
}
```

OrderVO

Remote clients use object OrderVO to transmit and receive data for an order. The web client is responsible for collecting data that constitutes an order and encapsulating it into an OrderVO object. This allows the CustomerSession EJB to create the actual entity beans (and thus persist the information to permanent datastore). The OrderVO object contains not only information about a specific order that we store in an Order EJB, but it also has information relating to a particular customer and all of its line item data. The CustomerSession EJB uses the customer information to create an Order EJB (thus initializing the Order EJB's CMR customer field). It will also use the line item data to create the LineItem EJBs for the order.

Listing 7.18 contains the source for **OrderVO.java**.

Listing 7.18 OrderVO.java

```java
// OrderVO.java
import java.util.*;

public class OrderVO implements java.io.Serializable
{
  private double totalAmount;
  private int orderStatus;
  private Calendar orderDate;
  private Calendar shipDate;
  private String customerName;
  private Collection lineItems;

  public OrderVO(double amount, int status,
      Calendar orderDate, Calendar shipDate,
      String name, Collection lineItems)
  {
    setTotalAmount(amount);
    setOrderStatus(status);
    setOrderDate(orderDate);
    setShipDate(shipDate);
    setCustomerName(name);
    setLineItems(lineItems);
  }

  // getters
  public double getTotalAmount() { return totalAmount; }
  public int getOrderStatus() { return orderStatus; }
  public Calendar getOrderDate() {
    return (Calendar)orderDate.clone();
  }
  public Calendar getShipDate() {
    return (Calendar)shipDate.clone();
  }
  public String getCustomerName() { return customerName; }
  public Collection getLineItems() { return lineItems; }

  // setters
  public void setTotalAmount(double amount) {
    totalAmount = amount;
  }
  public void setOrderStatus(int status) {
    orderStatus = status;
  }
```

Listing 7.18 OrderVO.java *(continued)*

```
public void setOrderDate(Calendar d) {
  orderDate = (GregorianCalendar)new GregorianCalendar(
    d.get(Calendar.YEAR),
    d.get(Calendar.MONTH),
    d.get(Calendar.DATE)); }

public void setShipDate(Calendar d) {
  shipDate = (GregorianCalendar)new GregorianCalendar(
    d.get(Calendar.YEAR),
    d.get(Calendar.MONTH),
    d.get(Calendar.DATE)); }

public void setCustomerName(String name) {
  customerName = name;
}

public void setLineItems(Collection items) {
  lineItems = items;
}
}
```

CustomerSession EJB

Now that we've specified how the remote client sends and receives information to the session facade bean, it's time to show you this workhorse in detail.

Home Interface

The CustomerSession EJB is a stateless session bean with a single `create()` method, as shown in Listing 7.19. (This file is unchanged from Listing 6.16 on page 252.)

Listing 7.19 CustomerSessionHome.java

```
// CustomerSessionHome.java
import java.io.Serializable;
import java.rmi.RemoteException;
import javax.ejb.CreateException;
import javax.ejb.EJBHome;
```

Listing 7.19 CustomerSessionHome.java *(continued)*

```java
public interface CustomerSessionHome extends EJBHome {
    CustomerSession create() throws RemoteException,
        CreateException;
}
```

Remote Interface

The remote interface contains the business methods that manipulate our three
entity beans. Because we have added the Order EJB and LineItem EJB to our
Customer EJB, we require additional business methods to create an order and
build a collection of line items. Listing 7.20 contains the remote interface, CustomerSession.

Listing 7.20 CustomerSession.java

```java
// CustomerSession.java
import javax.ejb.*;
import java.rmi.RemoteException;
import java.util.*;

public interface CustomerSession extends EJBObject {

    public int getTotalCustomers()
        throws RemoteException;

    public void createCustomer(CustomerVO customer)
        throws CreateException, FinderException,
        RemoteException;

    public void changePassword(String name, String password)
        throws CustomerIdentityException, CustomerException,
        FinderException, RemoteException;

    public void changeEmail(String name, String email)
        throws CustomerIdentityException, CustomerException,
        FinderException, RemoteException;

    public void identifyCustomer(String name,
        String password) throws CustomerIdentityException,
        FinderException, RemoteException;
```

Listing 7.20 CustomerSession.java *(continued)*

```
public boolean getOrdersPending(String name)
    throws CustomerIdentityException,
    FinderException, RemoteException;

public Collection getOrders(String name)
    throws CustomerIdentityException,
    FinderException, RemoteException;

public void createOrder(OrderVO order)
    throws CreateException, CustomerIdentityException,
    FinderException, RemoteException;

public Collection buildItems(Collection items)
    throws RemoteException;

public Collection getCustomers()
    throws FinderException, RemoteException;

public void shipOrdersByDate(Calendar orderDate)
    throws FinderException, RemoteException;
}
```

Method getOrders() returns a collection of OrderVO objects belonging to a customer identified by name. Method createOrder() creates a new Order EJB using information provided in the OrderVO object argument. Method build-Items() takes the collection of RecordingVO objects produced by the client and returns a collection of LineItemVO objects (eliminating duplicate titles by incrementing the corresponding quantity for that title).

The shipOrdersByDate() method "ships" all orders in the system that have not yet been shipped and have an order date that is equal to or earlier than the Calendar argument.

Design Guideline

A use case is a description of how someone would use your system. If you build use case diagrams for your enterprise application, then the Session Facade's remote interface should contain all the methods that implement each use case.

Bean Implementation

Since CustomerSession EJB is a stateless session bean, the bulk of the code is the implementation of the business methods we defined in the remote interface. Some of the methods we presented in an earlier version from Chapter 6 (see Listing 6.20 on page 256). For example, the methods that deal solely with the Customer EJB are unchanged. These include `createCustomer()`, `changePassword()`, `changeEmail()`, `identifyCustomer()`, `getOrders-Pending()`, and `getCustomers()`. New to this implementation are the business methods that manipulate the Order EJBs and LineItem EJBs. These include `getOrders()`, `createOrder()`, `buildItems()`, and `shipOrdersBy-Date()`.

You'll also note that `ejbCreate()` initializes instance variables `customer-Home`, `orderHome`, and `lineItemHome`. These hold the local home interfaces to the three entity beans. Since CustomerSession EJB is stateless, the container may use the same instance among multiple clients and share these (client-independent) instance variables.

A few methods deserve special mention here. Let's look at `getOrders()` first (see page 343.) Method `getOrders()` returns a collection of `OrderVO` objects for the customer named in the argument. We first access the customer local home interface and invoke customer finder method `findByCustomerName()`. This returns a `CustomerLocal` object (within the collection), which provides access to the business methods of the Customer EJB. We then access the Customer EJB business method `getOrders()`, which returns a collection of `OrderLocal` objects. This in turn provides access to the Order EJB business methods. (Customer EJB method `getOrders()` returns the CMR field `orders`.) The Order EJB contains relationship access method `getLineItems()`, which returns a collection of `LineItemLocal` objects. We now begin to build the `OrderVO` object to transmit back to the client.

Since an `OrderVO` object contains a collection of `LineItemVO` objects, we build these first. We then extricate the details of the Order EJB to put into the `OrderVO` object. Note that we convert the date from a `long` to a `Calendar` object as part of this process.

CMP Limitation

In the EJB 2.0 specification, the EJB Query Language does not currently support SQL date objects. Therefore, we store Calendar objects by converting them to `long` *data types using* `Calendar.getTime()` *(which returns a* Date*) and* `Date.getTime()` *(which returns a* `long`*), as shown below. To convert a* `long` *to a* `Calendar` *object, we create a* Date *object with a* `long` *and call* Calendar's `setTime()` *with a* Date *object.*

```
// convert Calendar object to long
long dateAsLong =
      myCalendarObject.getTime().getTime();

// convert long to Calendar object
Calendar myCalendarObject =
      new GregorianCalendar();
myCalendarObject.setTime(new Date(dateAsLong));
```

Each `OrderVO` object that we build contains information from the Order EJB, as well as information from the related Customer EJB and the LineItem EJBs.

The second method that deserves special attention is `createOrder()` (see page 346). Here we show you how to construct an Order EJB, as well as how to set its relationship fields. We pass an `OrderVO` object to `createOrder()` and extract the customer name. We can then identify the Customer EJB using finder method `findByCustomerName()`.

After successfully finding the relevant Customer EJB, we create a new Order EJB using the `OrderLocalHome`'s `create()` method. We include the `Customer-Local` object (`cust`) with the arguments to the Order's `create()` call. We then build the LineItem EJBs using the `LineItemLocalHome` object and invoke the `create()` method. As we build the LineItem EJBs, we associate each LineItem EJB with the newly created OrderEJB by including `OrderLocal` object `myorder` with the LineItem EJB `create()` call.

Design Guideline

*Even though we implement **two-way** navigation with all our entity bean relationships, the entity bean create process must only initialize **one end** of the relationship. The container initializes the other end for you during the current transaction context. The container's involvement here guarantees the referential integrity of CMR fields.*

Finally, look at method `shipOrdersByDate()` (see page 344). We provide a `Calendar` object as a target date, requesting all orders that have not yet been shipped with an order date that is equal to or earlier than the target date. This method uses a custom finder to obtain a collection of `OrderLocal` objects. After acquiring the collection, we can invoke business method `shipOrder()` in Order EJB for each order.

Listing 7.21 shows the bean implementation code in file **CustomerSession-Bean.java**.

Listing 7.21 CustomerSessionBean.java

```java
// CustomerSessionBean.java
import java.rmi.RemoteException;
import javax.ejb.*;
import javax.naming.*;
import java.util.*;

public class CustomerSessionBean implements SessionBean {

    // initialize in ejbCreate()

    private CustomerLocalHome customerHome;
    private OrderLocalHome orderHome;
    private LineItemLocalHome lineItemHome;

    // Business methods

    // Return the number of Customers in the database

    public int getTotalCustomers() throws FinderException {
        return customerHome.getTotalCustomers();
    }
```

Listing 7.21 CustomerSessionBean.java *(continued)*

```java
// Create a new Customer in the CustomerDB
// verify that the name is unique and the password
// is non-empty.

public void createCustomer(CustomerVO customer)
    throws CreateException, FinderException {
  if (customer.getName() == null
      || customer.getPassword() == null
      || customer.getEmail() == null) {
    throw new CreateException("Customer data is null");
  }

  if (customer.getName().equals("")
      || customer.getPassword().equals("")
      || customer.getEmail().equals("")) {
    throw new CreateException(
          "Customer fields cannot be empty.");
  }

  Collection c =
    customerHome.findByCustomerName(customer.getName());
  if (c.size() == 0) {
    customerHome.create(
      customer.getName(),
      customer.getPassword(),
      customer.getEmail());
  }

  else {
    throw new CreateException(
        "Customer name already in use.");
  }
}

// Change the password for the customer.
// Make sure customer is in the database
// Throws CustomerIdentityException if no match.
// Throws CustomerException if other problems.
```

Listing 7.21 CustomerSessionBean.java *(continued)*

```java
public void changePassword(String name, String password)
    throws CustomerIdentityException, CustomerException,
    FinderException {
  if (password.equals("")) {
    throw new CustomerException(
        "Password cannot be empty");
  }

  Collection c = customerHome.findByCustomerName(name);
  if (c.size() == 1) {
    Iterator i=c.iterator();
    CustomerLocal cust = (CustomerLocal)i.next();
    cust.setPassword(password);
  }
  else {
    throw new CustomerIdentityException(
          "Cannot find customer " + name);
  }
}

// Change the email for the customer.
// Make sure customer is in the database
// Throws CustomerIdentityException if no match.
// Throws CustomerException if other problems.

public void changeEmail(String name, String email)
    throws CustomerIdentityException, CustomerException,
    FinderException {
  if (email.equals("")) {
    throw new CustomerException(
        "Email cannot be empty");
  }

  Collection c = customerHome.findByCustomerName(name);
  if (c.size() == 1) {
    Iterator i=c.iterator();
    CustomerLocal cust = (CustomerLocal)i.next();
    cust.setEmail(email);
  }
```

Listing 7.21 CustomerSessionBean.java *(continued)*

```
    else {
      throw new CustomerIdentityException(
            "Cannot find customer " + name);
    }
  }

  // Given a customer name, make sure the password
  // matches the customer's name in the database
  // Throws CustomerIdentityException if no match.

  public void identifyCustomer(String name,
        String password) throws CustomerIdentityException,
        FinderException {
    Collection c = customerHome.findByCustomerName(name);
    if (c.size() == 1) {
      Iterator i=c.iterator();
      CustomerLocal cust = (CustomerLocal)i.next();
      if (!cust.getPassword().equals(password)) {
        throw new CustomerIdentityException(
            "Incorrect Password for customer " + name);
      }
    }
    else {
      throw new CustomerIdentityException(
            "Cannot find customer " + name);
    }
  }

  // Given the customer name,
  // get the OrdersPending flag

  public boolean getOrdersPending(String name)
      throws CustomerIdentityException, FinderException {
    Collection c = customerHome.findByCustomerName(name);
    if (c.size() == 1) {
      Iterator i=c.iterator();
      CustomerLocal cust = (CustomerLocal)i.next();
      return cust.getOrdersPending();
    }
```

Listing 7.21 CustomerSessionBean.java *(continued)*

```java
    else {
      throw new CustomerIdentityException(
            "Cannot find customer " + name);
    }
}

// Given the customer name,
// return ArrayList of OrderVOs
// for that customer

public Collection getOrders(String name)
    throws CustomerIdentityException, FinderException {

  Collection c = customerHome.findByCustomerName(name);

  if (c.size() == 1) {
    Iterator i=c.iterator();
    CustomerLocal cust = (CustomerLocal)i.next();

    // create an ArrayList of OrderVOs
    ArrayList orderList = new ArrayList();

    Collection a = cust.getOrders();
    i = a.iterator();

    while (i.hasNext()) {
      OrderLocal orderEJB = (OrderLocal)i.next();

      // get orderEJB's ArrayList of LineItem EJBs
      // and put them in a new ArrayList of LineItemVOs

      ArrayList lineItems = new ArrayList();
      Iterator lineIt =
              orderEJB.getLineItems().iterator();
      while (lineIt.hasNext()) {
        LineItemLocal item =
                (LineItemLocal) lineIt.next();
        lineItems.add(new LineItemVO(
                item.getTitle(), item.getQuantity()));
      }
```

Listing 7.21 CustomerSessionBean.java *(continued)*

```
            // convert OrderEJB longs to Calendar objects
            Calendar orderDate = new GregorianCalendar();
            orderDate.setTime(new Date(
                    orderEJB.getOrderDate()));
            Calendar shipDate = new GregorianCalendar();
            shipDate.setTime(new Date(
                    orderEJB.getShipDate()));

            // create OrderVO object and add to orderlist
            OrderVO order =
              new OrderVO(orderEJB.getTotalAmount(),
                orderEJB.getOrderStatus(),
                orderDate,
                shipDate,
                cust.getName(),
                lineItems);
            orderList.add(order);
        }
        return orderList;
    }

    else {
      throw new CustomerIdentityException(
              "Cannot find customer " + name);
    }
}

// Ship all Order EJBs with an orderDate that
// is equal to or earlier than argument orderDate

public void shipOrdersByDate(Calendar orderDate)
      throws FinderException {
    // convert Calendar object to long
    long when = orderDate.getTime().getTime();

    // use finder to get orders
    try {
    Collection orders =
      orderHome.findByOrderDatePrevious(when,
        OrderLocalHome.InProcess);

    Iterator i = orders.iterator();
```

Listing 7.21 CustomerSessionBean.java *(continued)*

```java
    // use today's date for the ship date
    Date now = new Date();
    while (i.hasNext()) {
      OrderLocal orderEJB = (OrderLocal)i.next();
      orderEJB.shipOrder(now.getTime());
      System.out.println("Shipped order for " +
          orderEJB.getCustomer().getName());
    }

  } catch (Exception ex) {
    ex.printStackTrace();
    throw new EJBException(
        "shipOrdersByDate: " + ex.getMessage());
  }
}

// Get the shoppingList of RecordingVOs and build
// an ArrayList of LineItemVOs with no duplicates.
// Increment the quantity when we find duplicates.

public Collection buildItems(Collection items) {
  try {
    ArrayList itemList = new ArrayList();
    Iterator i = items.iterator();

    while (i.hasNext()) {
      RecordingVO r = (RecordingVO) i.next();
      LineItemVO thisItem =
              new LineItemVO(r.getTitle(), 1);
      // is LineItemVO already in itemList?
      int index = itemList.indexOf(thisItem);

      if (index < 0) {
        // not a duplicate;
        // just add this one
        itemList.add(thisItem);
      }

      else {
        // Duplicate LineItemVO--
        // Get the duplicate & increment quantity
```

Listing 7.21 CustomerSessionBean.java *(continued)*

```
                LineItemVO l = (LineItemVO) itemList.get(index);
                int q = l.getQuantity() + 1;
                l.setQuantity(q);

                // Replace with updated quantity field
                itemList.set(index, l);
              }
            }
            return itemList;

        } catch (Exception ex) {
          ex.printStackTrace();
          throw new EJBException(
              "buildItems: " + ex.getMessage());
        }
    }

    public void createOrder(OrderVO order)
        throws CustomerIdentityException, CreateException,
        FinderException {

      Collection c = customerHome.findByCustomerName(
            order.getCustomerName());
      if (c.size() == 1) {
        // get CustomerEJB
        Iterator i = c.iterator();
        CustomerLocal cust = (CustomerLocal)i.next();

        try {
          // get the LineItemVO ArrayList
          Collection items = order.getLineItems();
          if (items.isEmpty()) {
            throw new CreateException(
                "createOrder: LineItems cannot be empty.");
          }

          // create Order EJB
          // include Customer EJB with create arguments
          OrderLocal myorder = orderHome.create(
            order.getTotalAmount(),
            order.getOrderStatus(),
```

Listing 7.21 CustomerSessionBean.java *(continued)*

```java
        // convert Calendar objects to longs
      order.getOrderDate().getTime().getTime(),
      order.getShipDate().getTime().getTime(),
      cust);

    // create LineItem EJBs
    // include Order EJB with create arguments
    Iterator lineIt = items.iterator();
    while (lineIt.hasNext()) {
      LineItemVO lineItem =
            (LineItemVO) lineIt.next();
      LineItemLocal myLineItem = lineItemHome.create(
        lineItem.getTitle(),
        lineItem.getQuantity(),
        myorder);
    }

    cust.setOrdersPending(true);
  }

  catch (Exception ex) {
    System.out.println(ex.getMessage());
    ex.printStackTrace();
    throw new EJBException(
        "CustomerSessionBean: createOrder");
  }
}

else {
  throw new CustomerIdentityException(
      "Cannot find customer " +
      order.getCustomerName());
}
}

// Get all the customers in the customer database
// Return an ArrayList of CustomerVOs

public Collection getCustomers()
              throws FinderException {

  // return an ArrayList of CustomerVOs
  ArrayList customerList = new ArrayList();
```

Listing 7.21 CustomerSessionBean.java *(continued)*

```java
    Collection a = customerHome.findAll();
    Iterator i = a.iterator();

    while (i.hasNext()) {
      CustomerLocal customerEJB = (CustomerLocal)i.next();

      CustomerVO customer =
        new CustomerVO(customerEJB.getName(),
          customerEJB.getPassword(),
          customerEJB.getEmail());
      customerList.add(customer);
    }

    return customerList;
  }

  // EJB Methods
  public CustomerSessionBean() {}

  public void ejbCreate() {
    try {
      Context initial = new InitialContext();
      System.out.println("CustomerSession ejbCreate()");

      // Find LocalHome Interface to CustomerEJB
      Object objref =
            initial.lookup("java:comp/env/ejb/Customer");
      customerHome = (CustomerLocalHome)objref;

      // Find LocalHome Interface to OrderEJB
      objref = initial.lookup("java:comp/env/ejb/Order");
      orderHome = (OrderLocalHome)objref;

      // Find LocalHome Interface to LineItemEJB
      objref =
            initial.lookup("java:comp/env/ejb/LineItem");
      lineItemHome = (LineItemLocalHome)objref;
    } catch (Exception ex) {
      ex.printStackTrace();
      throw new EJBException(ex.getMessage());
    }
    System.out.println("CustomerSessionBean: ejbCreate");
  }
```

Listing 7.21 CustomerSessionBean.java *(continued)*

```
    public void ejbRemove() {}
    public void ejbActivate() {}
    public void ejbPassivate() {}
    public void setSessionContext(SessionContext sc) {}

} // CustomerSessionBean
```

Deployment Descriptor

Listing 7.22 shows portions of the deployment descriptor for the EJB JAR file containing the CustomerSession EJB. The CustomerSession EJB is a stateless session bean with container-managed transactions. It has remote (Customer-Session) and remote home (CustomerSessionHome) interfaces and references the Customer, Order, and LineItem entity beans through their local and local home interfaces. Under the <assembly-descriptor> tag, the deployment descriptor lists all of its transactional methods, along with the transaction attribute we assign (in all cases, attribute **Required**). The <method> tag identifies methods with transactions. We show the <method> tags for createCustomer() and createOrder() only. We highlight the tag values for readability.

Listing 7.22 Generated XML Tags for CustomerSession EJB

```
  . . .
  <session>
   <display-name>CustomerSessionBean</display-name>
      <ejb-name>CustomerSessionBean</ejb-name>
      <home>CustomerSessionHome</home>
      <remote>CustomerSession</remote>
      <ejb-class>CustomerSessionBean</ejb-class>
      <session-type>Stateless</session-type>
      <transaction-type>Container</transaction-type>

      <ejb-local-ref>
        <ejb-ref-name>ejb/Customer</ejb-ref-name>
        <ejb-ref-type>Entity</ejb-ref-type>
        <local-home>CustomerLocalHome</local-home>
        <local>CustomerLocal</local>
        <ejb-link>CustomerBean</ejb-link>
      </ejb-local-ref>
```

Listing 7.22 Generated XML Tags for CustomerSession EJB *(continued)*

```
      <ejb-local-ref>
        <ejb-ref-name>ejb/Order</ejb-ref-name>
        <ejb-ref-type>Entity</ejb-ref-type>
        <local-home>OrderLocalHome</local-home>
        <local>OrderLocal</local>
        <ejb-link>OrderBean</ejb-link>
      </ejb-local-ref>

      <ejb-local-ref>
        <ejb-ref-name>ejb/LineItem</ejb-ref-name>
        <ejb-ref-type>Entity</ejb-ref-type>
        <local-home>LineItemLocalHome</local-home>
        <local>LineItemLocal</local>
        <ejb-link>LineItemBean</ejb-link>
      </ejb-local-ref>

      <security-identity>
        <description></description>
        <use-caller-identity></use-caller-identity>
      </security-identity>
    </session>
  </enterprise-beans>

  <assembly-descriptor>
    <container-transaction>
      <method>
        <ejb-name>CustomerSessionBean</ejb-name>
        <method-intf>Remote</method-intf>
        <method-name>createCustomer</method-name>
        <method-params>
          <method-param>CustomerVO</method-param>
        </method-params>
      </method>
      <trans-attribute>Required</trans-attribute>
    </container-transaction>

  <container-transaction>
      <method>
        <ejb-name>CustomerSessionBean</ejb-name>
        <method-intf>Remote</method-intf>
        <method-name>createOrder</method-name>
```

Listing 7.22 Generated XML Tags for CustomerSession EJB *(continued)*

```
            <method-params>
                <method-param>OrderVO</method-param>
            </method-params>
          </method>
          <trans-attribute>Required</trans-attribute>
      </container-transaction>
      .  .  .
  </assembly-descriptor>
</ejb-jar>
```

Entity Beans and Session Beans Revisited

The three entity beans that we described and coded reflect business data. While we can add custom finders or business methods to these entity beans, we expect the underlying database to be stable and for the entity beans to be highly reusable components.

In contrast, as we add requirements or use cases to our system, our CustomerSession bean may expand. Or, we may implement a second session facade to handle a different set of use cases. Thus, a flexible, scalable system should have a stable backbone entity bean structure upon which we can build use cases within a session facade. Adding custom finder methods or business methods to the entity bean does not affect the underlying entity bean or database structure.

This approach again points to the efficiency and flexibility of the Session Facade Pattern and its importance in a well-designed enterprise system.

7.4 Web Component Client

In Chapter 5, "Stateful Session Beans," our web component allows users to select recording titles from a music database and place them in a virtual shopping cart. We represent the virtual shopping cart with a stateful session bean. In Chapter 6, "Entity Beans with BMP," we add true database lookup for returning customers and the ability to sign up as a new customer using a Customer EJB and a session facade to provide the interface between the web component and the entity bean. In this chapter our online shopping application can create orders and add them to an underlying database. To do this, we enhance the session facade with the underlying support of entity beans Order EJB and LineItem EJB. Also, we include relationship fields so that our Customer EJB, Order EJB, and LineItem EJB entity beans are properly connected. (And we re-implement Customer EJB using CMP.)

Now it's time to show you the enhanced web component that allows a customer to "check out" an order from the virtual shopping cart. Figure 7–6 shows the new web JSP files (shown with white background) we use to accomplish this, **processOrder.jsp** and **submitOrder.jsp**, and their relationship to the JSP files presented previously (see Figure 6-8 on page 263.)

Figure 7–7 shows the screen displayed by **musicCart.jsp**. When a customer is ready to submit an order, he or she selects "Process Shopping Cart Order." This invokes JSP file **processOrder.jsp**, which allows the customer to confirm orders in the shopping cart. We show this screen in Figure 7–8. The customer can then either continue shopping without submitting any orders or choose to

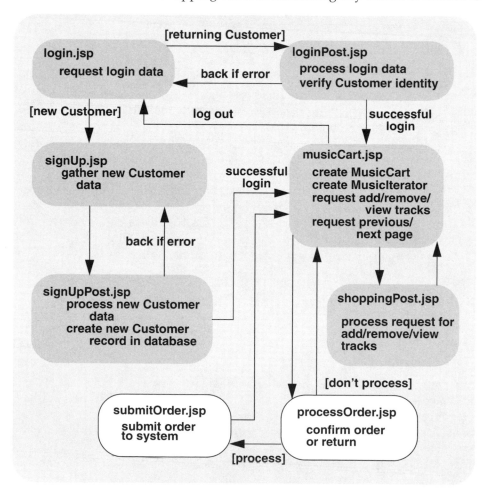

Figure 7–6 Relationship Among JSP Files After Adding the Ability to Process and Submit the Customer's Order

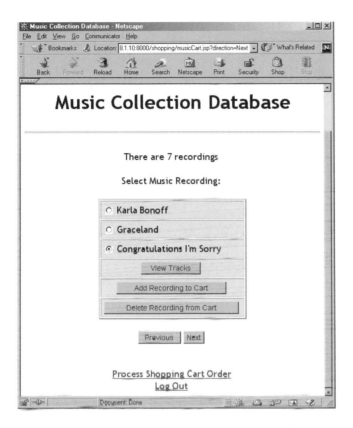

Figure 7–7 Screen Shot Showing the "Process Shopping Cart Order" Link

submit an order. The latter choice invokes JSP file **submitOrder.jsp**, which in turn invokes CustomerSession EJB business method `createOrder()`.

processOrder.jsp

Listing 7.23 shows the source for **processOrder.jsp**. After checking to make sure there's at least one item in the shopping cart, the program builds a table of the items and gives the customer a choice between submitting the order or not. It obtains the MusicCart EJB instance from the `session` object. Note that this program does not access the CustomerSession EJB. As is common with many JSP programs, the bulk of this code is presentation logic.

Figure 7–8 Screen Shot After Selecting the "Process Shopping Cart Order" Link

---

Listing 7.23 processOrder.jsp

```
<%--
  processOrder.jsp
--%>

<%--
  Use a page directive to import needed classes and
  packages for compilation. Specify "error.jsp"
  as the page's errorPage.
--%>

<%@ page import="MusicCart,CustomerVO,
RecordingVO,java.util.*, javax.naming.Context,
javax.naming.InitialContext,
javax.rmi.PortableRemoteObject" errorPage="error.jsp" %>
```

Listing 7.23 processOrder.jsp *(continued)*

```jsp
<%--
  Declare and initialize variables.
--%>

<%
  ArrayList shoppingList;
  String requestURI =
    (String)session.getValue("musicURL");
  MusicCart cart =
    (MusicCart)session.getValue("musicCart");
%>

<html>
<head>
<title>Music Collection Database Process Orders Page
</title>
</head>
<body bgcolor=white>
<center>
<h1>Process Orders Page</h1>
<hr>
<p>

<%
  shoppingList = cart.getShoppingList();

  // make sure the cart isn't empty
  if (shoppingList.size() == 0) {
    // it's empty, tell user
%>

<p STYLE="background:#e0e0e0;color:red;
font-weight:bold;border:double thin;padding:5">
Your shopping cart is currently empty.
</font>
<br><br><a href="<%= requestURI %>">Continue Shopping</a>

<%
  }
  else {
    // it's not empty, proceed
%>
```

Listing 7.23 processOrder.jsp *(continued)*

```
<table bgcolor="#e0e0e0" border=2 cellpadding=5>
<tr>
    <th>Current Shopping List for
        <%= cart.getCustomer().getName() %>
    </th>
</tr>

<%
    // Use a combination of scriptlet code,
    // html and JSP expressions to build the table
    Iterator i = shoppingList.iterator();
    while (i.hasNext()) {
      RecordingVO r = (RecordingVO)i.next();
%>
    <tr><td> <%= r.getTitle() %></td></tr>
<%
    } // end while
%>

</table>
<br><br><a href="<%= requestURI %>">
  Continue Shopping (Do Not Process Order)</a>
<br><br><a href="submitOrder.jsp">
  Submit Order</a>

<%
  } // end else
%>
</body></html>
```

---

submitOrder.jsp

If a customer chooses to submit their order, we invoke our next JSP program, **submitOrder.jsp** in Listing 7.24. Now access to the session facade is necessary, so the `jspInit()` method initializes the CustomerSession EJB. Variable `mysession` is shareable among all threads of **submitOrder.jsp**.

Next we obtain the shopping cart (MusicCart EJB) from the session object and build a table to display its contents. Before we build an `OrderVO` object, we make sure the shopping cart is not empty. For simplicity, we make the price of each recording the same (ten dollars). We invoke method `createOrder()` in CustomerSession EJB and then clear out the virtual shopping cart. At this point, the customer's orders have been submitted to the system (we've built the Order EJB and its related LineItem EJBs, and everything is written to persistent store).

Listing 7.24 submitOrder.jsp

```jsp
<%--
  submitOrder.jsp
--%>

<%--
  Use a page directive to import needed classes and
  packages for compilation. Specify "error.jsp"
  as the page's errorPage.
--%>

<%@ page import="OrderVO,MusicCart,RecordingVO,
OrderLocalHome,OrderLocal,CustomerSession,
CustomerSessionHome,CustomerVO,java.util.*,
javax.ejb.CreateException, javax.ejb.EJBException,
javax.naming.Context, javax.naming.InitialContext,
javax.rmi.PortableRemoteObject" errorPage="error.jsp" %>

<%!
  CustomerSession mysession = null;

  public void jspInit() {
    try {
      Context initial = new InitialContext();
      Object objref = initial.lookup(
          "java:comp/env/ejb/CustomerSession");
      CustomerSessionHome home = (CustomerSessionHome)
          PortableRemoteObject.narrow(
          objref, CustomerSessionHome.class);
      mysession = home.create();
    } catch (Exception ex) {
      System.out.println("Unexpected Exception: " +
          ex.getMessage());
    }
  }
%>
```

Listing 7.24 submitOrder.jsp *(continued)*

```
<%--
  Declare and initialize variables.
--%>

<%
  ArrayList shoppingList;
  String errorString = null;
  String requestURI =
    (String)session.getValue("musicURL");
  MusicCart cart =
    (MusicCart)session.getValue("musicCart");
%>

<html>
<head>
<title>Music Collection Database Submit Orders Page</title>
</head>
<body bgcolor=white>
<center>
<h1>Submit Orders Page</h1>
<hr>
<p>

<table bgcolor="#e0e0e0" border=2 cellpadding=5>
<tr>
<th>Current Shopping List for
<%= cart.getCustomer().getName() %></th>
</tr>
<%
  // Use a combination of scriptlet code,
  // html and JSP expressions to build the table
  shoppingList = cart.getShoppingList();
  Iterator i = shoppingList.iterator();
  while (i.hasNext()) {
    RecordingVO r = (RecordingVO)i.next();
%>

    <tr><td> <%= r.getTitle() %></td></tr>
<%
  }
%>
```

Listing 7.24 submitOrder.jsp *(continued)*

```
</table>
<p>
Thank you
  <%= cart.getCustomer().getName() %> for your order!

<%
  // Every item costs $10.00
  if (shoppingList.size() > 0) {
    try {
      OrderVO order = new OrderVO(
        shoppingList.size() * 10.0,
        OrderLocalHome.InProcess, new GregorianCalendar(),
        new GregorianCalendar(),
        cart.getCustomer().getName(),
        mysession.buildItems(shoppingList));
      mysession.createOrder(order);
      // clear the shopping list
      cart.clearShoppingList();

    } catch (Exception ex) {
      errorString = ex.getMessage();
    } // end catch handler
  }
  else {
    errorString = "Shopping cart is empty.";
  }

  if (errorString != null) {
%>

<p STYLE="background:#e0e0e0;color:red;
font-weight:bold;border:double thin;padding:5">
There was a problem submitting your order.
<%= errorString %>
</font>

<%
  }
%>

<br><br><a href="<%= requestURI %>">Continue Shopping</a>
</body></html>
```

7.5 Administrator Client

Once we deploy our enterprise application and folks visit the web site, they will create a lot of Customer EJBs, Order EJBs, and LineItem EJBs. An administrator client program is often handy for inspecting a growing database. We'd also like to test our beans as we develop the system, as well as check the integrity of the CMP and CMR fields managed by the container behind the scenes on our behalf.

AdminClient.java

To this end, we've written a stand-alone Java client (AdminClient) that we use to inspect our database. As we add features to the CustomerSession EJB, we can also add methods to this program to test any new business methods.

Our program simply instantiates a CustomerSession EJB and uses the bean to find all customers and print out their orders. However, you could easily expand this program to test other aspects of the system.

Listing 7.25 contains the source for **AdminClient.java**, our stand-alone Java test client.

Listing 7.25 AdminClient.java

```java
// AdminClient.java
import java.util.*;
import java.text.*;
import javax.naming.Context;
import javax.naming.InitialContext;
import javax.rmi.PortableRemoteObject;
import javax.ejb.CreateException;

public class AdminClient {

  public static void main(String[] args) {
    DecimalFormat money =
        new DecimalFormat("$###,###.00");
    SimpleDateFormat dateformat =
        new SimpleDateFormat("MMM dd, yyyy");

    try {
      Context initial = new InitialContext();
      Object objref = initial.lookup(
          "java:comp/env/ejb/CustomerSession");
```

Listing 7.25 AdminClient.java *(continued)*

```java
// Get a home interface object
CustomerSessionHome home = (CustomerSessionHome)
        PortableRemoteObject.narrow(objref,
        CustomerSessionHome.class);

CustomerSession mysession = home.create();
int count = mysession.getTotalCustomers();
System.out.println("Total customers in database = "
        + count);

// Get all the customers
Collection customers = mysession.getCustomers();
Iterator i = customers.iterator();

while (i.hasNext()) {
  CustomerVO cust = (CustomerVO)i.next();
  System.out.println(cust.getName() +
    "\t" + cust.getPassword() +
    "\t" + cust.getEmail());

  if (mysession.getOrdersPending(cust.getName())) {
  // print any orders associated with customer
    Collection orders =
            mysession.getOrders(cust.getName());

    if (orders.size() > 0) {
      System.out.println("Orders for Customer "
          + cust.getName());
    }
    Iterator t = orders.iterator();

    while (t.hasNext()) {
      OrderVO myorder = (OrderVO)t.next();
      System.out.println(
"\t" + money.format(myorder.getTotalAmount()) +
"\t" + dateformat.format(
        myorder.getOrderDate().getTime()) +
"\t" + dateformat.format(
        myorder.getShipDate().getTime()));
      Iterator items =
              myorder.getLineItems().iterator();
```

Listing 7.25 AdminClient.java *(continued)*

```
        while (items.hasNext()) {
          LineItemVO myItem =
              (LineItemVO) items.next();
          System.out.println("\t" + myItem.getTitle()
              + "\t" + myItem.getQuantity());
        }
      }
      System.out.println(
          "_____\n");
      }
    }

  } catch (Exception ex) {
    System.err.println(
          "Caught an unexpected exception." );
    System.err.println(ex.getMessage());
  } finally {
    System.exit(0);
  }
  }
} // AdminClient
```

We package this program as an application client. To run the program, we use the `runclient` utility under the Sun Microsystems reference implementation as follows.

$ **runclient -client OrderCMPApp.ear -name AdminClient**

Here's some sample output on the client screen. The output shows what you might see after manipulating the web component to create several customers and orders.

```
Total customers in database = 4
tess        clare           tess@asgteach.com
_____

lydia       benoni          lydia@asgteach.com
Orders for Customer lydia
  $10.00   Dec 22, 2001   Dec 22, 2001
  Rites of Passage                      1
_____
```

```
morpheus   neo              morpheus@matrix.com
Orders for Customer morpheus
   $30.00   Dec 22, 2001   Dec 22, 2001
   Imagine                                    1
   Congratulations I'm Sorry                  1
   Sgt. Pepper's Lonely Hearts Club Band      2
   _____


capitola   black            cap@asgteach.com
Orders for Customer capitola
   $20.00   Dec 22, 2001   Dec 22, 2001
   Orff: Carmina Burana                       1
   Sgt. Pepper's Lonely Hearts Club Band      1
   _____
```

7.6 Design Guidelines and Patterns

Along with CMP entity beans, we've also introduced entity beans that maintain relationships with other entity beans. With the EJB 2.0 specification, it is possible to implement these relationship fields with container-managed relationships (CMR). Let's review the design elements and patterns that characterize the enterprise application presented in this chapter.

Using CMP

Container-managed persistence adds portability to systems because bean developers do not have to write database access code. Compared to BMP, the amount of bean implementation code shrinks when using CMP. This is largely due to declarative information in the deployment descriptor, which allows the container to generate implementation code. The container also generates code from the abstract access methods used to define CMP and CMR fields.

Local Interfaces

Local interfaces change the way a bean developer designs entity beans. Without local interfaces, the fine-grained access methods for both persistent fields and relationship fields would quickly clog network throughput. Therefore, bean developers would be forced to use coarse-grained value objects to get and set entity bean data. Related entity beans would become dependent objects. For example, the LineItem EJB would be a candidate to be "demoted" to a dependent object of the Order EJB.

With local interfaces, we create entity beans that mirror the underlying database. We use fine-grained setters and getters to access the persistent data fields as well as the relationship fields. The design and implementation is more straightforward. The coarse-grained and dependent objects are artifacts of the overhead involved with remote access to entity beans. The bean developer benefits greatly from this enhancement to the EJB specification.

Transactions

The principals of transaction management from the previous chapter apply equivalently to CMP entity beans. We make our create, finder, and business methods execute within a transaction (again through declarative statements in the deployment descriptor). In addition, the business methods of the session facade session bean execute within a transaction. Thus, the multistep process of creating orders or customers is treated as a single unit of work (atomicity).

Session Facade Pattern

In the previous chapter, we presented a single entity bean, Customer EJB. We showed the importance of creating a session facade to isolate the entity bean from general remote clients. The same factors that motivate this design pattern apply to the triad of entity beans we developed in this chapter. In fact, the motivation is greater. Not only do we simplify access to all three entity beans, but we manage the relationships between the entity beans within the session facade. (Thus, the session facade collects all the necessary information to create an Order EJB, including the customer information passed to the Order EJB's create() method.) The session facade implements the business rules that govern the business processes of our system. The entity beans implement the maintenance of the business data.

Value Object Pattern

Once again the value object pattern conveniently bundles data for transmission between remote clients and the session facade. Value objects are "coarse-grained" data containers that simplify the interface between the session facade and the remote client. Note that we do not use value objects between the session facade and the entity beans, but instead use the fine-grained accessor methods with local interfaces.

Administrative Client

In the previous chapter we created an entity bean test program. In this chapter, we create a stand-alone Java client that manipulates the CustomerSession EJB. This program invokes business methods of the session facade to inspect the underlying data that remote clients create through JSP web components. It is always useful to create such a remote client along with a web component client. The Administrator Client can also perform consistency checks on the database.

7.7   Key Point Summary

This chapter not only introduces container-managed persistence (CMP), but it also stresses the importance of relationships between entity beans. Entity bean structure is similar, whether you're using CMP or BMP. However, with CMP, the container generates code based on abstract access methods and declarative information provided by the bean developer during deployment.

Here are the key points from this chapter.

- Entity beans model business data. Each entity bean in general maps to a corresponding row in a database.
- Entity beans have a unique primary key that maps to the underlying database primary key.
- If CMP entity beans are related (for example, the Customer EJB is related to zero or more Order EJBs), then we use container-managed relationship (CMR) fields to implement associations. With BMP, the bean developer must define and persist the relationship field. With CMP, the bean developer defines abstract access methods to "virtual" relationship fields, and the container persists the relationship data.
- Bean developers define an abstract schema which specifies CMP and CMR fields of an entity bean. The bean developer may access the abstract schema to define queries for database select methods.
- Bean developers define abstract access methods to an entity bean's CMP and CMR fields inside the bean implementation class.
- The bean implementation class of a CMP entity bean is always abstract.
- The multiplicity of an entity bean defines the number of beans associated with a related bean. Multiplicity can be one to one, one to many, many to one, and many to many. We define many to mean either one or more or zero or more. We define one to mean exactly one and optional to be zero or one.
- Relationship navigability can be one-way or two-way. Two-way navigation implies that you may access one entity bean from another in either direction (for example, you can obtain Order EJBs from a Customer EJB and vice versa). One-way navigation means that you may find a related entity bean in one direction only.

- To implement two-way (bidirectional) navigation, you define abstract access methods to the relationship field in both related entity beans. One-way (unidirectional) navigation means that you do not define abstract access methods in one class of the relationship.
- In two-way navigation, if you initialize or update a CMR field, the container initializes or updates the associated CMR field on the "other" end of the association for you (within the current transaction).
- The life cycle of entity bean relationships affects how we set or initialize relationship fields. For example, when creating an Order EJB, we initialize its `customer` CMR field during the create process. In contrast, when we create a Customer EJB, we do not yet have any Order EJBs to initialize the `orders` CMR field.
- Use `ejbPostCreate()` to initialize a CMR field during the create process. You cannot use `ejbCreate()` to access CMR fields because the entity bean is not yet fully instantiated.
- Cascading deletes apply to an entity bean that cannot exist by itself. For example, an Order EJB cannot exist without a related Customer EJB. Thus, when Customer EJB is removed, its related Order EJBs must also be deleted. You specify which relationships require cascading deletes in the deployment descriptor.
- You cannot apply cascading deletes to the "one" end of a one-to-many relationship. For example, we cannot specify that Customer EJB should be deleted when one (or more) of its related "many" Order EJBs are deleted.
- The EJB 2.0 specification includes an EJB Query Language. The EJB QL is a portable way for bean developers to specify how the container should generate SQL queries for custom finder and select methods.
- Like BMP entity beans, CMP entity beans have finder methods. CMP finder methods are generated by the EJB container from declarative information provided by the bean developer. The container generates the `findByPrimaryKey()` method using the persistent data field that corresponds to the bean's primary key. It generates the custom finder methods by interpreting the EJB QL queries provided by the bean developer in the deployment descriptor.
- Bean developers may define select methods to implement business methods that depend on custom database select statements. The EJB container generates code for `ejbSelectXXX()` methods by interpreting the EJB QL queries provided by the bean developer in the deployment descriptor.

- The Session Facade Pattern simplifies the client interface to our triad of entity beans and implements the business rules that apply to these entity beans. The session facade bean also helps maintain entity bean relationships. Finally, the session facade bean accesses the entity beans with local interfaces, allowing access to fine-grain setters and getters without a performance penalty.

MESSAGE-DRIVEN BEANS

Chapter 8

The previous chapters showed you how to design session and entity beans with business methods. When clients call these business methods, each caller blocks (or waits) until the method completes. Although this synchronous behavior certainly works well with many applications, it can become a problem with clients who cannot afford to wait around for lengthy business methods to complete their jobs. In situations like this, we need another way for clients to perform enterprise tasks without waiting.

The Java Message Service (JMS) allows objects to communicate with other objects asynchronously (no waiting). In this chapter we'll present an overview of JMS followed by a discussion of *message-driven beans*. You'll learn how to design a message-driven bean, how to send and receive messages with the bean, and why message-driven beans are important to enterprise programming. You'll also understand how to use message-driven beans with client applications and Enterprise JavaBeans.

8.1 Messaging Architectures

Let's begin with a discussion of how one might send data between clients in an enterprise application. Consider the architecture shown in Figure 8–1. All clients are tightly coupled. This arrangement makes each client aware of other clients in a many-to-many relationship. In a Remote Procedure Call (RPC)

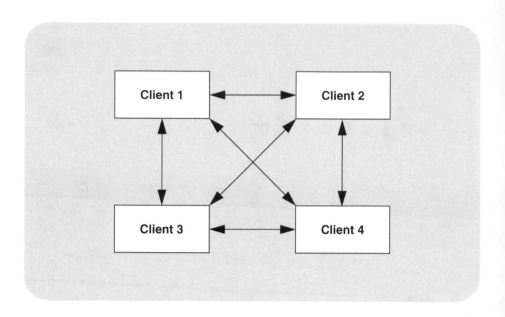

Figure 8–1 Synchronous Architecture

environment (such as Java RMI), each business method represents a call which may be remote across a network. Because these calls are synchronous, the client's thread blocks and cannot proceed until the business method completes.

Tightly coupled RPC architectures can have problems. If one client goes down, the effect can easily ripple through the system and make other clients wait for their synchronous calls to complete (which may never happen). In general, most client failures will have an immediate impact on the system. Perhaps the biggest problem with this arrangement is that it is difficult to administer. All clients must be informed if you add or delete another client, and upgrades to the system affect each client separately.

Figure 8–2 shows a loosely coupled architecture where clients send messages asynchronously through a message server. This hub-and-spoke arrangement represents a more flexible architecture for many enterprise applications. Instead of sending data directly from one client to another, the data is sent to a *destination* managed by a message server. Although we show only a single message server here, the centralized server is often implemented as a cluster of fault-tolerant machines. If one of the servers goes down, another server in the cluster can continue to handle client requests. In an asynchronous architecture, clients communicate only with a message server. Each client, therefore, is decoupled from the other clients in the system.

Loosely coupled architectures with a centralized message server have several advantages. Clients only see the message server; hence, they can be added

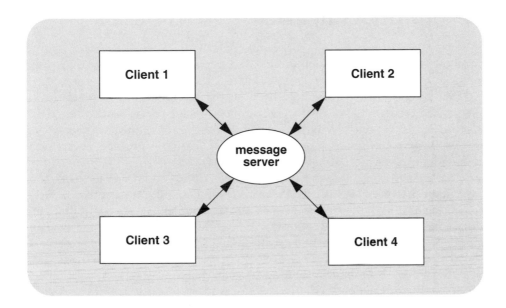

Figure 8–2 Asynchronous Architecture

or removed with minimal impact to the system. Data sent from a client does not require an immediate response from another application. Guaranteed delivery is also possible with a ***store-and-forward*** mechanism. This means that the message server saves a message in persistent storage if it is intended for a client that is temporarily down or unavailable. When the intended client comes back up, the message server delivers the message data automatically.

There are many examples of systems that use a loosely coupled architecture with a central message server. A stock quote system, for example, could broadcast stock quotes as asynchronous messages to any client that wants to be informed periodically. In a Business-to-Business (B2B) system, messaging allows business subsystems (accounting, inventory, sales, etc.) to communicate with each other without having to be tightly integrated. And with the worldwide web, messaging offers a safe and secure way to transmit data around the globe.

Although decentralized architectures with different server protocols are certainly possible with enterprise messaging, we will focus on the Java Message Service (JMS) in this chapter. JMS is part of the J2EE platform and works well with the hub-and-spoke architecture that we've shown you. Although JMS is a big subject by itself, we'll present an overview of JMS, so that you'll understand how to use it with message-driven beans.

8.2   Introducing JMS

If you are already familiar with the Java Message Service (JMS), you can skip this section.

JMS is a vendor-independent API that can be used on the J2EE platform for enterprise messaging. JMS abstracts access to message servers much like JDBC and JNDI abstract access to databases and naming services, respectively. When you use JMS for enterprise messaging, your application is portable and vendor independent with different message service providers.

Before we show you JMS programming, let's define some JMS terms. A Java application that uses JMS is a *JMS client*. The messaging system that handles the routing and delivery of messages is a *JMS provider*. A JMS client that generates a message is a *producer* and a JMS client that receives a message is a *consumer*. A JMS client can be both a provider (sender) and a consumer (receiver).

With JMS, a client sends a message asynchronously to a *destination*. JMS has two types of destinations: *topic* and *queue*. When a JMS client sends a message to a topic or queue, the client does not wait for a reply. The JMS provider is responsible for routing, and delivering the messages to the appropriate consumer. Providers are not dependent on consumers, and clients that send messages are decoupled from the clients that receive them.

Messaging Domains

How does the JMS provider know where to send messages? In JMS, a *message domain* defines how the JMS provider routes and delivers messages. There are two ways to set up message routing in a JMS message domain: *publish/subscribe* and *point-to-point*. You'll often hear the shorter terms "pub/sub" and "PTP" used for these message domains. Since choosing the right message domain is an important step in designing robust JMS applications and message-driven beans, let's discuss each one separately and show you how to apply them.

Publish/Subscribe

Figure 8–3 shows the two JMS messaging domains. The top half illustrates pub/sub messaging. This model applies to a *one-to-many* broadcast of messages. Think of it like a magazine publisher with a list of subscribers. A single publisher sends one message to *all* subscribers who register to be notified when a message is sent. Every subscriber receives a copy of the message.

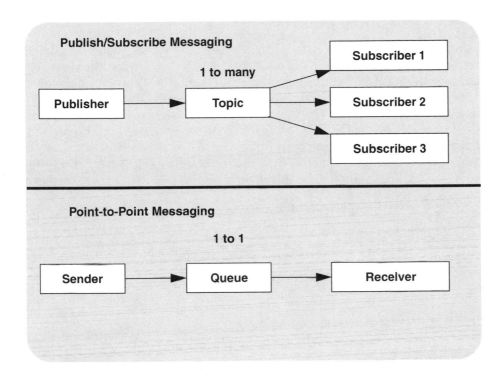

Figure 8–3 JMS Messaging Domains

Pub/sub messaging is a *push model*, which means that the JMS provider automatically broadcasts messages to consumers. This is an important aspect of publish/subscribe messaging, because it means that subscribers do not have to poll for messages or ask to receive them. Note that pub/sub messaging uses a *topic* destination for sending and receiving messages.

Point-to-Point

The lower half of Figure 8–3 illustrates PTP messaging. This model applies to a *one-to-one* conversation between a sender and a receiver. Think of it like a telephone call between two people. A sender transmits a message to *one* receiver who wants to listen. If there are multiple receivers, only one receiver gets the message (typically the first receiver that reads it).

Point-to-point messaging is a *pull model*, meaning that consumers must request messages from the JMS provider. This implies that PTP messaging guarantees that only one consumer will process each message. Note that PTP messaging uses a *queue* destination for sending and receiving messages.

JMS Building Blocks

JMS requires quite a few objects to make everything work. There are administrative objects (such as topic or queue destinations and connection factories), message producers and consumers, connections, and the messages themselves. Figure 8–4 shows these building blocks and how they relate to each other. This diagram augments the following sections as we explain in more detail the responsibilities of each object. Destinations (topic or queue) and the Connection Factory objects are created and maintained administratively by the J2EE application server. JMS clients access them through the JNDI Initial Context lookup. We shade them to show this difference. The other objects are created as indicated in the diagram.

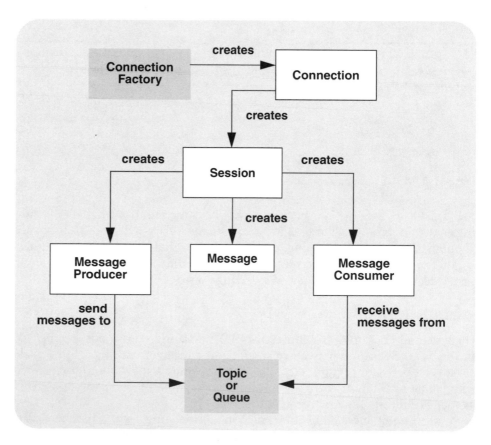

Figure 8–4 JMS Building Blocks

Topic Messaging

With pub/sub messaging, the publisher and subscriber send and receive messages through a *topic* destination managed by the JMS provider. Producers use a topic to publish messages, and subscribers use the topic to consume them. Remember that subscribers receive messages automatically after registering to listen, and each subscriber to a topic receives its own copy of the message that was published to that topic. You may add or remove subscribers and publishers dynamically at runtime, and a single message from one publisher can be sent to thousands of subscribers.

Let's go through the steps to create a topic destination and publish a message. We'll also show you how to receive messages from the topic destination. Table 8.1 shows the JMS objects required to publish and subscribe to topic destinations.

Table 8.1 JMS Objects Required for Topic Messaging

Object	How Created/ Initialized	Description
TopicConnection Factory	Initial Context	Used to obtain a TopicConnection
Topic	Initial Context	Destination/source for messages
TopicConnection	TopicConnection Factory	Connects to JMS provider
TopicSession	TopicConnection	Creates messages, publishers, and subscribers
TopicPublisher	TopicSession	Publishes messages "about" Topic
Message	TopicSession	Actual message
TopicSubscriber	TopicSession	Receives message "about" Topic

TopicConnectionFactory and Topic

The first step is to create a JMS connection factory object. After obtaining the context, a successful lookup of the JNDI name returns a TopicConnectionFactory object, as follows.

```
InitialContext jndi = new InitialContext();

TopicConnectionFactory factory =
    (TopicConnectionFactory)jndi.lookup
        ("java:comp/env/jms/MyTopicConnectionFactory");
```

This is the object we will use to make the actual connection to the JMS provider. Note that `TopicConnectionFactory` is similar to the JDBC `DataSource` object, which is used to connect to a database.

A topic destination is necessary for the message we intend to publish. This is also done with a JNDI lookup, which returns a `Topic` object.

```
Topic topic = (Topic)jndi.lookup
        ("java:comp/env/jms/MyTopic");
```

Design Guideline

When the JMS software detects a problem, it throws a JMSException. Therefore, you must either place JMS code inside a try block or within a method that includes JMSException in its throws *clause.*

TopicConnection and TopicSession

Once you have a `TopicConnectionFactory` object, you can connect to the JMS provider.

```
TopicConnection con = factory.createTopicConnection();
```

Next, you create a `TopicSession` object if the connection is successful.

```
TopicSession session = con.createTopicSession(false,
        Session.AUTO_ACKNOWLEDGE);
```

The `createTopicSession()` method has two arguments. The first argument is a boolean that determines whether transaction is enabled for the session or not. The second argument specifies the acknowledgement mode. As you will see later, the EJB container manages the transaction and acknowledgment modes for session objects; hence, we show only typical initial values here.

The `TopicSession` object is important because it's used to create messages, publishers, and subscribers. Typically, you'll have only one object in a single thread program, because sending and receiving messages is usually done with the same thread that creates the `TopicSession` object. It is possible, however, to create separate `TopicSession` objects in the same thread or with each thread in a multithreading application.

A `TopicConnection` object has `start()`, `stop()`, and `close()` methods to help JMS clients manage the connection. Consumers should call `start()` when ready to receive messages. The `stop()` method prevents new messages from being received until `start()` is called again.

Make sure you always close a topic connection when you are finished with the session. This makes the connection resource available to other clients, since the JMS provider maintains a pool of topic connections.

```
TopicConnection con = factory.createTopicSession();
. . .
con.start();      // start connection
. , .
con.close();      // close connection
```

TopicPublisher (Producer Side)

Now that we have a JMS connection and a session object, we create a publisher to send messages to a topic destination.

```
Topic topic = (Topic)jndi.lookup
      ("java:comp/env/jms/MyTopic");
TopicSession session = con.createTopicSession(false,
      Session.AUTO_ACKNOWLEDGE);
TopicPublisher publisher =
      session.createPublisher(topic);
```

To create a topic publisher with the `createPublisher()` method, we call it with a `TopicSession` object (`session`) and pass a `Topic` destination (`topic`) as an argument. The topic is determined by a JNDI lookup.

Message Types

Ok, we have a publisher, now what? It's time for the publisher to send a message to the topic destination. JMS has several different message types, but here's the simplest, a text message.

```
TextMessage textMsg = session.createTextMessage();
textMsg.setText("World Series Tickets for sale");
publisher.publish(textMsg);
```

All JMS messages are Java objects with a header and a message body. The header contains metadata, and the message body is data of a specific JMS type. JMS provides a wide variety of different types that apply to most applications. Five message types are available: TextMessage, StreamMessage, MapMessage, ObjectMessage, and BytesMessage. All are interface types extended from a generic Message interface.

We've already seen a TextMessage example, so let's look at the other JMS message types now. The following example is MapMessage, which handles key-value pairs. Here we use it to publish someone's e-mail address.

```
MapMessage mapMsg = session.createMapMessage();
mapMsg.setString("Robert", "BillyBob@company.com");
publisher.publish(mapMsg);
```

The StreamMessage type is handy for working with different types.

```
String name = "Bob"; int age = 25; float weight = 165;
StreamMessage streamMsg = session.createStreamMessage();
streamMsg.writeString(name);
streamMsg.writeInt(age);
streamMsg.writeFloat(weight);
publisher.publish(streamMsg);
```

Consumers need to read the data types from a StreamMessage in the same order they were written.

The ObjectMessage type handles Java serializable objects. Here we use it to publish a RecordingVO object from our Music Collection Database (see "RecordingVO Class" on page 96).

```
// albums is an ArrayList of RecordingVO objects
RecordingVO rec = (RecordingVO)albums.get(2);
ObjectMessage objectMsg = session.createObjectMessage();
objectMsg.setObject(rec);
publisher.publish(objectMsg);
```

The BytesMessage type is useful for byte-oriented data.

```
byte[] data = { 10, 20, 30, 40 };
BytesMessage byteMsg = session.createBytesMessage();
byteMsg.writeBytes(data);
publisher.publish(byteMsg);
```

JMS messages have acknowledgment modes and can be prioritized and time stamped. Messages do not expire by default, although you can assign an expiration time to a message if you want to. Likewise, a JMS message is *persistent* by default, which means a message cannot get lost. If the JMS provider fails, the message will be delivered after the server recovers. You can make a message's delivery mode nonpersistent, but there's no guarantee that the message will be delivered if the JMS provider fails.

TopicSubscriber (Consumer Side)

Messages aren't very useful if no one is around to receive them. Here's how a consumer subscribes to a topic destination.

```
Topic topic = (Topic)jndi.lookup
        ("java:comp/env/jms/MyTopic");
TopicSession receiver = con.createTopicSession(false,
        Session.AUTO_ACKNOWLEDGE);
TopicSubscriber subscriber =
        receiver.createSubscriber(topic);
```

To create a topic subscriber with the createSubscriber() method, we call it with a TopicSession object (receiver) and pass a Topic destination (topic) as an argument. Note that a topic subscriber would use the same JNDI lookup name as a topic publisher.

One important aspect of pub/sub messaging is that if a message is sent to a topic and a subscriber has disconnected from the JMS provider, the subscriber will *not* receive the message unless it has been set up with a *durable subscription*. If a durable subscriber is unavailable, the JMS provider saves all messages for that topic and redelivers them when the durable subscriber reconnects.

Design Guideline

A persistent message is not enough with topics and pub/sub messaging. To guarantee delivery and implement true store-and-forward messaging, a topic subscriber should be created with a durable subscription.

Here's how to create a durable subscriber.

```
TopicSubscriber subscriber =
        receiver.createDurableSubscriber(topic, "News");
```

The createDurableSubscriber() method is called with a TopicSession object (receiver). Its first argument is a topic destination, and the second argument is a subscription name. This string name can be useful in administrative tools that track the status of durable subscriptions.

Durable subscribers are very important to receivers who may not be able to stay connected to JMS servers all the time but still have to receive messages when they reconnect.

The onMessage() Method

All that's left is to show you how to receive messages. Suppose one client publishes a topic text message to another client, as shown in Figure 8–5. Client1, acting as a topic publisher, looks up the JNDI topic name, connects to the JMS server, and sends a message to the topic destination. Client2, acting as a topic subscriber, connects to the JMS server with the same JNDI lookup name as Client1. Client2, however, has to be set up properly to receive the message.

In JMS, both pub/sub and PTP messaging support a Java event model for handling incoming messages. This event mechanism is similar to what is used in Java applets and JavaBeans. Basically, a client class implements the MessageListener interface and registers itself with the TopicSubscriber object. The receiving client class must define an onMessage() method to handle incoming messages from the topic.

When a message is sent to a topic, the TopicSubscriber object calls the onMessage() method in any MessageListener object registered with the subscriber. This registration is typically done in the client constructor after creating the subscriber object.

The following skeletal code shows how all this is done for a text message.

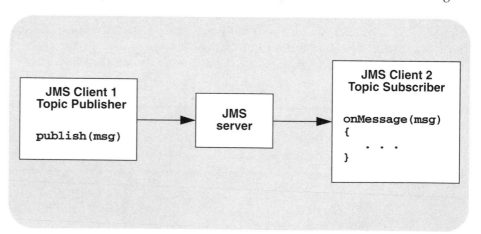

Figure 8–5 The onMessage() Method

```
import javax.jms.*;
public class Client2 implements MessageListener {

  public Class2() {
    try {
      . . .
      TopicSubscriber subscriber =
          receiver.createSubscriber(topic);
      subscriber.setMessageListener(this);
    }
    catch (JMSException ex) { . . . }
  }

  public void onMessage(Message message) {
    try {
      TextMessage msg = (TextMessage)message;
      String text = msg.getText();
      System.out.println(text);
    } catch (JMSException ex) { . . . }
  }
  . . .
}
```

Because Client2 implements the MessageListener interface, we must provide an onMessage() method in the Client2 class. To register with the subscriber, the constructor calls setMessageListener(this) with a TopicSubscriber object. Inside onMessage(), we print the message received as a string.

Queue Messaging

A message *queue* implements the point-to-point messaging model in JMS. Queues are similar to topics, except that a queue is a one-to-one connection rather than a one-to-many broadcast. Although JMS queues can perform synchronous messaging, we will discuss only how to send and receive messages asynchronously here. Remember that each message is guaranteed to be delivered to only one receiver.

Design Guideline

Messages delivered to a queue remain in the JMS server, even if a consumer is not connected. The JMS server delivers the message to the consumer when they reconnect. Note that this behavior is different from topics, which do not guarantee a message delivery unless the receiver is a durable subscriber.

Working with queues is similar to working with topics. Table 8.2 shows the JMS objects required to send and receive queue messages.

Table 8.2 JMS Objects Required for Queue Messaging

Object	How Created/ Initialized	Description
QueueConnection Factory	Initial Context	Used to obtain a QueueConnection
Queue	Initial Context	Destination/source for messages
QueueConnection	QueueConnection Factory	Connects to JMS provider
QueueSession	QueueConnection	Creates messages, senders, and receivers
QueueSender	QueueSession	Sends messages "to" Queue
Message	QueueSession	Actual message
QueueReceiver	QueueSession	Receives message "from" Queue

There is a QueueConnectionFactory object for the JNDI lookup name that connects to the JMS provider, and a QueueConnection object to create QueueSession objects. A QueueSession object can create QueueSender and QueueReceiver objects to deliver messages or receive messages from a queue. This is similar in concept to the TopicPublisher and TopicSubscriber objects in pub/sub messaging.

To demonstrate how point-to-point messaging is done with queues, let's examine a program that sends a text message to itself. This program could presumably be used to verify that a JMS server is operating properly. Listing 8.1 shows the program (**PingServerApp.java**). The example combines the separate steps for defining the producer and consumer that we showed you earlier with topics, only we use a queue for the messaging. (This example uses JMS, but it is not a message-driven bean.)

Listing 8.1 PingServerApp.java

```
// PingServerApp.java - JMS Message Queues
import java.io.*;
import javax.jms.*;
import javax.naming.*;
```

Listing 8.1 PingServerApp.java *(continued)*

```java
public class PingServerApp implements MessageListener {
  private QueueConnection connect = null;
  private QueueSession sender, receiver;
  private QueueSender qsender;
  private QueueReceiver qreceiver;

  public PingServerApp() {
    try {
      // Setup required by both JMS consumers & producers
      InitialContext jndi = new InitialContext();

      QueueConnectionFactory factory =
        (QueueConnectionFactory)jndi.lookup
        ("java:comp/env/jms/MyQueueConnectionFactory");
      connect = factory.createQueueConnection();
      Queue queue = (Queue)jndi.lookup
        ("java:comp/env/jms/MyQueue");

      // JMS producer setup
      sender = connect.createQueueSession(false,
          Session.AUTO_ACKNOWLEDGE);
      qsender = sender.createSender(queue);

      // JMS consumer setup
      receiver = connect.createQueueSession(false,
          Session.AUTO_ACKNOWLEDGE);
      qreceiver = receiver.createReceiver(queue);
      qreceiver.setMessageListener(this);
      connect.start();

    } catch (Exception ex) {
      ex.printStackTrace();
      System.exit(1);
    }
  }

  public void sendMessage(String message) {
    try {
      TextMessage msg = sender.createTextMessage();
      msg.setText(message);
      qsender.send(msg);
      System.out.println("Sent message: " + message);
```

Listing 8.1 PingServerApp.java *(continued)*

```java
    } catch (Exception ex) {
      ex.printStackTrace();
    }
  }

  public void onMessage(Message message) {
    try {
      TextMessage msg = (TextMessage)message;
      String text = msg.getText();
      System.out.println("Received message: " + text);
    } catch (Exception ex) {
      ex.printStackTrace();
    }
  }

  public void exit() {
    try {
      if (connect != null)
        connect.close();
    } catch (Exception ex) {
      ex.printStackTrace();
      System.exit(1);
    }
    System.exit(0);
  }

  public static void main(String args[]) {
    PingServerApp ping = new PingServerApp();
    try {
      BufferedReader stdin = new
        BufferedReader(new InputStreamReader(System.in));

      while (true) {
        System.out.println("type quit to exit");
        ping.sendMessage("Test Message");
        String cmd = stdin.readLine();
        if (cmd.equals("quit"))
          ping.exit();
      }
```

Listing 8.1 PingServerApp.java *(continued)*

```
    } catch (Exception ex) {
        ex.printStackTrace();
    }
  }
}
```

In the constructor, JNDI lookups yield the QueueConnectionFactory and Queue objects for connecting to the JMS provider with a queue destination. After creating separate QueueSession objects (sender and receiver), the constructor attaches the same queue to the sender and receiver objects (qsender and qreceiver). Note that PingServerApp implements the MessageListener interface and registers itself as a listener with the qreceiver object. This means we'll need an onMessage() method in PingServerApp to receive messages.

The main() method creates an instance of PingServerApp to send and receive messages. Inside the while loop, we send a text string message to ourself. The readLine() method blocks program execution until the user types input followed by a return. When a messages arrives, the event handler invokes method onMessage(). The exit() method terminates the program when the user types "quit". Otherwise, the message is sent again in the loop.

The sendMessage() method creates a TextMessage from its string argument and sends the message via the qsender object. When it's available by the JMS provider, the onMessage() method receives the message and converts it to a String for display. The exit() method closes the queue connection.

JMS Deployment Descriptors

Listing 8.2 shows the deployment descriptor for our application client (PingServerApp), which uses JMS resources.

Listing 8.2 Deployment Descriptor for PingServerApp

```xml
<application-client>
  <display-name>PingServerApp</display-name>
  <resource-ref>
     <res-ref-name>jms/MyQueueConnectionFactory
     </res-ref-name>
     <res-type>javax.jms.QueueConnectionFactory
     </res-type>
     <res-auth>Container</res-auth>
     <res-sharing-scope>Shareable</res-sharing-scope>
  </resource-ref>
```

Listing 8.2 Deployment Descriptor for PingServerApp *(continued)*

```
  <resource-env-ref>
     <resource-env-ref-name>jms/MyQueue
     </resource-env-ref-name>
     <resource-env-ref-type>javax.jms.Queue
     </resource-env-ref-type>
  </resource-env-ref>
</application-client>
```

The `<resource-ref>` for the JMS `QueueConnectionFactory` specifies a JNDI name, interface type, and container authorization for the resource. This format makes the descriptor similar to a JDBC `DataSource`. Likewise, the `<resource-env-ref>` specifies a JNDI name and type for the `Queue` used by the program. The deployer maps the JMS `QueueConnectionFactory` and `Queue` elements to JMS factory and queue objects at deployment time.

8.3 Designing Message-Driven Beans

Now that we've introduced you to JMS, let's learn about message-driven beans. Simply put, a message-driven bean is an asynchronous *consumer* of JMS messages. Message-driven beans are stateless, server-side, transaction-aware components that receive messages from a JMS topic or queue. Like stateless session beans, message-driven beans do not store conversational state. They do not have a home or remote interface, nor do they have any business methods.

Figure 8–6 shows how a client interacts with a message-driven bean. When a message is sent from the client to a topic or queue destination in the JMS server, the EJB container fetches a bean instance from the message-driven bean pool. The container reads the message from the destination and calls the bean's `onMessage()` method with the message as an argument. The `onMessage()` method can then act on the message, since this is the data from the client.

Note that the EJB container acts as a message receiver. To do this, the container performs all the consumer-side steps we showed you in our earlier discussion of JMS message processing. First, the container connects to the JMS server and associates the bean with the same topic or queue destination that was used by the client. Next, it creates a `TopicSubscriber` or `QueueReceiver` to receive the message. Finally, the container registers the message listener and sets the message acknowledgment mode. The fact that the container does all this setup work is a major advantage for message-bean developers.

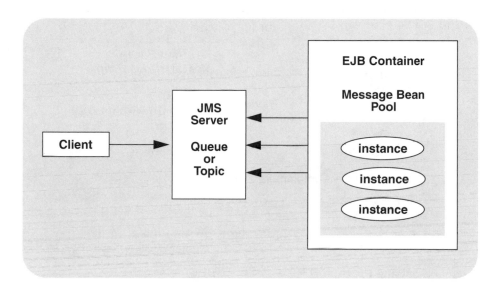

Figure 8–6 Message-Driven Bean, JMS, and EJB Container Architecture

There is another reason why message-driven beans are appealing. Because a message-driven bean is stateless, bean pool instances can concurrently consume hundreds, even thousands of messages delivered to the bean. This makes message-driven beans highly scalable. Message-driven beans can also forward tasks to other beans when they receive messages and model business processes by accessing database resources.

Let's take you through all the steps you'll need to know to apply message-driven beans to an enterprise design. We'll begin with how to create a message-driven bean.

Message Bean Structure

A message-driven bean is very simple to implement. Figure 8–7 shows the approach for a message bean called MusicMessageBean. This bean class implements two interfaces: MessageListener and MessageDrivenBean. The Music-MessageBean class, therefore, must provide implementations for ejbCreate(), ejbRemove(), setMessageDrivenContext(), and onMessage(). (The ejbCreate() method is required for a message bean, but is not inherited from either interface.) Note that the container does not invoke these methods as a result of client calls through either a home or remote interface; message beans do not have home or remote interfaces like session and entity beans. In particular, the EJB container calls the onMessage() method in the bean when a message arrives at a specific topic or queue destination.

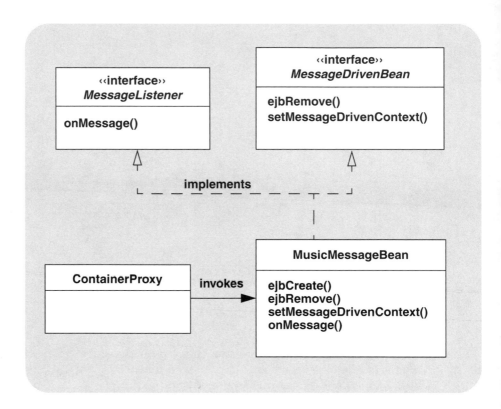

Figure 8–7 Class Diagram Showing the EJB Classes for a Message-Driven Bean

Now let's look at how we might apply these methods to the design of the MusicMessageBean, which reads data from a Music database. The idea is that clients send SQL select statements to the message bean, which the bean uses to access the database. Listing 8.3 shows the partial source code for **MusicMessageBean.java**.

Listing 8.3 MusicMessageBean.java

```
public class MusicMessageBean implements
    MessageListener, MessageDrivenBean {

    private Connection connect = null;
    private DataSource ds;
```

Listing 8.3 MusicMessageBean.java *(continued)*

```java
public void
setMessageDrivenContext(MessageDrivenContext mdc) { }

public void ejbCreate() {
  String dbName = "java:comp/env/jdbc/MusicDB";
  try {
    InitialContext jndi = new InitialContext();
    ds = (DataSource)jndi.lookup(dbName);
    . . .
  } catch (Exception ex) { . . . }
}

public void ejbRemove() { }

public void onMessage(Message message) {
  PreparedStatement stmt = null;
  ResultSet rs = null;
  try {
    TextMessage msg = (TextMessage)message;
    String selectQuery = msg.getText();
    connect = ds.getConnection();
    stmt = connect.prepareStatement(selectQuery);
    rs = stmt.executeQuery();
    . . .
  } catch (Exception ex) { . . .
  } finally {
    if (connect != null) connect.close();
    . . .
  }
}
}
```

In `ejbCreate()`, we obtain the `DataSource` object from the initial context. Inside `onMessage()`, we use the incoming message as an SQL select query String. A JDBC prepared statement uses this query command to read the database into a result set. Consistent with our other JDBC examples, we obtain a database connection only right before accessing the database, and release it in the `finally` block when we're finished.

The argument to `setMessageDrivenContext()` is analogous to the session and entity context classes.

Design Guideline

Note that receiving a message within a Message Bean is much simpler than using vanilla JMS. With JMS, we must connect to the message queue or topic, create the message receiver or subscriber, and register the object that implements MessageListener. With a Message Bean, the EJB container performs these steps for you.

Message Bean Life Cycle

It's important to understand the life cycle of a message-driven bean so that your bean is designed properly. Figure 8–8 is a sequence diagram that describes the life cycle of a message-driven bean. This is another way of looking at the state diagram that we showed you in Chapter 2 (see Figure 2–7 on page 28).

A message-driven bean has only two states: a *Does Not Exist* state and a *Ready* state. The container creates an instance of a message bean, which begins in the *Does Not Exist* state. To transition to the *Ready* state, the sequence dia-

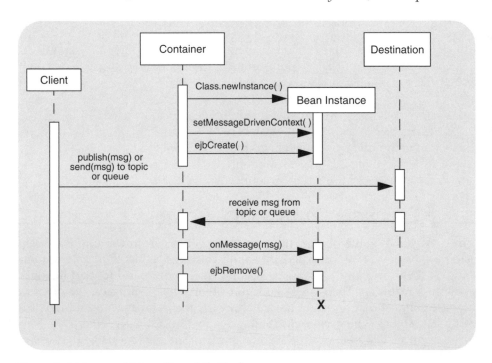

Figure 8–8 Message-Driven Bean Life Cycle

gram shows three steps. First, the container calls the `Class.newInstance()` method to create an instance of the bean. Second, it calls `setMessageDriven-Context()` in the bean with a context object. Third, the container calls the beans's `ejbCreate()` method. At this point, the bean is in the *Ready* state and is ready to receive messages.

The bean stays in the *Ready* state as long as the client sends messages. For each received message, the container calls `onMessage()` with the message as an argument. The container calls `ejbRemove()` when the container no longer requires the bean instance. This makes the bean leave the *Ready* state and return to the *Does Not Exist* state. Note that the container does not activate or passivate message beans since they are stateless.

The sequence diagram shows the client producer publishing a topic or sending a message to a queue destination. How is this set up for the message bean? The answer is that the container obtains the JMS specifications from the message bean's *deployment descriptor*. A message bean's deployment descriptor determines which receiver object (`TopicSubscriber` or `QueueReceiver`) the container will create to handle a message. The container will also use this receiver object to register itself (the container) as a `MessageListener`. (Note that in message-driven beans, the *container* intercepts and then forwards the message to the message bean. Thus, the container must be the registered listener for the JMS server.) We'll take a look at deployment descriptors for message-driven beans a little later in this chapter.

Back to life cycles. Why is it important to understand them? Let's return to our `MusicMessageBean` design for a moment. Recall that the `ejbCreate()` method creates the `DataSource` object for the connection. The `DataSource` reference (`ds`) is an instance variable. Inside `onMessage()`, we open and close the database connection *each time* the database is read. This helps scalability, since we do not tie up connection resources in the container between incoming messages. Also, we release the connection inside a `finally` block in case the system throws an exception while the connection is open.

Exceptions with Message Beans

Message-driven beans have different rules from session and entity beans regarding exceptions. Recall that application exceptions are nonfatal errors that are generally recoverable, whereas system exceptions are runtime errors that indicate a more serious problem. Methods in session and entity beans may throw either an application exception or a system exception because clients call these methods synchronously and can respond to thrown exceptions.

Message-driven beans, on the other hand, have no clients and respond to messages asynchronously. Application exceptions, therefore, are *not* allowed in message-driven beans because no client is known to the bean. The only exception that may be thrown from a message-driven bean is a ***system exception***.

The container handles system exceptions by removing the bean instance and rolling back any transactions started by the bean or by the container.

Here's an example of exception handling in the `ejbCreate()` method of our `MusicMessageBean`.

```
public void ejbCreate() {
   String dbName = "java:comp/env/jdbc/MusicDB";
   try {
      InitialContext jndi = new InitialContext();
      ds = (DataSource)jndi.lookup(dbName);
   } catch (Exception ex) {
      throw new EJBException("Cannot find DataSource: " +
        ex.getMessage());
   }
   . . .
}
```

If an error occurs from the JNDI lookup, we throw system exception `EJBException` from the catch handler with a descriptive error message.

8.4   Student Message-Driven Bean

Now let's move to an example that uses both publish/subscribe and point-to-point messaging. The example is a Student message-driven bean responding to topic messages broadcast from a School client. The idea is that the School publishes a list of new course topics to students who wish to be notified. Each new course has a name, course code, and price. Suppose a student who is interested in a new course uses a JSP program to "sign up" by recording his or her name and e-mail address in a database. When the School publishes a list of new courses, the Student bean checks the price of each course. If it's affordable, the Student bean reads the database and sends e-mail to each student with the new course information. The Student message bean also sends a reply back to the School. We won't show you the Student JSP program or the database code in this example, but we will show you how to design a message bean that receives a message and sends a reply.

Figure 8–9 shows the approach. The School JMS client is a stand-alone application that creates a topic for pub/sub messaging (as a producer) and a queue for PTP messaging (as a consumer). The Student bean is a message-driven bean that subscribes to a new course topic and replies to the School with a message queue. When the School publishes a new course, it also sends the queue identity to the Student bean. If the Student bean is interested in the course, it sends

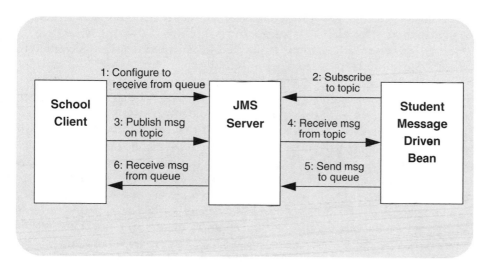

Figure 8–9 Sequence of Events for School Client and Student Message-Driven Bean

a reply back to the School using the queue identity that was sent from the School.

From the School's perspective, pub/sub messaging allows one School to broadcast new course topics to many Student beans. From the Student bean's standpoint, PTP messaging implements the reply from one Student bean to one School. Note that the School client and the Student bean must *both* be message consumers in this design.

Design Guideline

Make sure that you choose your messaging approach carefully. Using PTP instead of pub/sub or vice versa can result in lost messages and inappropriate message deliveries.

School Client

Listing 8.4 shows the School client application (SchoolApp). The first part of SchoolApp is a constructor which sets up the JMS resources (topic and queue), a publishCourses() method to publish course topics, and an onMessage() method to receive messages from a Student bean (StudentBean). Note that SchoolApp implements the MessageListener interface so that it can receive messages. There's also an exit() method to close JMS resources and a main() method to get the ball rolling. To run the program, you supply a course name, code, and price as command-line arguments.

The constructor creates a topic destination to publish course topics and a queue destination to receive messages. After calling `createPublisher()` to initialize a `TopicPublisher` object (`publisher`), the constructor calls `createReceiver()` to initialize a `QueueReceiver` object (`q`). `SchoolApp` also registers itself as a `MessageListener` with the `QueueReceiver` object before starting the topic and queue connections. When a message arrives in the queue from a Student bean, the `onMessage()` method accesses the information.

The `main()` method creates an instance of the `SchoolApp` client and calls `publishCourses()` with course information supplied on the command line. Inside the while loop, we call `readLine()` to block program execution until the user types input followed by a return. When a message arrives, the event handler calls `onMessage()`. The program exits when the user types "quit."

Inside `publishCourses()`, a `StreamMessage` is useful for encoding different data types into the message (here, `String` and integer). Before publishing the course topic, we call `setJMSReplyTo()` with a `message` object and a `receiveQueue` as an argument. This indicates which queue the Student bean should use when sending back a reply. Since the queue destination is now part of the message, a JNDI lookup in the Student bean for a queue destination will not be necessary.

Design Guideline

If replies are necessary, call `setJMSReplyTo()` with a topic or queue argument before publishing or sending a message. This allows the subscriber/ receiver to reply without looking up the destination through the Initial Context.

The `onMessage()` method displays course information received by the Student bean, and the `exit()` method closes the topic and queue connections.

Listing 8.4 SchoolApp.java

```
// SchoolApp.java - Client program for Student MDB
import java.io.*;
import javax.jms.*;
import javax.naming.*;

public class SchoolApp implements MessageListener {
   private TopicConnection topicConnect = null;
   private Topic courseTopic = null;
   private TopicPublisher publisher = null;
   private TopicSession publishSession = null;
```

Listing 8.4 SchoolApp.java *(continued)*

```java
private QueueConnection queueConnect = null;
private Queue receiveQueue = null;
private QueueSession queueSession = null;

/**********************************************************
 *    Sets up topic connection and topic session objects
 *    for publisher-subscribe messaging
 *    Sets up queue connection and queue session objects
 *    for point-to-point reply messaging
 *    Creates publisher for course topics
 *    Creates receive queue for student replies
 *    Registers as a listener for queue messages
 *    Starts the topic and queue connections
 */

public SchoolApp() {
  try {
    InitialContext jndi = new InitialContext();
    TopicConnectionFactory factory =
      (TopicConnectionFactory)jndi.lookup
      ("java:comp/env/jms/MyTopicConnectionFactory");
    topicConnect = factory.createTopicConnection();
    publishSession =
      topicConnect.createTopicSession(false,
        Session.AUTO_ACKNOWLEDGE);

  courseTopic = (Topic)jndi.lookup
      ("java:comp/env/jms/NewCourseTopics");
  QueueConnectionFactory queueFactory =
      (QueueConnectionFactory)jndi.lookup
      ("java:comp/env/jms/MyQueueConnectionFactory");
  queueConnect = queueFactory.createQueueConnection();

  queueSession =
      queueConnect.createQueueSession(false,
        Session.AUTO_ACKNOWLEDGE);
  receiveQueue = (Queue)jndi.lookup
      ("java:comp/env/jms/QueueStudents");
  publisher =
      publishSession.createPublisher(courseTopic);
  QueueReceiver q =
      queueSession.createReceiver(receiveQueue);
```

Listing 8.4 SchoolApp.java *(continued)*

```java
        q.setMessageListener(this);
        topicConnect.start();
        queueConnect.start();
      } catch (Exception ex) {
        ex.printStackTrace();
        System.exit(1);
      }
    }

/*****************************************************
 *   Publish course names, course codes, and
 *   course pricing to student subscribers
 */
    private void publishCourses(String name,
          String code, int price) {
      try {
        StreamMessage message =
          publishSession.createStreamMessage();
        message.writeString(name);
        message.writeString(code);
        message.writeInt(price);

        message.setJMSReplyTo(receiveQueue);
        publisher.publish(message);
      } catch (JMSException ex) {
        ex.printStackTrace();
        System.exit(1);
      }
    }

/*****************************************************
 *   Called when queue message arrives from StudentBean
 */
    public void onMessage(Message message) {
      try {
        TextMessage msg = (TextMessage)message;
        String text = msg.getText();
        System.out.println("Client received PTP message");
        System.out.println("\t" + text);
```

Listing 8.4 SchoolApp.java *(continued)*

```
    } catch (Exception ex) {
      ex.printStackTrace();
      System.exit(1);
    }
  }

/**********************************************
 *   Close topic and queue connections
 */
  public void exit() {
    try {
      if (topicConnect != null)
        topicConnect.close();
      if (queueConnect != null)
        queueConnect.close();
    } catch (JMSException ex) {
      ex.printStackTrace();
      System.exit(1);
    }
    System.exit(0);
  }

/*****************************************************
 *   Main program to read Course info from the command
 *   line and publish to student subscribers
 *   Loop until User types quit to exit program
 */
  public static void main(String args[]) {
    String courseName, courseCode;
    int price;
    if (args.length == 3) {
      courseName = args[0];
      courseCode = args[1];
      price = Integer.parseInt(args[2]);
    } else {
      System.out.println("Usage: Course Code Price");
      return;
    }
    SchoolApp school = new SchoolApp();
```

Listing 8.4 SchoolApp.java *(continued)*

```
  try {
    BufferedReader stdin = new
      BufferedReader(new InputStreamReader(System.in));
    school.publishCourses(courseName,
        courseCode, price);
    System.out.println("Published " +
      courseName + " " + courseCode +
        " Course, waiting for response");

    while (true) {
      System.out.println("type quit to exit");
      String cmd = stdin.readLine();
      if (cmd.equals("quit"))
        school.exit();
    }
  } catch (Exception ex) {
    ex.printStackTrace();
  }
  }
}
```

Student Message Bean

In Listing 8.5, the Student message bean (StudentBean) consists of an ejbCreate() method to set up a JMS queue connection, and an ejbRemove() method to close the connection. StudentBean also has an empty setMessageDriven-Context() method (there is nothing to do here), and an onMessage() method to receive published course topics from the SchoolApp client. Note that StudentBean must implement the MessageListener interface to receive messages.

Inside ejbCreate(), the bean establishes a queue factory connection with the same JNDI name as the SchoolApp client. There is no JNDI lookup of a queue name, however. Instead, ejbCreate() calls createSender(null) with a QueueSession object to specify that a destination queue will be named later. Recall that SchoolApp calls setJMSReplyTo() in its publishCourses() method to send a queue destination address along with the course topic message to the StudentBean. This queue destination address is what the bean uses to reply back to the SchoolApp client. The bean's onMessage() method, therefore, calls getJMSReplyTo() with a message object to access this queue address. When onMessage() calls send() with the course code message, it also specifies the queue address (sendQueue) as its first argument. This technique makes a JNDI lookup for a queue name unnecessary in the StudentBean.

Note that the StudentBean only replies to the SchoolApp client with a course code if the price is no more than $500. Although we set this price value directly in onMessage(), the bean could easily access this information from a database or even from the deployment descriptor. The bean also sends e-mail to the students in the database with the course name, code, and price, although we do not show this here.

Listing 8.5 StudentBean.java

```java
// StudentBean.java - Student Message-Driven Bean
import java.io.*;
import java.rmi.*;
import javax.ejb.*;
import javax.naming.*;
import javax.jms.*;

public class StudentBean implements
    MessageDrivenBean, MessageListener {

  private QueueConnection queueConnect = null;
  private QueueSession queueSession = null;
  private QueueSender qSender = null;

  public void
  setMessageDrivenContext(MessageDrivenContext mdc) { }

/************************************************
 *   Set up queue connection and queue session objects
 *   Create queue sender object for onMessage()
 */
  public void ejbCreate() {
    try {
      InitialContext jndi = new InitialContext();
      QueueConnectionFactory queueFactory =
        (QueueConnectionFactory)jndi.lookup
        ("java:comp/env/jms/MyQueueConnectionFactory");
      queueConnect =
        queueFactory.createQueueConnection();
      queueSession =
        queueConnect.createQueueSession(false,
          Session.AUTO_ACKNOWLEDGE);
```

Listing 8.5 StudentBean.java *(continued)*

```java
      // The null argument means the destination queue
      // will be specified by send() in onMessage()
      qSender = queueSession.createSender(null);
    } catch (Exception ex) {
      throw new EJBException(ex);
    }
  }

  public void ejbRemove() {
    try {
      if (queueConnect != null)
        queueConnect.close();
    } catch (Exception ex) {
      throw new EJBException(ex);
    }
  }

/**************************************************
 *   Read message for course name, code, price
 *   Reply to publisher only if price is right
 *   Send course code back to publisher
 */
  public void onMessage(Message message) {
    int MaxPrice = 500;        // Max price allowed
    try {
      StreamMessage msg = (StreamMessage)message;
      String name = msg.readString();
      String code = msg.readString();
      int price = msg.readInt();

      System.out.println
        ("MDB received published message");
      System.out.println("\t" + name + " " +
        code + " " + price);

      if (price <= MaxPrice) {
        TextMessage textMsg =
          queueSession.createTextMessage();
        textMsg.setText(code);      // store course code
```

Listing 8.5 StudentBean.java *(continued)*

```
        // Get Queue object sent from the publisher
        // Use QueueSender object created in ejbCreate()
        Queue sendQueue = (Queue)message.getJMSReplyTo();
        qSender.send(sendQueue, textMsg);

        // Read student database and send emails
        // to students with course name,
        // course code, and course price
        . . .
      }
    } catch (Exception ex) {
      throw new EJBException(ex);
    }
  }
}
```

Deployment Descriptors

Listing 8.6 shows the deployment descriptor for the SchoolApp client. The
<resource-ref> tag defines the connection factories for the topic and queue
destinations, and the <resource-env-ref> tag names the topic and queue
objects used for messaging.

Listing 8.6 SchoolApp Deployment Descriptor

```
<application-client>
  <display-name>SchoolApp</display-name>
  <resource-ref>
    <res-ref-name>jms/MyTopicConnectionFactory
    </res-ref-name>
    <res-type>javax.jms.TopicConnectionFactory
    </res-type>
    <res-auth>Container</res-auth>
    <res-sharing-scope>Shareable</res-sharing-scope>
  </resource-ref>

  <resource-ref>
    <res-ref-name>jms/MyQueueConnectionFactory
    </res-ref-name>
    <res-type>javax.jms.QueueConnectionFactory</res-type>
```

Listing 8.6 SchoolApp Deployment Descriptor *(continued)*

```
<res-auth>Container</res-auth>
   <res-sharing-scope>Shareable</res-sharing-scope>
</resource-ref>

<resource-env-ref>
   <resource-env-ref-name>jms/NewCourseTopics
   </resource-env-ref-name>
   <resource-env-ref-type>javax.jms.Topic
   </resource-env-ref-type>
</resource-env-ref>

<resource-env-ref>
   <resource-env-ref-name>jms/QueueStudents
   </resource-env-ref-name>
   <resource-env-ref-type>javax.jms.Queue
   </resource-env-ref-type>
</resource-env-ref>
</application-client>
```

Listing 8.7 shows the deployment descriptor for the Student message bean. The `<message-driven>` and `</message-driven>` tags define descriptor information for the message-driven enterprise bean. This includes the bean name, class, transaction type, security, and resource information.

The bean deployment descriptor also has a `<message-driven-destination>` tag, which includes a durable subscription for the topic destination. This means the JMS provider saves topic messages if a `StudentBean` is unavailable. When the bean is deployed, the container generates the code to register the Student message bean as a durable subscriber.

The bean deployment descriptor also names a factory for the queue connection in a `<resource-ref>` tag. The descriptor does not have to name a queue destination because the bean gets this information in the message sent from the client.

Listing 8.7 StudentBean Deployment Descriptor

```
<enterprise-beans>
  . . .
 <message-driven>
  <display-name>StudentEJB</display-name>
  <ejb-name>StudentEJB</ejb-name>
  <ejb-class>StudentBean</ejb-class>
  <transaction-type>Container</transaction-type>
```

Listing 8.7 StudentBean Deployment Descriptor *(continued)*

```
<message-driven-destination>
  <destination-type>javax.jms.Topic</destination-type>
  <subscription-durability>Durable
    </subscription-durability>
</message-driven-destination>

<security-identity>
  <description></description>
  <run-as>
    <description></description>
    <role-name></role-name>
  </run-as>
</security-identity>

<resource-ref>
  <res-ref-name>jms/MyQueueConnectionFactory
    </res-ref-name>
  <res-type>javax.jms.QueueConnectionFactory</res-type>
  <res-auth>Container</res-auth>
  <res-sharing-scope>Shareable</res-sharing-scope>
</resource-ref>
</message-driven>
   .  .  .
</enterprise-beans>
```

8.5 ShipOrder Message-Driven Bean

Asynchronous messages are useful for instigating tasks that take a long time to complete. The sender doesn't have to wait for a message to be delivered or for a receiver to carry out the subsequent request. Furthermore, loose coupling between senders and receivers makes systems more flexible as requirements change.

In this section we'll show you a JMS client producer that uses PTP messaging to interact with our online Music Collection Order processing system. This client, OrderApp, sends a message to a ShipOrder message-driven bean (ShipOrderBean). Upon receipt, the message-driven bean invokes a business method (shipOrdersByDate()) in our CustomerSession EJB. Recall that this method ships all orders with an order date equal to or earlier than its Calendar argument. The message bean invokes shipOrdersByDate() with an order date received from the client in the message.

Figure 8–10 shows the component diagram. The client and ShipOrder message bean use a queue for the PTP messaging. In this diagram we don't show any web components or any of our other EJBs (MusicCart, MusicPage, MusicIterator), since they do not interact with the message bean.

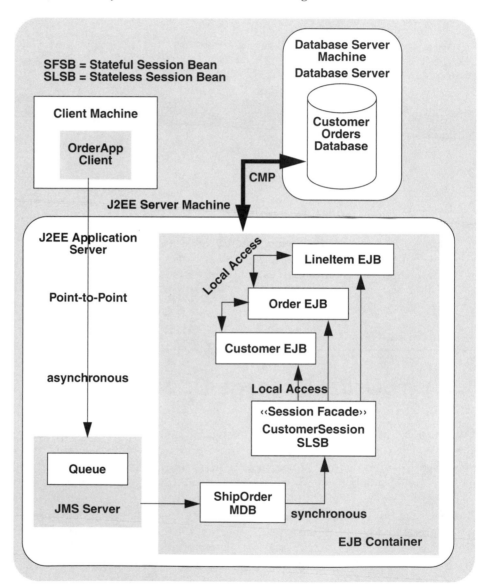

Figure 8–10 Architectural Overview of the Music Shopping Cart Enterprise Application with Added Components ShipOrder MDB and OrderApp JMS Client (Producer)

Note that the client is *completely* decoupled from these EJB components. The client also has no knowledge of the CustomerSession EJB, no knowledge of any entity beans (Customer EJB, Order EJB, or LineItem EJB), and doesn't interact with any underlying database structures. This decoupling is a direct result of having the client interact with the JMS server asynchronously. The message bean, on the other hand, invokes the EJB business method shipOrdersBy-Date() synchronously. Although our message bean doesn't do anything that takes a long time, it could easily be extended to perform more lengthy tasks, like sending e-mails to customers or writing data to log files.

OrderApp Client

The OrderApp producer is a stand-alone Java application client. In its constructor, OrderApp sets up a queue as the message destination and connects to the JMS server with a QueueConnection. Its sendMessage() method creates an ObjectMessage containing a Calendar object argument before sending it to the queue destination. Inside main(), OrderApp creates a Calendar object with today's date and calls sendMessage() with the date as an argument. Listing 8.8 contains the source code for **OrderApp.java**.

Listing 8.8 OrderApp.java

```
// OrderApp.java - Client for ShipOrder Bean
import java.io.*;
import java.util.*;
import javax.jms.*;
import javax.naming.*;

public class OrderApp {
    private QueueConnection connect = null;
    private QueueSession sender;
    private QueueSender qsender;


    public OrderApp() {
        try {
            InitialContext jndi = new InitialContext();
            QueueConnectionFactory factory =
                (QueueConnectionFactory)jndi.lookup
                    ("java:comp/env/jms/MyQueueConnectionFactory");
            connect = factory.createQueueConnection();
            Queue queue = (Queue)jndi.lookup
                ("java:comp/env/jms/MyQueue");
```

Listing 8.8 OrderApp.java *(continued)*

```java
        sender = connect.createQueueSession(false,
            Session.AUTO_ACKNOWLEDGE);

        qsender = sender.createSender(queue);
      } catch (Exception ex) {
        ex.printStackTrace();
        System.exit(1);
      }
    }

    public void sendMessage(Calendar date) {
      try {
        ObjectMessage msg = sender.createObjectMessage();
        msg.setObject(date);
        qsender.send(msg);
        System.out.println("Sent Ship date: " +
                date.getTime());
      } catch (Exception ex) {
        ex.printStackTrace();
      }
    }

    public void exit() {
      try {
        if (connect != null)
          connect.close();
      } catch (Exception ex) {
        ex.printStackTrace();
        System.exit(1);
      }
      System.exit(0);
    }

    public static void main(String args[]) {
      OrderApp order = new OrderApp();
      try {
        Calendar date = new GregorianCalendar();
        order.sendMessage(date);
        order.exit();
```

Listing 8.8 OrderApp.java *(continued)*

```
        } catch (Exception ex) {
            ex.printStackTrace();
        }
    }
}
```

ShipOrder Message Bean

The ShipOrder message bean (**ShipOrderBean.java**) is shown in Listing 8.9. ShipOrderBean has two tasks. First, it must implement the onMessage() method to receive messages. Second, the bean must create a CustomerSession object to call the shipOrdersByDate() method in the Customer EJB.

The ejbCreate() method invokes the necessary lookup() and PortableRemoteObject.narrow() methods to obtain a CustomerSessionHome object. It also creates a CustomerSession remote interface object in instance variable customer. Since CustomerSession EJB is a stateless session bean, we don't have to worry about tying up client-specific resources. Note that ejbCreate() does *not* perform a JNDI lookup for the queue used by the bean. The container performs this task by reading the message bean's deployment descriptor, as you will see shortly.

Inside onMessage(), ShipOrderBean extracts the Calendar object from the received message and calls shipOrdersByDate() with the date as an argument. (See page 344 for the source for CustomerSession EJB's shipOrdersByDate() method.)

Recall that message beans cannot throw application exceptions, since there are no clients that use a message bean directly. If errors occur while processing the message, a message bean could use the JMSReplyTo destination (queue or topic) to report errors. This type of error handling is left as an exercise for the reader.

Listing 8.9 ShipOrderBean.java

```
// ShipOrderBean.java - Ship Order Message-Driven Bean
import java.io.*;
import java.util.*;
import java.rmi.*;
import javax.ejb.*;
import javax.naming.*;
import javax.jms.*;
import javax.rmi.PortableRemoteObject;
```

Listing 8.9 ShipOrderBean.java *(continued)*

```java
public class ShipOrderBean implements
    MessageDrivenBean, MessageListener {

  private CustomerSession customer;
  private MessageDrivenContext messageContext;

  public void
  setMessageDrivenContext(MessageDrivenContext mdc) {
    messageContext = mdc;
  }

  public void ejbCreate() {
    try {
      InitialContext jndi = new InitialContext();
      Object objref = jndi.lookup(
              "java:comp/env/ejb/CustomerSession");

      // Get Customer EJB home interface object
      CustomerSessionHome home = (CustomerSessionHome)
              PortableRemoteObject.narrow(objref,
              CustomerSessionHome.class);
      customer = home.create();     // create Customer EJB
    } catch (Exception ex) {
      throw new EJBException(ex);
    }
  }

  public void ejbRemove() { }

  public void onMessage(Message message) {
    try {
      ObjectMessage msg = (ObjectMessage)message;
      Calendar shipDate = (Calendar)msg.getObject();

      System.out.println("MDB received message");
      System.out.println("\t" + shipDate.getTime());
```

Listing 8.9 ShipOrderBean.java *(continued)*

```
        // call shipOrdersByDate() in Customer EJB
        customer.shipOrdersByDate(shipDate);
        System.out.println("Shipped Orders.");

    } catch (Exception ex) {
        throw new EJBException(ex);
    }
  }
}
```

Deployment Descriptors

Let's examine the deployment descriptor for the application client (OrderApp) first. Listing 8.10 contains the XML file. The deployment descriptor contains the necessary resource references and resource environment references for the message queue used by the OrderApp client and the ShipOrderBean.

Listing 8.10 Deployment Descriptor for OrderApp Client

```
<application-client>
  <display-name>OrderApp</display-name>
  <resource-ref>
     <res-ref-name>jms/MyQueueConnectionFactory
     </res-ref-name>
     <res-type>javax.jms.QueueConnectionFactory</res-type>
     <res-auth>Container</res-auth>
     <res-sharing-scope>Shareable</res-sharing-scope>
  </resource-ref>
  <resource-env-ref>
     <resource-env-ref-name>jms/MyQueue
     </resource-env-ref-name>
     <resource-env-ref-type>javax.jms.Queue
     </resource-env-ref-type>
  </resource-env-ref>
</application-client>
```

Listing 8.11 shows the deployment descriptor for ShipOrderBean, whose display name is ShipOrderEJB. We use container-managed transactions and assign transaction attribute **Required** for method onMessage(). This assures that all messages are received and handled within a transaction. The container uses the queue destination type (javax.jms.Queue) to create a queue receiver for the message. The `ShipOrderBean` also references the CustomerSession EJB using the remote and remote home interfaces.

Listing 8.11 Deployment Descriptor for ShipOrderBean

```
<ejb-jar>
 <display-name>ShipOrderJAR</display-name>
 <enterprise-beans>
    <message-driven>
       <display-name>ShipOrderEJB</display-name>
       <ejb-name>ShipOrderEJB</ejb-name>
       <ejb-class>ShipOrderBean</ejb-class>
       <transaction-type>Container</transaction-type>
       <message-driven-destination>
          <destination-type>javax.jms.Queue
          </destination-type>
       </message-driven-destination>

       <ejb-ref>
          <ejb-ref-name>ejb/CustomerSession</ejb-ref-name>
          <ejb-ref-type>Session</ejb-ref-type>
          <home>CustomerSessionHome</home>
          <remote>CustomerSession</remote>
          <ejb-link>CustomerSessionBean</ejb-link>
       </ejb-ref>

      <security-identity>
         <description></description>
         <run-as>
            <description></description>
            <role-name></role-name>
         </run-as>
      </security-identity>
    </message-driven>
  </enterprise-beans>

  <assembly-descriptor>
     <container-transaction>
       <method>
          <ejb-name>ShipOrderEJB</ejb-name>
          <method-intf>Bean</method-intf>
          <method-name>onMessage</method-name>
          <method-params>
```

Listing 8.11 Deployment Descriptor for ShipOrderBean *(continued)*

```
<method-param>javax.jms.Message</method-param>
        </method-params>
      </method>
      <trans-attribute>Required</trans-attribute>
    </container-transaction>
  </assembly-descriptor>
</ejb-jar>
```

8.6 Design Guidelines and Patterns

Java Message Service (JMS)

JMS is an excellent solution for asynchronous data transfers in enterprise programming. JMS is appropriate with architectures requiring either a one-to-many broadcast (publish/subscribe), a point-to-point communication (PTP), or both. Because JMS is a centralized message server, JMS client components are loosely coupled.

Publish/Subscribe Pattern

The publish/subscribe pattern allows one client to broadcast information to multiple recipients. This pattern is an integral part of a JMS messaging domain. With message-driven beans, the EJB container uses the bean's deployment descriptor to subscribe the bean. Publishers and subscribers use topic destinations for messages.

Point-to-Point Pattern

The point-to-point (PTP) pattern allows a client producer to send a message to a single receiver. PTP is also part of the JMS messaging domain. As with publish/subscribe, the EJB container creates a receiver for you from the bean's deployment descriptor. Senders and receivers use queue destinations for messages.

Publish/Subscribe vs. Point-to-Point

One key difference between pub/sub and PTP is the number of receivers. pub/sub broadcasts messages to multiple message consumers. With PTP, a message is sent to only one receiver. Another key difference is the status of a receiver's connection. With PTP queues, a message consumer does not have to be currently connected to receive messages. With pub/sub topics, however, this is only true for durable subscribers.

Pub/sub delivers messages without subscribers requesting them. In our example where the school broadcasts course topics to students, the school doesn't really care if anyone is listening. From the publisher's standpoint, information is broadcast out to anyone who wants to listen. Pub/sub messaging is therefore a "push-based" model. This means you may consider using pub/sub messaging when it's not a strict requirement for information to be read. If it's important that a listener receive a message, make sure that the consumer is a durable subscriber.

With PTP, a message is always delivered to a receiver. When a message is sent, it doesn't matter if the receiver is connected or not. When the receiver reconnects, the message is received (assuming another receiver hasn't already read it from the same queue). PTP is therefore a "pull-based" model, meaning messages are requested from a queue instead of being pushed by the client. This means you should consider using PTP messaging with one-on-one communications, where it is important that the recipient receives your message.

Message-Driven Beans

Message-driven beans combine the features of EJB and JMS. Each bean has a deployment descriptor enabling the container to deploy a message bean as a JMS consumer. Message beans may receive messages from multiple producers but do not store conversational state, so in this respect they are similar to stateless session beans. Message beans, however, do not have direct clients, nor do they have a local or remote interface with business methods. Message beans are easy to implement and deploy because the container does most of the setup work. They are highly scalable and can respond to a large number of concurrent messages.

When to Use Message-Driven Beans

When designs require asynchronous data transfers, you should consider using a message-driven bean in your architecture. This approach decouples clients from EJBs and other programs, since clients only interact with a JMS server.

A message bean can use a topic with pub/sub messaging or a queue for PTP processing. Message beans are good candidates for off-loading tasks. Instead of having the client call a remote method of an EJB and wait for it to complete, you can have a message bean perform this task. Message beans, on the other hand, are limited to what they can do based on the fact that they are stateless. This is, however, their strong point, since message beans are highly scalable.

Transactions

One of the key advantages of using message-driven beans is that the `onMessage()` method can execute within a transaction. This allows the message-driven bean to invoke one or more methods from an entity or session bean within a single transaction. Because a message-driven bean executes under the auspices of the EJB container, we can use the services (such as transactional support) that the container provides.

8.7   Key Point Summary

This chapter shows you how to design message-driven beans with the Java Message Service (JMS). In enterprise systems, message-driven beans communicate with other objects asynchronously (no waiting). Designs with message beans are scalable because message beans are stateless. The container uses instance pooling to handle a large number of messages concurrently.

Here are the key points from this chapter.

- In a synchronous architecture, clients are tightly coupled with each other. A client's thread blocks until a method completes. Adding or removing clients is difficult.
- In an asynchronous architecture, clients are loosely coupled and communicate through a centralized server. Method calls return without blocking. Adding or removing clients is easy.
- Centralized message servers can implement a store-and-forward mechanism to guarantee delivery of data to clients that are temporarily unavailable.
- JMS is a vendor-independent API that can be used on the J2EE platform for enterprise messaging.
- A JMS client that generates a message is a producer, and a JMS client that receives a message is a consumer.
- With JMS, a client producer sends a message asynchronously to a topic or queue destination.
- JMS has two messaging domains: publish/subscribe (pub/sub) and point-to-point (PTP). Pub/sub messaging is a one-to-many broadcast and PTP is a one-to-one communication. Pub/sub uses topic destinations, whereas PTP uses queues.
- Message delivery to one receiver is guaranteed for queues. With topics and multiple subscribers, you must be a durable subscriber to guarantee message delivery.
- Message-driven beans combine the features of EJB and JMS. The container deploys a message bean as a JMS consumer.

- Message-driven beans are stateless and highly scalable. They can forward tasks to other beans or model business processes.
- Every message-driven bean has an `onMessage()` method which receives messages from topic or queue destinations.
- The life cycle of a message-driven bean alternates between two states. The container does not activate or passivate a message-driven bean because it is stateless.
- Message-driven beans do not have interfaces for direct client access. Because there is no client, application exceptions are not allowed in message-driven beans. The only exception that may be thrown from a message-driven bean is a system exception (which the container receives).
- The `SchoolApp` client application is a JMS producer that uses pub/sub messaging to broadcast course topics to Student message beans. If a Student is interested in a course, the `StudentBean` uses PTP messaging to send a reply back to the `SchoolApp` client.
- The `JMSReplyTo` destination can be useful with message-driven beans for sending replies. It is also helpful for sending error messages.
- The container uses a message bean's deployment descriptor to generate code and configure the bean. In particular, making a bean a durable subscriber is specified in the deployment descriptor.
- The OrderApp client is a JMS producer that uses point-to-point messaging to send `Calendar` objects to a queue destination. The ShipOrder MDB is a JMS consumer and a registered listener for the queue destination. It implements the `onMessage()` method which invokes the CustomerSession EJB business method `shipOrdersByDate()` with a `Calendar` object as an argument.

Appendix A

We present the complete source listing for the Swing application discussed in Chapter 4.

A.1 MusicApp Swing Application

Listing A.1 contains the source for **MusicApp.java**, the Java Swing application client presented in Chapter 4 (see "A Java Swing Application Client" on page 106). Also refer to Figure 4–3 on page 106 and Figure 4–4 on page 109 for screen shots captured during execution of this program.

Listing A.1 MusicApp.java

```
// MusicApp.java
// Swing application to read the Music Collection Database
// using the Music EJB stateless session bean
// Puts recording titles into a Swing JList component
// so that user can select the title
// Upon selection (ListSelectionEvent),
// displays additional information about the recording
// When user clicks "View Tracks" JButton (ActionEvent),
// displays track list for the selected recording title.

import java.awt.*;
import java.awt.event.*;
import java.util.*;
import javax.swing.*;
import javax.swing.event.*;
import javax.naming.Context;
import javax.naming.InitialContext;
import javax.rmi.PortableRemoteObject;

public class MusicApp extends JFrame implements
    ActionListener, ListSelectionListener {

    private MusicHome musicHome;// Music EJB home interface
    private Music mymusic;       // Music EJB remote interface

    // Swing components
    private JList musicTitle;    // Display music titles
    private JTextArea data;      // Display data/track titles
    private JPanel statusbar;    // Hold status text field
    private JPanel display;      // Hold music/track titles
    private JLabel helpline;     // How to use the program
    private JPanel helpPanel;    // Panel to hold helpline
    private JTextField status;   // Status/error messages
    private JButton goButton;    // Button to view tracks

    // Keep track of various lists
    private ArrayList albums;    // RecordingVO objects
    private ArrayList tracks;    // TrackVO objects
    private Vector titles;       // Recording titles
```

```java
// Given a RecordingVO, get the tracklist
private void getTracks(RecordingVO rec) {
  try {
    // access MusicEJB
    tracks = mymusic.getTrackList(rec);
    TrackVO t;
    Iterator i = tracks.iterator();
    while (i.hasNext()) {
      t = (TrackVO)i.next();
      // put track info into data JTextArea
      data.append("\n" + t.getTrackNumber() + "\t" +
        t.getTrackLength() + "\t" + t.getTitle());
    }

  // Check separately for NoTrackListException
  } catch (NoTrackListException ex) {
    status.setText("NoTrackListException Exception: " +
        ex.getMessage());
  } catch (Exception ex) {
    status.setText("Unexpected Exception: " +
        ex.getMessage());
    ex.printStackTrace();
  }
}

// Get recording information
private void getRecordings() {
  try {
    // access MusicEJB
    albums = mymusic.getMusicList();
  } catch (Exception ex) {
    status.setText("Unexpected Exception: " +
        ex.getMessage());
    ex.printStackTrace();
  }
```

Listing A.1 MusicApp.java *(continued)*

```
        RecordingVO r;
        Iterator i = albums.iterator();
        while (i.hasNext()) {
          r = (RecordingVO)i.next();
          // put Recording titles into titles Vector,
          // which is displayed in the JList Swing component
          titles.add(r.getTitle());
        }
    }

    public MusicApp() {
      // Set up Swing components
      getContentPane().setLayout(new BorderLayout());
      getContentPane().setBackground(Color.lightGray);
      setSize(800, 200);

      helpPanel = new JPanel();
      helpPanel.setLayout(new FlowLayout(
              FlowLayout.CENTER,5,5));

      // Put the help panel at the top
      getContentPane().add("North", helpPanel);
      helpline = new JLabel(
        "Select recording & click button to View Tracks");
      helpPanel.add(helpline);

      display = new JPanel();
      display.setLayout(new GridLayout(1,2,15,15));

      // Set up the musicTitle JList
      // Initialize it with titles vector
      // Make 7 rows visible and add a scrollbar
      // Add the ListSelectionListener
      // to allow user to select titles
      titles = new Vector();
      musicTitle = new JList(titles);
      musicTitle.setBackground(Color.white);
      musicTitle.setVisibleRowCount(7);
      musicTitle.addListSelectionListener(this);
      display.add( new JScrollPane( musicTitle ));
```

Listing A.1 MusicApp.java *(continued)*

```java
// Set up the data JTextArea
// Turn off editing and add a scrollbar
data = new JTextArea(12,40);
data.setBackground(Color.white);
data.setEditable(false);
display.add( new JScrollPane( data ));
// Put the display JPanel in the Center
getContentPane().add("Center", display);

// Set up the statusbar JPanel
// Put the statusbar JPanel at the bottom
// Give it a flow layout
// Add the goButton JButton and the status JTextField
// Add the Action Listener to goButton
statusbar = new JPanel();
statusbar.setLayout(new FlowLayout(
        FlowLayout.LEFT,5,5));
goButton = new JButton("View Tracks");
goButton.addActionListener(this);
statusbar.add(goButton);

status = new JTextField(60);
status.setEditable(false);
statusbar.add(status);
getContentPane().add("South", statusbar);
setTitle("Music Collection - Using EJB with JDBC");

try {
  // Create Music EJB
  Context initial = new InitialContext();
  Object objref = initial.lookup(
          "java:comp/env/ejb/MyMusic");
  musicHome = (MusicHome)PortableRemoteObject.narrow(
            objref, MusicHome.class);
  mymusic = musicHome.create();
} catch (Exception ex) {
  System.out.println("Unexpected Exception: " +
        ex.getMessage());
  ex.printStackTrace();
}
```

Listing A.1 MusicApp.java *(continued)*

```java
// Access the EJB to read the Music Collection database
// and put the title names in the JList swing component
getRecordings();
status.setText("There are " + albums.size() +
      " recordings");
pack();
show();

// Set up the WindowListener object
this.addWindowListener(new WindowAdapter() {
  public void windowClosing(WindowEvent e)
    { dispose(); }
  public void windowClosed(WindowEvent e)
    { System.exit(0); }
});
}

public MusicApp(String title) {
    this();
    setTitle(title);
}

  public void actionPerformed(ActionEvent e) {

    // Event handler for ActionEvent
    // (user clicks "View Tracks" button)

    if (e.getSource() instanceof JButton) {

    // make sure the user has selected a music title
    if (musicTitle.getSelectedValue() == null) {
      status.setText(
          "You must select a recording title first.");
    }

    else {
      // Tell the user what title
      // we're getting track info for
      status.setText("Displaying track list for " +
        musicTitle.getSelectedValue());
      // Using setText() wipes out any text previously
      // written to JTextArea
      data.setText("Track information for " +
        musicTitle.getSelectedValue());
```

```
      // getTracks() calls Music EJB
      // business method getTrackList()
      // getTracks() puts track info into the
      // JTextArea component
      getTracks(
        (RecordingVO)albums.get(
          musicTitle.getSelectedIndex())));

      // In case there are more tracks than visible
      // lines, position caret to top of component
      data.setCaretPosition(0);
    }
  }
}

public void valueChanged(ListSelectionEvent e) {

  // Event handler for ListSelectionEvent
  // (user changes selection in musicTitle
  // JList component)

  if (!e.getValueIsAdjusting()) {
    // Tell user which title was selected
    // Method getSelectedValue() returns a String
    status.setText("You selected " +
      musicTitle.getSelectedValue());

    // Access the RecordingVO object at the index
    // of the selected music title.
    // Method getSelectedIndex() returns the index of
    // the selected list item,
    // which corresponds to the same
    // index value in the albums ArrayList collection.
    RecordingVO r =
        (RecordingVO)albums.get(
            musicTitle.getSelectedIndex());

    // Display information from the RecordingVO object
    // in the JTextArea.
    // Use method setText() to clear previously written
    // text, then use method append().
    // Set caret position to top in case text causes
    // JTextArea to scroll.
```

Listing A.1 MusicApp.java *(continued)*

```java
        data.setText("RecordingID = " +
                r.getRecordID() + ",\n");
        data.append("Title = " + r.getTitle() + ",\n");
        data.append("Artist is " +
                r.getArtistName() + ",\n");
        data.append("Music Category is " +
                r.getMusicCategory() + ",\n");
        data.append("Label is " + r.getLabel() + ",\n");
        data.append("Number of Tracks = " +
                r.getNumberOfTracks());
        data.setCaretPosition(0);
    }
  }

static public void main(String args[]) {
    MusicApp acs = new MusicApp();
  }
} // MusicApp
```

Index

W

WAR file 77
web component client, *See* JSP client
web container 18
Where clause, EJB QL 296

X

XML
    deployment descriptor 53, 82

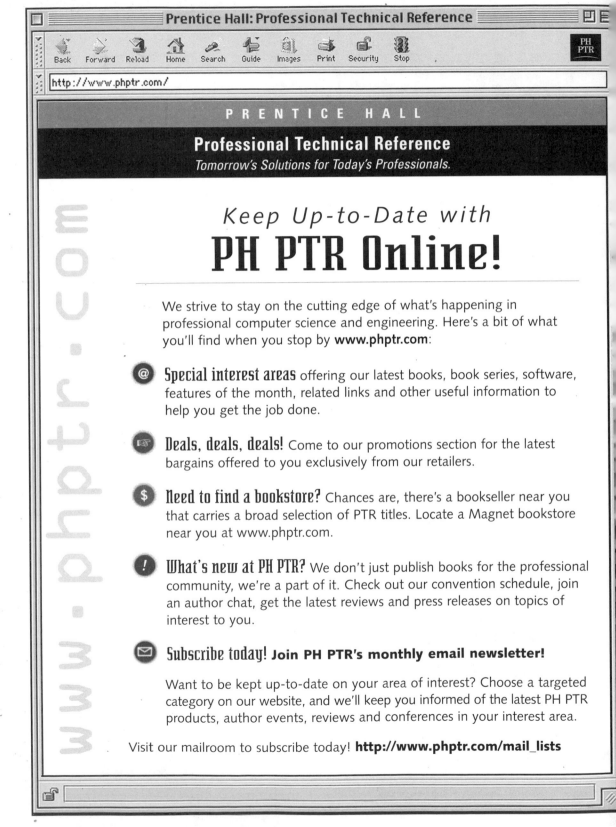